USB
System
Architecture

The PC System Architecture Series

The PC System Architecture Series is a crisply written and comprehensive set of guides to the most important PC hardware standards. Each title illustrates the relationship between the software and hardware, and thoroughly explains the architecture, features, and operation of systems built using one particular type of chip or hardware specification.

MindShare, Inc. is one of the leading technical training companies in the computer industry,

providing innovative courses for dozens of companies, including Intel, IBM, and Compaq.

> *"There is only one way to describe the series of PC hardware and architecture books written by Tom Shanley and Don Anderson: INVALUABLE."*
> —*PC Magazine*'s "Read Only" column

ISBN 0-201-40994-1

ISBN 0-201-70069-7

ISBN 0-201-40997-6

ISBN 0-201-40995-X

ISBN 0-201-48535-4

ISBN 0-201-40996-8

ISBN 0-201-30974-2

ISBN 0-201-40991-7

ISBN 0-201-30973-4

ISBN 0-201-40992-5

ISBN 0-201-41013-3

ISBN 0-201-40990-9

ISBN 0-201-55447-X

ISBN 0-201-46137-4

http://www.awl.com/cseng/series/mindshare/   ♦ Addison-Wesley

USB
System
Architecture

MindShare, Inc.

Don Anderson

ADDISON-WESLEY
An imprint of Addison Wesley Longman, Inc.

Reading, Massachusetts • Harlow, England • Menlo Park, California
Berkeley, California • Don Mills, Ontario • Sydney
Bonn • Amsterdam • Tokyo • Mexico City

Library of Congress Cataloging-in-Publication Data

Anderson, Don.
    USB system architecture / MindShare, Inc., Don Anderson.
       p.   cm. -- (PC system architecture series)
    Includes index.
    ISBN 0-201-46137-4
    1. USB (Computer bus) 2. Computer architecture. I. MindShare, Inc.
  II. Title. III. Series.
    TK7895.B87A53 1997   96-52321
    004.6'4--dc   CIP

Sponsoring Editor: Kathleen Tibbetts
Project Manager: Sarah Weaver
Cover Design: Barbara T. Atkinson
Set in 10-point Palatino by MindShare, Inc.

7 8 9 101112 MA   02 01 00 99

7th Printing   November 1999

For my stepson Ryan, the brightest kid on the block

Contents

About This Book

The MindShare Architecture Series 1
Cautionary Note 2
Organization of This Book 2
    Part I: The Emergence of USB 2
    Part II: The USB Solution 2
    Part III: USB Configuration 3
    Part IV: USB Host Software 4
    Part V: USB Device Class 4
    Part VI: Host Controllers and Hub: Example Implementations 4
Who This Book Is For 5
Prerequisite Knowledge 5
Documentation Conventions 5
    Hexadecimal Notation 5
    Binary Notation 5
    Decimal Notation 6
    Bits Versus Byte Notation 6
Identification of Bit Fields 6
Visit Our Web Page 7
We Want Your Feedback 7

Part I: The Emergence of USB

Chapter 1: The Need for USB

Shortcomings of the Existing PC IO Paradigm 11
Technical Issues 11
    Interrupts 12
    IO Addresses 14
    Non-Shareable Interfaces 14
End User Concerns 14
    Cable Crazed 14
    Installation and Configuration of Expansion Cards 15
    No Hot Attachment of Peripheral 15
Cost 16

Contents

Chapter 2: Solutions

Design Goals..17
Challenges of the New Solution 17
    Enhanced System Performance..18
    Plug and Play Support 18
    Hot Attachment..18
    Room for Growth/Expandability..19
    Legacy Hardware/Software Support 19
    Low Cost 19
Analysis of Potential Solutions..19
    Access Bus 21
    GeoPort..21
    IEEE 1394 21
USB - The Right Balance..21
The USB Paradigm..24
How to Get the USB Specifications...24

Part II: The USB Solution

Chapter 3: The Big Picture

Overview..27
The Players 29
    USB Device Drivers 30
    USB Driver 31
    USB Host Controller Driver 31
    USB Host Controller/Root Hub 32
        The Host Controller...32
        The Root Hub 33
    USB Hubs 34
        Hub Controller...36
        Hub Repeater...36
        Hub's Role in Configuration 37
    USB Devices...38
        High-Speed Devices...38
        Low-Speed Devices 38
USB Communications Model 38
    Communications Flow 39
    Transfers, IRPs, Frames, and Packets..41
        Transfers..41
        The USB Driver, IRPs and Frames 41

Contents

The Host Controller Driver and Transactions.. 42
The Host Controller and Packets.. 44
Device Framework (how devices present themselves to software).................... **45**
Device Descriptors... 45
Device Framework.. 47
USB Bus Interface Layer 47
USB Device Layer 48
Function Layer 49
USB Peripheral Connection **50**
Topology **51**

Chapter 4: The Physical Environment

The Connectors... **53**
Series A Connectors... 54
Series B Connectors... 55
Cables **55**
Low-Speed Cables.. 55
Full-Speed Cables... 56
Cable Power.. 57
Electrical and Mechanical Specifications **57**

Chapter 5: The Signaling Environment

Overview.. **59**
Detecting Device Attachment and Speed.. **60**
NRZI Encoding... **62**
Bit Stuffing.. **63**
Differential Pair Signaling.. **64**
Differential Drivers... 65
Low-Speed Drivers.. 66
Full-Speed Drivers... 66
Differential Receivers... 68
Single-Ended Receivers.. 68
Summary of USB Signaling States **69**

Chapter 6: USB Transfers

Overview.. **71**
Client Initiates Transfer.. **72**
Frame-Based Transfers.. **74**
Transfer Types.. **75**
Isochronous... 76
Direction of Transfers... 77

Contents

Service Period 78
Bandwidth Allocation 78
Error Recovery 78
Interrupt Transfers 78
Service Period 78
Bus Bandwidth Allocation 80
Error Recovery 80
Control Transfers 80
Bus Bandwidth Allocation 81
Error Recovery 81
Bulk Transfers **81**
Bus Bandwidth Allocation 81
Error Recovery 82

Chapter 7: USB Transactions

Overview **83**
Packets — The Basic Building Blocks of USB transactions **85**
Synchronization Sequence 86
Packet Identifier 87
Packet-Specific Information 88
Cyclic Redundancy Checking (CRC) 88
End of Packet (EOP) 88
Token Packets **89**
SOF Packet 90
IN Packet 91
OUT Packet 92
SETUP Packet 93
Data Packets — Data0 and Data1 .... **94**
Handshake Packets **95**
Preamble Packet **97**
Transactions **98**
IN Transactions 98
IN Transaction without Errors 98
IN Transaction with Errors 99
IN Transaction with No Interrupt Pending/Target Busy 100
IN Transaction with Target Stalled 101
IN Transaction during Isochronous Transfer 101
OUT Transactions 102
OUT Transaction without Data Packet Errors 102
OUT Transaction with Errors/Target Busy 103
OUT Transaction — Target Unable to Accept Data 103
OUT Transaction with Target Stalled 104

Contents

OUT Transaction during Isochronous Transfer 104
Setup Transactions/Control Transfers 105
Two Stage Control Transfer 106
Three Stage Control Transfer with IN Data Stage 107
Three Stage Control Transfer with OUT Data Stage 108
Control Transfers with Errors 108

Chapter 8: Error Recovery

Overview 109
Packet Errors 110
PID Checks 110
CRC Errors 111
Bit Stuff Errors 112
Packet-Related Error Handling 112
Token Packet Errors 112
IN Packet Errors 112
OUT or Setup Packet Errors 112
Data Packet Errors 113
During OUT or Setup Transactions 113
During IN Transactions 113
Handshake Packet Errors 113
During OUT Transactions 113
During IN Transactions 113
Bus Time-Out 114
False EOPs 115
False EOP during Host Transmission 115
False EOP during Target Transmission 116
Data Toggle Errors 116
Data Toggle Procedure without Errors 116
Data Toggle during OUT Transactions 117
Data Toggle during IN Transactions 118
Data Toggle Procedure with Data Packet Errors 120
Data Toggle and Data Packet Errors — OUT Transactions 120
Data Toggle and Data Packet Errors — IN Transactions 122
Data Toggle with Handshake Packet Errors 124
Data Toggle and Handshake Errors — OUT Transactions 125
Data Toggle with Handshake Packet Error — IN Transaction 126
Special Case: Data Toggle During Control Transfer 128
Babble 129
Loss of Activity (LOA) 130
Babble/LOA Detection and Recovery 130
Frame Timer 130

Contents

Host to Hub Skew 131
Hub Repeater State Machine 132
Isochronous Transfers (Delivery Not Guaranteed) **133**
Interrupt Transfer Error Recovery **133**
Bulk Transfer Error Recovery **134**
Control Transfer Error Recovery **134**

Chapter 9: USB Cable Power Distribution

USB Power **135**
Hubs **135**
Current Budget 136
Over-Current Protection 137
Voltage Drop Budget 137
Power Switching 138
Bus-Powered Hubs **139**
Power During Hub Configuration 139
Bus-Powered Hub Attached to 500ma Port 140
Bus-Powered Hub Attached to 100ma Port 140
Bus-Powered Hub Attached to Port with >100ma but <500ma 140
Current Limiting 141
Bus-Powered Devices **142**
Low-Power Devices 142
High-Power Devices 143
Power During Configuration 143
Insufficient Port Power 143
Self-Powered Hubs **145**
Power During Configuration 146
Locally Powered Bus Interface 146
Hybrid-Powered Device 146
Current Limiting 147
Self-Powered Devices **148**
Power During Configuration 148
Locally Powered Bus Interface 148
Hybrid Powered Device 148

Chapter 10: USB Power Conservation

Power Conservation-Suspend **151**
Device Response to Suspend 152
Hub Response to Suspend 152
Global Suspend **153**
Initiating Global Suspend 153

Contents

Resume from Global Suspend.. 153
    Resume Initiated By Host 153
    Remote Wakeup from Device 155
    Remote Wakeup via Device Attachment and Detachment 157
Selective Suspend **157**
  Initiating Selective Suspend 157
  Resume from Selective Suspend 157
    Host Initiated Selective Resume 157
    Selective Wakeup from Device 158
  Selective Suspend When Hub is Suspended.. 160
    Device Signals Resume 160
    Port Receives Connect or Disconnect 162
Selective Suspend Followed by Global Suspend................................... **162**
Resume Via Reset.. **162**
  Hub Frame Timer after Wakeup.. 164

Part III: USB Configuration

Chapter 11: Configuration Process

Overview.. **167**
The Configuration Model.. **169**
Root Hub Configuration... **170**
  Each Device is Isolated for Configuration... 171
  Reset Forces Device to Default Address (zero).................................... 172
  Host Assigns a Unique Device Address.. 172
  Host Software Verifies Configuration.. 172
    Power Requirements 172
    Bus Bandwidth.. 173
  Configuration Value is Assigned... 173
  Client Software is Notified 173

Chapter 12: Hub Configuration

Configuring the Hub... **175**
  The Default Pipe.. 176
  The Status Change Pipe 176
Reading the Hub's Descriptors **176**
  Hub Device Descriptor.. 178
  Hub Configuration Descriptor.. 180
    Number of Interfaces... 180
    Configuration Value.. 181
    Bus- or Self-Powered Hub 181

Contents

Maximum Bus Power Consumed 181
Hub Interface Descriptor 182
Status Endpoint Descriptor 184
Status Change Endpoint Address/Transfer Direction............................. 184
Transfer Type 185
Maximum Data Packet Size... 185
Polling Interval.. 185
Hub Class Descriptor 186
Power Switching Mode Implemented 187
Compound Device or Hub Only 187
Over-current Protection Mode... 187
Power On to Power Good Delay 187
Maximum Bus Current for Hub Controller 188
Device Removable/Non-removable.. 188
Port Power Mask.. 188
Powering the Hub 191
Checking Hub Status... 191
Detecting Hub Status Changes 191
Reading the Hub Status Field... 192
Reading Port Status Field 193
Enabling the Device 193
Summary of Hub Port States 194

Chapter 13: Hub Requests

Overview.. 197
Hub Request Types 198
Standard Requests and Hub Response.. 199
Hub Class Requests 200
Get/Set Descriptor.. 202
Get Hub Status Request.. 202
Hub Status Fields 203
Local Power Status 203
Over-Current Indicator.. 203
Hub State Change Fields... 204
Local Power Status Change 204
Over-Current Indicator Change 204
Set/Clear Hub Feature Request 205
Hub Local Power Change Request.. 206
Hub Over Current Change Request... 206
Get Port Status Request 206
Port Status Fields... 207
Current Connect Status Field 207

Contents

Port Enabled/Disabled 207
Suspend 208
Over-Current Indicator 208
Reset... 208
Port Power 208
Low Speed Device Attached 209
Port Change Fields 209
Current Status Change... 209
Port Enabled/Disable Change... 210
Suspend Change (Resume Complete) 210
Over-Current Indicator Change 210
Reset Complete... 210
Set/Clear Port Feature **211**
Get Bus State **212**

Chapter 14: USB Device Configuration

Overview.. **213**
Reading and Interpreting the USB Descriptors **214**
Device Classes **215**
Device Descriptors.. **216**
Class Code Field.. 216
Maximum Packet Size 0 217
Manufacturer, Product, Serial Number 217
Number of Configurations 218
Configuration Descriptors... **221**
Number of Interfaces.. 221
Configuration Value 221
Attributes and Maximum Power.. 222
Interface Descriptors **223**
Interface Number and Alternate Setting 223
Number of Endpoints 225
Interface Class and Sub Class... 225
Protocol.. 225
Endpoint Descriptors **227**
Device States **229**
Attached State.. 229
Powered State.. 229
Default State... 229
Addressed State... 230
Configured State 230
Suspended State 230

Contents

Chapter 15: Device Requests

Overview.. 233
Standard Device Requests... 234
Set/Clear Feature.. 237
    Device Remote Wakeup.. 237
    EndPoint Stall... 237
Set/Get Configuration.. 238
Set/Get Descriptor.. 238
Set/Get Interface.. 239
Get Status.. 240
    Device Status... 240
        Self Powered Bit... 240
        Remote Wakeup Bit.. 241
    Endpoint Status.. 241
Sync Frame.. 241

Part IV: USB Host Software

Chapter 16: USB Host Software

USB Software.. 245
    Function Layer... 246
    Device Layer... 246
    Interface Layer... 247
    The Software Components.. 248
USB Driver (USBD).. 250
Configuration Management... 250
    USB Elements Requiring Configuration...................................... 250
    Allocating USB Resources.. 251
        Verifying Power.. 251
        Tracking and Allocating Bus Bandwidth.............................. 252
        Bus Bandwidth Reclamation.. 253
Bus Management... 253
Data Transfer Management... 254
Providing Client Services (The USB Driver Interface)................... 254
    Pipe Mechanisms.. 254
        Client Pipe Requirements.. 255
    Command Mechanisms... 255

Contents

Part V: USB Device Class

Chapter 17: Device Classes

Overview 259
Device Classes 262
Audio Device Class 262
    Standard Audio Interface Requirements 264
    Synchronization Types 264
    Audio Class-Specific Descriptors 265
    Audio Class-Specific Requests 265
Communication Device Class 266
    Communications Device Interfaces 267
    Communications Class-Specific Descriptors 267
    Communications Class-Specific Requests 267
Display Device Class 268
    The Standard Display Device Class Interface 268
    Display Device-Specific Descriptors 269
    Device-Specific Requests 269
Mass Storage Device Class 269
    Standard Mass Storage Interface 271
        Control Endpoint 271
        Bulk Transfer Endpoints 271
        Interrupt Endpoint 271
    General Mass Storage Subclass 271
    CD-ROM Subclass 272
    Tape Subclass 273
    Solid State Subclass 273
    Class and Device-Specific USB Requests 273
Human Interface Device Class 274

Part VI: Host Controllers and Hub: Example Implementations

Chapter 18: Universal Host Controller

Overview 277
Universal Host Controller Transaction Scheduling 278
    Universal Host Controller Frame List Access 278
    UHC Transfer Scheduling Mechanism 280
    Bus Bandwidth Reclamation 280

Contents

Transfer Descriptors 281
    Queue Heads 285
UHC Control Registers 287

Chapter 19: Open Host Controller

Overview 289
Open Host Controller Transfer Scheduling 289
    The Open Host Controller Transfer Mechanism 290
    The ED and TD List Structure 292
        Interrupt and Isochronous Transfer Processing 292
        Control and Bulk Transfer Processing 292
        The Done Queue 293
    Interrupt Transfer Scheduling 293
EndPoint Descriptors 295
Transfer Descriptors 298
    General Transfer Descriptor 298
    Isochronous Transfer Descriptor 301
The Open Host Controller Registers 304

Chapter 20: The TUSB2040 Hub

Overview 307
Power Control 309
    Self-Powered with Individual Port Control 309
    Self-Powered Hub with Ganged Port Control 310
    Bus-Powered Hub with Ganged Port Control 311

Appendix: FuturePlus USB Preprocessor

Overview 313
Capabilities 313
Implementation 314
    State Analysis Mode 314
    Timing Analysis Mode 314
    Cross-Domain Analysis 315

Index 317

Figures

1-1   System Resources Used by Legacy Peripheral Devices 12

1-2   Connectors at Backplane.. 15

2-1   USB Device Connections 22

3-1   USB System Implemented in a PCI-based Platform............................. 28

3-2   Communication Flow in a USB System.. 30

3-3   Block Diagram of Major Root Hub Functions 34

3-4   USB Hub Types.. 35

3-5   Primary Hub Functions 36

3-6   Hub Repeater Performing Downstream and Upstream Connectivity 37

3-7   The Communications Model.. 40

3-8   USB Devices Performing Transfers during Frame.............................. 43

3-9   Relationship Between IRPs, Transfers, Frames, and Packets 44

3-10   Standard Device Descriptors.. 46

3-11   Device Framework — Software's View of Hardware 48

3-12   USB's Tiered Star Topology 51

4-1   Cross Section of a Low Speed Cable Segment..................................... 56

4-2   Cross Section of High Speed Cable Segment....................................... 57

5-1   Transfer Across USB Cables Employ NRZI
Encoding and Differential Signaling.. 60

5-2   Resistor Connections for Hub and Devices 61

5-3   Device Attachment and Detachment... 62

5-4   NRZI Encoded Data 63

5-5   Stuffed Bit.. 64

5-6   Signaling Interface Between Hub and Device 65

5-7   Example Full-Speed CMOS Differential Driver 67

5-8   Full-Speed Drive Waveforms... 68

5-9   USB Signaling Levels... 70

6-1   Communication Pipe Between Client Software's
Memory Buffer and Device Endpoint.. 73

6-2   Client Request Converted to USB Transactions..................................... 74

6-3   Isochronous Application Using USB CD-ROM and Speakers 77

7-1   The Layers Involved in USB Transfers 84

7-2   Many USB Transactions Consist of Three Phases.............................. 85

7-3   Packet Format.. 86

7-4   Synchronization Sequence.. 86

7-5   Packet Identifier Format 88

7-6   End of Packet Signalling 89

7-7   Format of a SOF Packet... 91

7-8   IN Token Packet Format 92

7-9   OUT Token Packet Format 93

7-10   SETUP Token Packet Format 94

7-11   Data0 Packet Format 95

Figures

7-12   Data1 Packet Format 95
7-13   Handshake Packet Formats 96
7-14   Preamble Packet Format 98
7-15   IN Transaction without Errors 99
7-16   IN Transaction with Data Phase Errors 100
7-17   IN Transaction with Target Temporarily Unable to Return Data 100
7-18   IN Transaction with Target Stalled 101
7-19   IN Transaction during Isochronous Transfer 102
7-20   OUT Transactions without Errors 103
7-21   OUT Transaction with Data Packet Errors 103
7-22   OUT Transaction to Target That is Unable to Accept Data 104
7-23   OUT Transaction to Stalled Endpoint 104
7-24   OUT Transaction during Isochronous Transfer 105
7-25   Format of a Two-Stage Control Transfer 107
7-26   Control Transfer Requesting Data from Target 107
7-27   Control Transfer Issuing a Command to a Target's Control Endpoint 108
8-1   PID Check 110
8-2   Total Trip Delay 115
8-3   OUT Transaction with Data Toggle Sequence and No Error 118
8-4   IN Transactions with Data Toggle Sequence and No Errors 120
8-5   OUT Transaction with Data Toggle and Data Packet Errors 121
8-6   IN Transactions with Data Toggle and Data Packet Errors 123
8-7   OUT Transaction with Data Toggle and Handshake Errors 126
8-8   IN Transaction with Data Toggle and Handshake Errors 128
8-9   Data Toggle During Control Transfers 129
8-10   Hub EOF Points 130
8-11   EOF Timing Ranges 131
8-12   Hub Repeater State Diagram 133
9-1   Minimum Cable Voltage and Voltage Drop Budget 138
9-2   Bus-Powered Hub with Embedded Function and Four Ports 141
9-3   Low-Power USB Function 142
9-4   High-Power/Bus Powered Function 144
9-5   Self-Powered Hub with Embedded Function 147
9-6   Self-Powered Device 149
10-1   Host Initiated Resume 154
10-2   Global Resume Signaling Due to Wakeup from Target Device 156
10-3   Selective Resume Signaled by Target Device 159
10-4   Device Initiated Selective Resume to Suspended Hub 161
10-5   Resume with Selective and Global Suspend 163
11-1   The Configuration Software Model 169
11-2   Root Hub's Control and Status Change Endpoints 171
12-1   Required Hub Endpoints 177

Figures

12-2   Standard Hub Descriptors.. 178

12-3   Hub and Port Status Change Bitmap.. 192

13-1   Format of Setup Transaction that Specifies
        the Device Request Being Performed 198

14-1   Descriptor Tree Containing Alternate Interface Settings................... 224

15-1   Format of Setup Transaction that Specifies the
        Device Request Being Performed 234

16-1   Device Framework — Software's View of Hardware 247

16-2   Software Layers.. 249

17-1   CD-ROM Supporting Mass Storage and Audio Interfaces................. 261

18-1   Universal Host Controller Transfer Scheduling................................. 278

18-2   Frame List Access 279

18-3   Transfer Mechanism and Execution Order.. 281

18-4   Transfer Descriptor Format 282

18-5   The Queue Head Link and Element Link Pointers............................. 285

19-1   USB Transfer Scheduling 290

19-2   The Transfer Scheduling Mechanism 291

19-3   Transfer Queues.. 293

19-4   Interrupt Scheduling 294

19-5   Endpoint Descriptor Format 295

19-6   Transfer Descriptor Format 298

19-7   Isochronous Transfer Descriptor 302

19-8   Open Host Controller Registers... 305

20-1   Block Diagram of TUSB2040 Hub 308

20-2   TUSB2040 Implemented as Self-Powered Hub with Individual
        Port Power Switching and Over-current Protection............................ 310

20-3   Self-Powered Hub Implemented with Ganged Power
        Switching and Over-Current Protection. 311

20-4   TUSB2040 Configured for Bus-Powered Operation and
        Ganged Power Switching 312

Tables

1-1	Typical Legacy Interrupt Lines used by Standard Devices	13
2-1	Applications, Relative Performance Required and Desired Attributes	20
2-2	Various Solutions with Relative Performance and Complexity	20
2-3	Key USB Features	23
4-1	Connector pin designations	54
4-2	Cable Propagation Delay	56
5-1	USB Bus States	69
6-1	Endpoint Descriptor Transfer Type Definition	75
6-2	Endpoint Descriptor's Interrupt Polling Interval Definition	79
7-1	USB Tokens	90
7-2	Direction of Data Packets	94
7-3	Format of Setup Transaction Data Phase	106
8-1	Packet Type and CRC	111
9-1	Source of Hub Power Defined in Configuration Descriptor	136
9-2	Power Switching Mode Supported is Defined by the Hub Class Descriptor	139
9-3	Maximum Power Defined in Device's Configuration Descriptor	145
12-1	Hub's Device Descriptor	179
12-2	Hub Configuration Descriptor	181
12-3	Hub Interface Descriptor	183
12-4	Hub Status Endpoint Descriptor	185
12-5	Hub Class Descriptor	188
12-6	Hub Port States	194
13-1	Format of Setup Transaction Data Phase	199
13-2	Hub's Response to Standard Device Requests	200
13-3	Hub Class Request Codes	201
13-4	Hub Class-Specific Requests	201
13-5	Format of Hub Status Fields Returned During the Get Hub Status Request	204
13-6	Format of Hub Change Field Returned During Hub Status Request	205
13-7	Feature Selector and Index Values for Hub-Specific Requests	205
13-8	Format of Port Status Fields Returned During the Get Port Status Request	207
13-9	Format of Port Change Fields Returned During the Get Port Status Request	209
13-10	Feature Selector and Index Values for Port Specific Requests	211
13-11	Format of the Bus State Returned During the Get Bus State Request	212
14-1	Descriptor Type Values	215
14-2	Definition of Get Descriptor Request Used to Read the String Descriptors	218
14-3	Device Descriptor Definition	218
14-4	Configuration Descriptor Definition	222
14-5	Interface Descriptor Definition	225
14-6	Endpoint Descriptor Definition	227
14-7	Device States	230
15-1	Format of Data Payload during Setup Transactions	235
15-2	Standard Device Requests	236

Tables

15-3   Feature Selectors 237

15-4   Contents of Setup Transaction During Get Descriptor Requests 239

15-5   Descriptor Types That Can Be Specified Via Standard Get/Set
Descriptor Request 239

15-6   Device Status Information Returned during Get Status Request 240

15-7   Endpoint Status Information Returned during Get Status Request 241

17-1   Audio Subclasses and Protocols 263

17-2   Telephony Protocol Types and Codes Used by Telephony Devices 266

17-3   Display Class Standard Device Descriptor Definition 268

17-4   Mass Storage Class Code and Subclass Code 270

18-1   Definition of Fields (DW0) 282

18-2   Definition of DW1 283

18-3   Definition of DW2 284

18-4   Definition of DW3 285

18-5   Queue Head Link Pointer Definition 286

18-6   Queue Head Element Link Pointer Definition 286

18-7   UHC I/O Registers 287

19-1   Definition of Endpoint Descriptor Fields (DW0) 295

19-2   Definition of Endpoint Descriptor Fields (DW1) 296

19-3   Definition of Endpoint Descriptor Fields (DW2) 297

19-4   Definition of Endpoint Descriptor Fields (DW3) 297

19-5   Definition of Transfer Descriptor Fields (DW0) 299

19-6   Definition of Transfer Descriptor Fields (DW1) 300

19-7   Definition of Transfer Descriptor Fields (DW2) 300

19-8   Definition of Transfer Descriptor Fields (DW3) 300

19-9   Definition of Isochronous Transfer Descriptor Field (DW0) 302

19-10 Definition of Isochronous Transfer Descriptor Fields (DW1) 303

19-11 Definition of Isochronous Transfer Descriptor Fields (DW2) 303

19-12 Definition of Isochronous Transfer Descriptor Fields (DW3) 304

19-13 Definition of Isochronous Transfer Descriptor Fields (DW4-7) 304

Acknowledgments

Thanks to the engineers who attended MindShare's USB pilot courses. Their suggestions and insight were invaluable. Thanks also to Don Coston for his contributions and to Kathleen Tibbetts, our editor at Addison-Wesley, who has been extremely patient and supportive during the long writing process.

Special thanks to Tom and Nancy Shanley for their friendship and support.

About This Book

The MindShare Architecture Series

The MindShare Architecture book series includes: *ISA System Architecture, EISA System Architecture, 80486 System Architecture, PCI System Architecture, Pentium System Architecture, PCMCIA System Architecture, PowerPC System Architecture, Plug-and-Play System Architecture, CardBus System Architecture, Protected Mode Software Architecture, Pentium Pro System Architecture,* and *USB System Architecture.* The book series is published by Addison-Wesley.

Rather than duplicating common information in each book, the series uses the building-block approach. *ISA System Architecture* is the core book upon which the others build. The figure below illustrates the relationship of the books to each other.

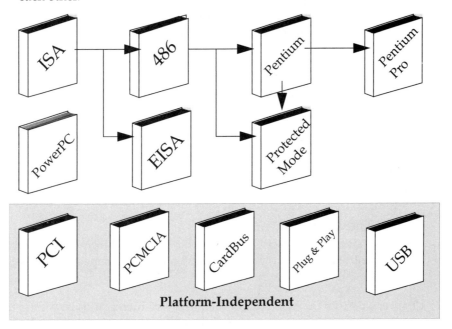

Cautionary Note

The reader should keep in mind that MindShare's book series often deals with rapidly-evolving technologies. This being the case, it should be recognized that the book is a "snapshot" of the state of the targeted technology at the time that the book was completed. We attempt to update each book on a timely basis to reflect changes in the targeted technology, but, due to various factors (waiting for the next version of the spec to be "frozen," the time necessary to make the changes, and the time to produce the books and get them out to the distribution channels), there will always be a delay.

Organization of This Book

The book is divided into seven parts and contains the chapters listed below:

Part I: The Emergence of USB

Part I discusses the need for and origins of USB, including potential solutions. It also provides a brief introduction to USB.

Chapter 1 describes how current PC peripherals are designed and how software typically interacts with these devices. This discussion points out the shortcomings associated with existing PC I/O paradigm and describes attributes of the ideal solution.

Chapter 2 describes the rationale for establishing USB as the solution to address the shortcomings of the existing PC I/O implementations. This chapter analyzes the possible solutions that are based on existing or emerging standards, and introduces USB.

Part II: The USB Solution

Part II introduces and describes the USB hardware and introduces the role of USB host software. The physical, electrical, and logical aspects of USB are discussed.

Chapter 3 defines the USB environment by introducing and describing the key hardware and software elements and the interaction between them. It defines the USB topology, bus speed and communications model, and introduces the USB devices descriptors.

Chapter 4 describes the physical environment, including the cables and connectors defined by the USB specification.

Chapter 5 discusses the signaling environment used by USB. This chapter explains the rationale behind USB's differential pair signaling and NRZI encoding mechanisms and discusses their operation. This chapter also discusses maximum cable length, cable delay, and other pertinent electrical constraints. The appendix contains a reference listing of the electrical specifications.

Chapter 6 covers the nature of USB transfers. Frame based transfers are described, along with the transfer types supported and the related applications that use each transfer type.

Chapter 7 details individual transactions that comprise the transfer types discussed in Chapter six. It defines the various packet types and how they are used to perform the requested transfers.

Chapter 8 focuses on the error detection and recovery supported by USB. Each transfer type is discussed and the error detection and correction mechanism is defined for each type.

Chapter 9 discusses both bus-powered and self-powered USB hubs and devices. Power distribution via the USB bus is also discussed. This chapter also discusses power conservation techniques employed by USB. Namely, the suspend mode defined by the USB specification and its operation.

Chapter 10 USB devices support power conservation by entering their suspend state. Chapter ten discusses the USB implementation of power management.

Part III: USB Configuration

Part III of the book details the automatic configuration process. It describes the hardware and software interaction required to recognize and configure USB hubs and devices. It details the device descriptor structures and describes how host software utilizes the descriptor information to establish transfers to/from a USB device.

Chapter 11 overviews the USB configuration process by reviewing the steps that take place when the system boots and when a device is determined to be attached to the USB bus. The hardware and software actions are described to provide an overall view of the configuration procedures.

Chapter 12 focuses the hub configuration process. Hub descriptors are detailed along with the action taken by software to configure hubs.

Chapter 13 discusses the standard USB requests used to configure hubs and also details the hub class requests used to access hubs to detect the attachment or detachment of devices and control hub port features.

Chapter 14 focuses on non-hub device configuration. The process of detecting and configuring USB devices is detailed. This chapter also defines the descriptors included within USB devices to describe themselves to the host system. The various states that a device may go through from attachment to the point it is ready to be used are also defined.

Chapter 15 discusses the standard USB requests that are used to detect the attachment or detachment of devices, and for configuring and accessing devices.

Part IV: USB Host Software

This part of the book reviews the role of the USB host software and discusses the specific requirements of the USB Driver software and the Host Controller Driver.

Chapter 16 discusses the three types of USB host software components: the USB Device Drivers, the USB Driver, and the Host Controller Driver. This chapter discusses the role of each software layers and describes the requirements of their programming interface.

Part V: USB Device Class

Part V discusses the device class definitions.

Chapter 17 introduces the concept of device classes and discusses their role within the USB. The device class discussion provides the reader with a sense of the information defined for each class and the USB mechanisms that they use.

Part VI: Host Controllers and Hub: Example Implementations

This part of the book provides example solutions for the USB host controller/ root hub and includes an example implementation of a standard hub.

Chapter 18 defines the implementation of the Universal HCI. It details the programming interface and the mechanisms used to generate transactions over the USB. It also describes the interaction between the Universal HCI driver and controller.

Chapter 19 defines the implementation of Open HCI. It details the programming interface and the mechanisms used to generate transactions over the USB. It also describes the interaction between the Open HCI driver and controller.

Chapter 20 discusses the implementation of the Texas Instruments TUSB2040 hub.

Who This Book Is For

This book is intended for use by hardware and software design and support personnel. Due to the clear, concise explanatory methods used to describe each subject, personnel outside of the design field may also find the text useful.

Prerequisite Knowledge

The reader should be familiar with PC architectures and legacy hardware and software issues. MindShare's *ISA System Architecture* book provides foundation material that describes the legacy issues.

Documentation Conventions

This document contains conventions for numeric values as follows.

Hexadecimal Notation

This section defines the typographical convention used throughout this book. All hex numbers are followed by an "h." Examples:

```
9A4Eh
0100h
```

Binary Notation

All binary numbers are followed by a "b." Examples:

```
0001 0101b
01b
```

Decimal Notation

Numbers without any suffix are decimal. When required for clarity, decimal numbers are followed by a "d." The following examples each represent a decimal number:

```
16
255
256d
128d
```

Bits Versus Byte Notation

The Univeral Serial Bus as its name implies transmits serial data, resulting in numerous discussions of bit-related issues. This book employs the standard notation for differentiating bits versus bytes as follows.

All abbreviations for "bits" use lower case. For example:

1.5Mb/s
2Mb

All references to "bytes" are specified in upper case. For example:

10MB/s
1KB

Identification of Bit Fields (logical groups of bits or signals)

All bit fields are designated in little-endian bit ordering as follows:

[X:Y],

where "X" is the most-significant bit and "Y" is the least-significant bit of the field.

Visit Our Web Page

Our web site contains a listing of all of our courses and books. In addition, it contains errata for a number of the books, a hot link to our publisher's web site, as well as course outlines.

www.mindshare.com

Our publisher's web page contains a listing of our currently-available books and includes pricing and ordering information. Their home page is accessible at:

www.aw.com/devpress/

We Want Your Feedback

MindShare values your comments and suggestions. You can contact us via mail, phone, fax or internet email.

Phone: (972) 231-2216 and, in the U.S., (800) 633-1440

Fax: (972) 783-4715

E-mail: mindshar@interserv.com

For information on MindShare seminars, please check our web site.

Mailing Address:

MindShare, Inc.
2202 Buttercup Drive
Richardson, Texas 75082

Part I

The Emergence
of USB

1 *The Need for USB*

This Chapter

Most PCs designed today still implement peripheral devices based on interfaces used in the original IBM PC designs of the early 1980s. These implementations have numerous shortcomings that cause both designers and users considerable frustration. This chapter reviews these shortcomings, many of which led directly to the need for a better solution for attaching peripherals.

The Next Chapter

The next chapter discusses the possible solutions to the peripheral attachment problems discussed in this chapter and introduces the USB solution.

Shortcomings of the Existing PC IO Paradigm

USB emerged as a result of the difficulties associated with the cost, configuration, and attachment of peripheral devices in the personal computer environment. In short, USB creates a method of attaching and accessing peripheral devices that reduces overall cost, simplifies the attachment and configuration from the end-user perspective, and solves several technical issues associated with old style peripherals. The following sections detail the various problems associated with PC peripherals today and investigate the challenges that the USB standard faces.

Technical Issues

Figure 1-1 on page 12 illustrates the legacy IO paradigm where peripheral devices were typically mapped into the CPU's IO address space and assigned a specific IRQ line, and in some cases a DMA channel. These system resources were assigned to particular peripheral devices by IBM and other manufacturers and became the standard IO locations, IRQs, and DMA channels used by software developers to access a given device.

As illustrated in Figure 1-1, peripheral devices consume many system resources in the PC environment, making many of the system resources scarce and conflict free configuration a real challenge.

Figure 1-1: System Resources Used by Legacy Peripheral Devices

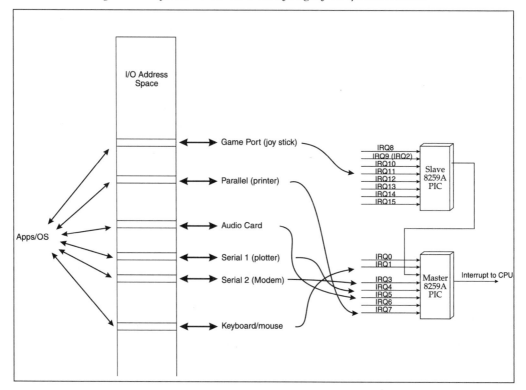

Interrupts

Perhaps the most critical system resource problem revolves around the allocation of interrupts required by the myriad of devices that are typically implemented in PCs. This is particularly true of peripheral devices that attach via the ISA bus, since the ISA bus does not reliably support sharable interrupts. Table 1-1 lists each IRQ line and the devices that typically use them. As can be seen many of the IRQ lines are dedicated to particular devices based on legacy conventions, while other IRQ lines may be used by a variety of peripheral devices. In PCI-based systems that also contain an ISA or EISA bus, the interrupt shortage can become a major problem, because several of the IRQ lines ideally should be left available for ISA expansion cards that might require them.

Table 1-1: Typical Legacy Interrupt Lines used by Standard Devices

IRQ Line	Devices
IRQ0	system timer (dedicated on system board)
IRQ1	keyboard (dedicated on system board0
IRQ2	cascade channel for slave interrupt controller (not available for peripheral devices)
IRQ3	serial mouse, modem, plotter, serial printer, game port, pen, Infrared port
IRQ4	serial mouse, modem, plotter, serial printer
IRQ5	bus mouse, parallel printer, sound card, LAN adapter, tape drive, game port
IRQ6	floppy drive
IRQ7	parallel printer
IRQ8	RTC Alarm (dedicated on system board)
IRQ9	LAN adapter, video adapter, tape drive, game port,
IRQ10	LAN adapter, sound card
IRQ11	LAN adapter, SCSI controller, PCMCIA controller
IRQ12	PS/2 mouse, PCMCIA controller
IRQ13	numeric coprocessor errors (dedicated on system board)
IRQ14	hard drive
IRQ15	SCSI controller, PCMCIA controller

IO Addresses

IO address conflicts are also quite common in the PC environment. Note that Peripheral devices usually require a block of IO address locations to report status information and to issue commands to the device. While its true that x86 processors have the ability to access 64KB of IO address locations (more than enough for all peripheral devices), legacy ISA expansion cards typically decode only 10 of the 16 address lines available. This yields a maximum 1KB block of address space that is usable by ISA expansion devices. Furthermore, the limited decode creates the well known aliasing effect that renders the upper 768 bytes of each aligned 1KB of IO space unusable by other devices. See MindShare's *ISA System Architecture* book, published by Addison-Wesley, for details.

Non-Shareable Interfaces

Standard PC peripheral interfaces (e.g., serial and parallel connections) support the attachment of a single device. Since only one peripheral device can be attached at any given time, the flexibility of such connections is minimized. This limitation frequently leads to the costly decision of building an expansion card that plugs into an expansion bus (e.g., ISA/EISA or PCI) to create an attachment point for a new peripheral design.

End User Concerns

End users are faced with a variety of problems when connecting peripheral to their PCs as discussed in the following sections.

Cable Crazed

Dedicated cables are required for the mouse, keyboard, printer, external modem, Zip drive, plotter, etc. most of which are completely different. Figure Figure 1-2 on page 15 illustrates the backplane of a typical PC before USB. The variety of different connectors and cables required to connect particular peripheral devices makes many users a little crazy.

Figure 1-2: Connectors at Backplane

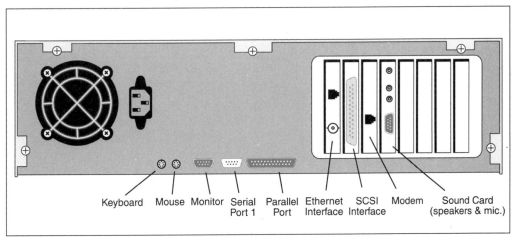

Installation and Configuration of Expansion Cards

When peripherals are purchased many of them require the installation of expansion cards. This of course may involved removing the cover of the PC (#!*&%^! it still won't come off. Go get me that **big** screw driver), setting the switches and jumpers to configure the card (what the heck does 03F8h mean?), inserting the card, and replacing the cover. The trouble only begins there. Once the system is powered up the software for this device may have to be installed from diskette, which can also be a frustrating process for novice and experienced user alike. After all this the device may or may not work due to hardware or software conflicts.

No Hot Attachment of Peripheral

Ever forget to plug in your mouse before powering up your system? After the boot process completes, your mouse of course won't work. Time to reboot! Since software checks for the presence of hardware and installs software for only those devices it detects, most peripheral devices are not usable without rebooting the system so that software can detect the device just attached and load the necessary software to access it.

When a device is attached the user is also faced with having to install new software and restart the system. In the process, system resources must be selected and assigned to the new device (e.g., IO space, IRQ line, and DMA channel) in order for them to work correctly, and ensure that the resource selected is not already being used by another device in the system.

Cost

The cost of implementing systems and peripheral devices based on the original PC design is fairly expensive due to the high cost of the standard peripheral connectors and associated cables. Since most of the standard connectors on the PC are already used by a wide variety of peripheral devices, it may be necessary to build an expansion card to provide a way to attach your peripheral device to the system, making the solution quite costly.

The next chapter reviews the possible solutions to solve these problems.

2 *Solutions*

The Previous Chapter

The first chapter identifies the problems associated with attaching peripheral devices in PCs before the advent of USB. It also identifies the features that a new method of attaching peripheral devices should include.

This Chapter

This chapter discusses the potential solutions that would satisfy the requirements of a new peripheral attachment mechanism for the PC environment.

The Next Chapter

The next chapter provides an overview of the USB environment. It defines the USB communications model and describes all the hardware and software elements in a USB implementation and describes the interaction between each element.

Design Goals

The design goals of a new peripheral attachment scheme should overcome the existing shortcoming perceived by manufacturers and users, while providing for further growth and expansion. The shortcomings are summarized below:

Challenges of the New Solution

A new solution should clearly be designed to overcome the perceived shortcomings and to provide new capabilities. As a result, the design goals include:

- a single connector type to connect any PC peripheral
- ability to attach many peripheral devices to the same connector
- a method of easing the system resource conflicts
- automatic detection and configuration of peripheral devices

- low cost solution for both system and peripheral implementations
- enhanced performance capability
- support for attaching new peripheral designs
- support for legacy hardware and software
- low power implementation

The design goals are discussed in the following sections.

Enhanced System Performance

A new standard that replaces legacy peripheral devices should provide improved system performance. Many systems based on the PCI bus suffer performance problems when accessing legacy peripheral devices that reside on the ISA bus. USB peripheral devices provide ample performance without adversely affecting the overall performance of the system.

Plug and Play Support

Automatic configuration is crucial to satisfying end user requirements. The new solution should eliminate the need to set switches and jumpers to configure the device and should eliminate the need to install software when a new peripheral device is attached. The device should simply be attached by the user and be ready for immediate use.

Hot Attachment

When most legacy IO devices are attached to the system, they will not work without first restarting the system. Restarting the system is required so that the new peripheral can be detected by software. The new solution should provide a method of detecting that a new peripheral has been attached and automatically install the relevant software needed to access the device.

Room for Growth/Expandability

The new solution should provide for additional growth to support a whole new generation of peripheral devices. Support should be provided to ease the implementation of telephony into the PC. The new solution should also provide flexibility for newer "smart" peripheral devices: interactive peripherals (e.g., games), home automation, digital audio, telephony, compressed video, etc.

Legacy Hardware/Software Support

Support should also be added for legacy hardware and software. Applications that communicate with old style legacy peripherals should continue working with the newer peripherals. Support must also be maintained for older style legacy peripherals to smooth the transition to the new implementation.

Older operating systems will have no knowledge of USB, nor will the applications designed for the systems. The choice may be to discontinue support of older operating systems such as DOS on new machines that implement the USB solution. Alternatively, USB support may be added with newer versions of such operating systems of USB support may be added via installable devices drivers.

Low Cost

A new method of attaching peripherals should provide the above features, but should not significantly increase the cost of peripheral devices, nor the cost of the system. For example, if the cost of a legacy mouse is appreciably less expensive than a USB mouse, users would likely reject the USB keyboard solution.

Analysis of Potential Solutions

Numerous solutions exist that might satisfy the requirements of a new method for attaching and accessing peripheral devices. The following sections briefly discuss various options that might be used. Presuming that all other features are supported by each solution and are more or less equal, a major factor in selecting a solution lies in evaluating cost versus performance. The range of applications that a new solution supports can be grouped as shown in Table 2-1. This table shows that some peripheral devices require little bandwidth, while others such as disk drives and video applications require considerably more.

Table 2-1: Applications, Relative Performance Required and Desired Attributes

Performance	Applications	Attributes
Low Speed: Interactive Devices 10-100 Kb/s	Keyboard, Mouse Stylus Game peripherals VR peripherals Monitor configuration	Lower cost Hot plug-unplug Ease of use Multiple peripherals
Medium Speed: Phone, Audio 500-10,000 Kb/s	ISDN PBX POTS Digital Audio Scanner/Printer	Low cost Ease of use Guaranteed latency Guaranteed Bandwidth Dynamic Attach/Detach Multiple devices
High Speed: Video, Disk, Lan 25-500 Mb/s	Desktop Hard Disk Drive Video Conferencing PnP LAN	High Bandwidth Guaranteed latency Ease of use

Table 2-2 lists possible solutions and compares performance versus cost.

Table 2-2: Various Solutions with Relative Performance and Complexity

Bus Name	Data Rate	Host Complexity	Peripheral Complexity
Access.bus	100 Kb/s	Simple HW or SW UART	Simple HW or SW UART
GeoPort	2.048 Mb/s	SCC USART	SCC USART
IEEE 1394 (Firewire)	400 Mb/s	12,000 - 20,000 gates	5,000 - 7,000 gates
USB	12 Mb/s	10,000 gates	1,500 - 2,000 gates

Access Bus

The host and peripheral complexity are extremely low, making the cost very reasonable. However, the lower bandwidth of 100Kb/second making this solution too slow to support all the desired peripheral devices.

GeoPort

The GeoPort is a proprietary solution implemented in Apple Computers. GeoPort is focused solely on telecommunications and does not support the range of PC peripheral desired.

IEEE 1394

This solution, commonly referred to as Firewire, provides ample bandwidth to accommodate all peripheral applications. However, the associated complexity makes cost undesirable, particularly when implementing the low performance/ low cost peripherals.

USB - The Right Balance

The Universal Serial Bus (USB) creates a solution for attaching PC peripherals that balances performance and cost. Devices attached to USB ports can incorporate additional connections for attaching other USB devices as illustrated in Figure 2-1 on page 22. These additional connections are provided via a USB hub. Hubs can be stand-alone devices, or can be integrated into other USB peripherals such as printers or keyboards.

Figure 2-1: USB Device Connections

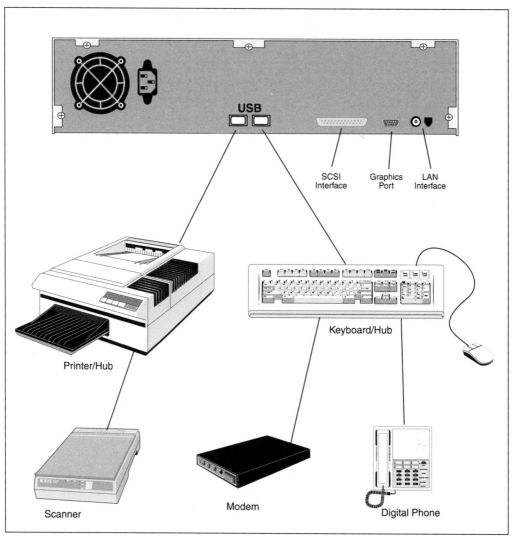

Table 2-3 lists the key features that comprise the USB implementation.

Table 2-3: Key USB Features

Feature	Description
Low Cost	The USB provides a low cost solution for attaching peripheral devices to PCs.
Hot Pluggable	Device attachment is automatically detected by the USB and software automatically configures the device for immediate use, without user intervention.
Single Connector Type	The USB defines a single connector used to attach any USB device. Additional connectors can be added with USB hubs.
127 Devices	Supports the attachment of 127 devices per USB.
Low Speed or Full Speed Devices	The USB supports two device speeds: 1.5Mb/s and 12Mb/s. The lower speed makes it possible to implement low speed/low cost USB devices. This is due to the reduced cost of the speed cables that can be designed without shielding.
Cable Power	Peripheral can be powered directly from the cable. 5.0vdc power is available from the cable. The current available can vary from 100ma - 500ma depending on the hub port.
System Resource Requirement Eliminated	USB devices, unlike their ISA, EISA, and PCI cousins require no memory or IO address space and need no IRQ lines.
Error Detection and Recovery	USB transactions include error detection mechanisms that are used to ensure that data is delivered without error. In the event of errors, transactions can be retried.
Power Conservation	USB devices automatically enter a suspend state after 3ms of no bus activity. During suspend devices can consume no more than 500µa of current.
Support for four types of transfers	The USB defines four different transfer types to support different transfer characteristics required by devices. Transfer types include: Bulk, Isochronous, Interrupt, and Control transfers.

USB System Architecture

The USB Paradigm

USB breaks away from the resource problems associated with legacy PC IO implementations. The resource constraints related to IO address space, IRQ lines, and DMA channels no longer exist with the USB implementation. Each device residing on the USB is assigned an address known only to the USB subsystem and does not consume any system resources. USB supports up to 127 addresses which limits the number of USB devices supported in a single USB implementation. USB devices typically contain a number of individual registers or ports that can be indirectly accessed by USB device drivers. These registers are known as USB device endpoints.

When a transaction is sent over the USB, all devices (except low speed devices) will see the transaction. Each transaction begins with a packet transmission that defines the type of transaction being performed along with the USB device and endpoint addresses. This addressing is managed by USB software, and other non-USB devices and related software within the system are not impacted by these addresses.

Every USB device must have an endpoint address zero that is reserved for configuration. Via endpoint zero, USB system software accesses USB device descriptors from the device. These descriptors provide information necessary for identifying the device, specifying the number of endpoints, and the purpose of each. In this manner, system software can detect the device type or class and determine how the device is intended to be accessed.

How to Get the USB Specifications

The USB specifications are available from the USB web site at:

www.usb.org

This web site has the 1.0 version of the USB specification and the Device Class specifications, along with other information related to USB.

Part II

The USB Solution

3 *The Big Picture*

The Previous Chapter

The previous chapter introduced the basic design goals needed to overcome the problems of legacy implementations and discussed the possible solutions. The USB solution was also introduced and its key features described.

This Chapter

This chapter provides an overview of the primary concepts of USB transfers and describes the interaction between USB system software, system hardware, and USB devices. The USB communications process is described, including the concept of the device framework. Each hardware and software element in a USB system is introduced and its primary functions are described.

The Next Chapter

USB defines a single connector type for attaching all USB peripherals to the host system. The next chapter describes the physical aspects of USB connectors and cables.

Overview

Figure 3-1 on page 28 provides a system view of USB implemented in a PCI-based system. The USB host controller residing on the PCI bus fetches a transaction list that describes the USB transactions that have been scheduled by system software for delivery over the USB. The host controller executes the transaction list by performing each transaction described in the list. This chapter provides an overview of the communications process and subsequent chapters detail the mechanisms and processes employed by the USB.

USB System Architecture

Figure 3-1: USB System Implemented in a PCI-based Platform

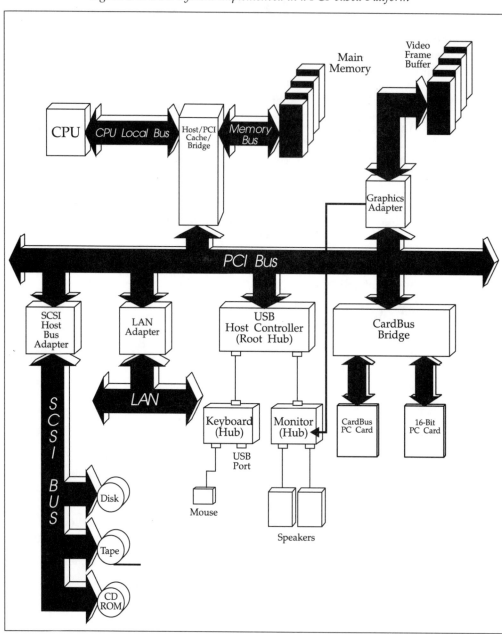

The Players

Figure 3-2 on page 30 illustrates the hardware and software elements involved in the USB system. All USB transactions are initiated by USB software. These accesses are typically originated by a USB device driver that wants to communicate with its device. The USB driver provides the interface between USB device driver and the USB host controller. This software is responsible for translating client requests into one or more transactions that are directed to or from a target USB device.

The primary hardware and software elements associated with a USB solution includes:

- USB Hardware
  - USB Host Controller/Root Hub
  - USB Hubs
  - USB Devices

- USB Software
  - USB Device Drivers
  - USB Driver
  - Host Controller Driver

The following sections describe the role of each component involved in USB transfers. Refer to Figure 3-2 on page 30 during the following discussions. More detail regarding the role of each hardware and software component can be found in subsequent chapters.

Figure 3-2: Communication Flow in a USB System

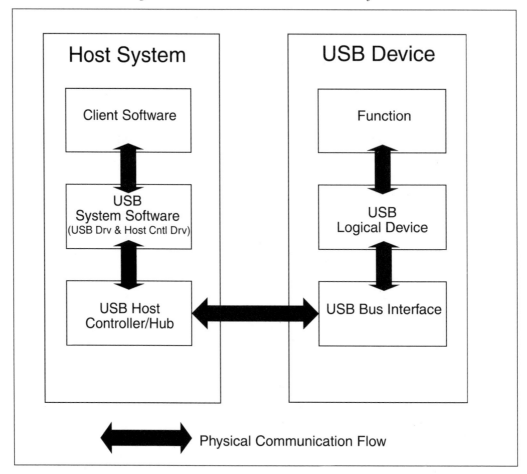

USB Device Drivers

USB device drivers (or client drivers) issue requests to the USB driver via IO Request Packets (IRPs). These IRPs initiate a given transfer to or from a target USB device. For example, a USB keyboard driver must initiate an interrupt transfer by establishing an IRP and supplying a memory buffer into which data will be returned from the USB keyboard. Note that the client driver has no knowledge of the USB serial transfer mechanisms.

USB Driver

The USB driver knows the characteristics of the USB target device and how to communicate with the device via the USB. The USB characteristics are detected by the USB driver when it parses the device descriptors during device configuration. For example, some devices require a specific amount of throughput during each frame, while others may only require periodic access every nth frame.

When an IRP is received from a USB client driver, the USB driver organizes the request into individual transactions that will be executed during a series of 1ms frames. The USB driver sets up the transactions based on its knowledge of the USB device requirements, the needs of the client driver, and the limitations/ capabilities of the USB.

Depending on the operating environment, the USB driver may be shipped along with the operating system or added as an extension via a loadable device driver.

USB Host Controller Driver

The USB host controller driver (HCD) schedules transactions to be broadcast over the USB. Transactions are scheduled by the host controller driver by building a series of transaction lists. Each list consists of pending transactions targeted for one or more of the USB devices attached to the bus. A transaction list, or frame list, defines the sequence of transactions to be performed during each 1ms frame. The USB host controller executes these transaction lists at 1ms intervals. Note that a single block transfer requested by a USB client may be performed as a series of transactions that are scheduled and executed during consecutive 1ms frames. The actual scheduling depends on a variety of factors including; the type of transaction, transfer requirements specified by the device, and the transaction traffic of other USB devices.

The USB host controller initiates transactions via its root hub or hubs. Each 1ms frame begins with a start of frame (SOF) transaction and is followed by the serial broadcast of all transactions contained within the current list. For example, if one of the requested transactions is a request to transfer data to a USB printer, the host controller would obtain the data to be sent from a memory buffer supplied by the client software and transmit the data over the USB. The hub portion of the controller converts the requested transactions into the low level protocols required by the USB.

USB Host Controller/Root Hub

All communication on USB originates at the host under software control. The host hardware consists the USB host controller, which initiates transactions over the USB system, and the root hub, which provides attachment points (or ports) for USB devices. Two USB host controller designs have been developed:

- Open Host Controller (OHC)
- Universal Host Controller (UHC)

Each of these controllers perform the same basic job although in slightly different ways. Chapter 19 and Chapter 18 respectively discuss the operation of the host controllers.

The Host Controller

The host controller is responsible for generating the transactions that have been scheduled by the host software. The host controller driver, or HCD, software builds a linked list of data structures in memory that defines the transactions that are scheduled to be performed during a given frame. These data structures, called transfer descriptors, contain all of the information the host controller needs to generate the transactions. This information includes:

- USB Device Address
- Type of Transfer
- Direction of Transfer
- Address of Device Driver's Memory Buffer

The host controller performs writes to a target device by reading data from a memory buffer (supplied by the USB device driver) that is to be delivered to the target device. The host controller performs a parallel to serial conversion on the data, creates the USB transaction, and forwards it to the root hub to send over the bus.

If a read transfer is required, the host controller builds the read transaction and sends it to the root hub. The hub transmits the read transaction over the USB. The target device recognizes that it is being addressed and that data is being requested. The device then transmits data back to the root hub, which forwards the data on to the host controller. The host controller performs the serial to parallel conversion on the data and transfers the data to the device driver's memory buffer.

Note that the USB root hub and target devices perform error checks during a transaction. Errors detected are recognized by the root hub, forwarded to the host controller to be logged and reported to the host software.

The Root Hub

Transactions generated by the host controller are forwarded to the root hub to be transmitted to the USB. Consequently, every USB transaction originates at the root hub. The root hub provides the connection points for USB devices and performs the following key operations:

- controls power to its USB ports
- enables and disables ports
- recognizes devices attached to each ports
- sets and reports status events associated with each port (when polled by host software)

The root hub consists of a hub controller and repeater as illustrated in Figure 3-3 on page 34. The hub controller responds to accesses made to the hub itself. For example, requests by the host software to apply or remove power to a port. The repeater forwards transactions to and from the USB and the host controller.

Figure 3-3: Block Diagram of Major Root Hub Functions

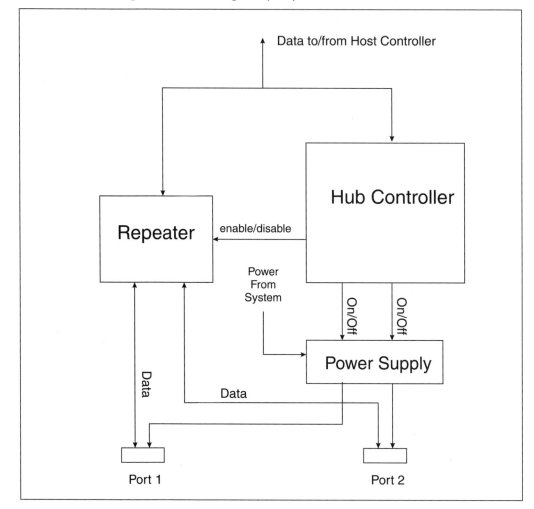

USB Hubs

In addition to the root hub, USB systems support additional hubs that permit extension of the USB system by providing one or more USB ports for attaching other USB devices. USB hubs may be integrated into devices such as keyboards or monitors (called compound devices), or implemented as stand-alone devices as illustrated in Figure 3-4. Furthermore, hubs may be bus powered (i.e. derive power for itself and all attached devices from the USB bus) or may be self-powered. Bus powered hubs are limited by the amount of power available from the bus and can therefore support a maximum of four USB ports. Chapter 9 discusses USB power issues.

Figure 3-4: USB Hub Types

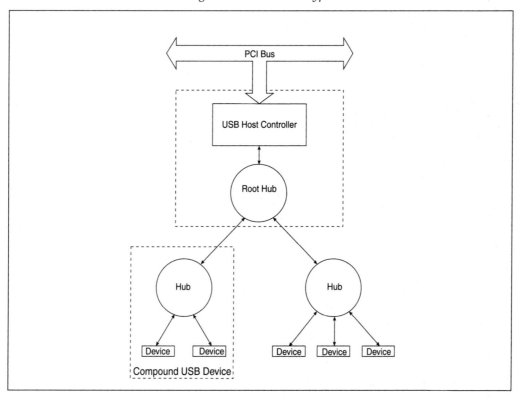

Hubs contain two major functional elements:

- hub controller
- repeater

Figure 3-5 on page 36 illustrates these functions.

Figure 3-5: Primary Hub Functions

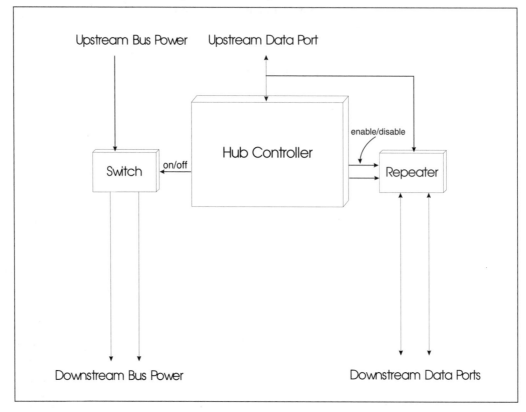

Hub Controller

The hub controller contains a USB interface, or serial interface engine (SIE). It also contains the descriptors that software reads to identify the device as a hub. The hub controller gathers hub and port status information also read by the USB host software to detect the connection and removal of devices and to determine other status information. The controller also receives commands from host software to control various aspects of the hub's operation (e.g., powering and enabling the ports).

Hub Repeater

Refer to Figure 3-6. Bus traffic arriving at the hub must be forwarded on in either the upstream (toward the host) or downstream (away from the host) direction. Transmissions originating at the host will arrive on the hub's root port and must be forwarded to all enabled ports. When a target device responds to a host-initiated transaction it must transmit a response upstream, which the hub must forward from the downstream port to the root port.

Figure 3-6: Hub Repeater Performing Downstream and Upstream Connectivity

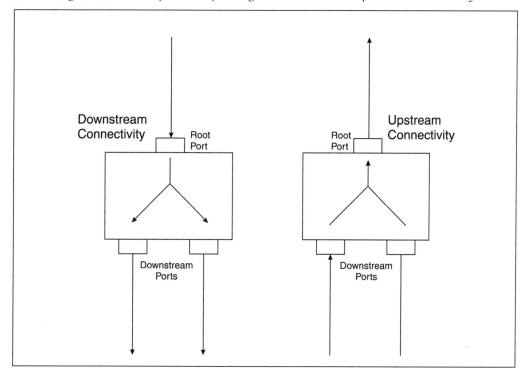

Hub's Role in Configuration

Hubs also play a pivotal role in the hot attachment/detachment (automatic detection and configuration during runtime) of USB devices. Hubs must recognize that a device has been attached or detached and report the event when host software polls the hub.

USB Devices

USB devices contain descriptors that specify a given devices attributes and characteristics. This information specifies to host software a variety of features and capabilities that are needed to configure the device and to locate the USB client software driver. The USB device driver may also use device descriptors to determine additional information needed to access the device in the proper fashion. This mechanism is referred to as the Device Framework and must be understood by software in order to configure and access the device correctly. See the section entitled, "Device Framework" on page 47 for a more complete discussion.

As mentioned previously, USB devices can be implemented either as full-speed or low-speed devices.

High-Speed Devices

High-speed devices see all transactions broadcast over the USB and can be implemented as full-feature devices. These devices accept and send serial data at the maximim 12Mb/s rate.

Low-Speed Devices

Low-speed devices are limited in not only throughput (1.5Mb/s) but feature support. Furthermore, low-speed devices only see USB transactions that follow a preamble packet. Low-speed hub ports remain disabled during full-speed transactions, preventing full-speed bus traffic from being sent over low-speed cables. Preamble packets specify that the following transaction will be broadcast at low speed. Hubs enable their low-speed ports after detecting a preamble packet, permitting low-speed devices to see the low-speed bus activity.

USB Communications Model

Unlike devices that reside on other common bus structures, USB devices do not directly consume system resources. That is, USB devices are not mapped into memory or IO address space, nor do they use IRQ lines or DMA channels. Furthermore, all transactions originate from the host system. The only system resources required by a USB system are the memory locations used by USB system software and the memory and/or IO address space and IRQ line used by the USB host controller. This eliminates much of the difficulty encountered with standard peripheral implementations that require a considerable amount of IO space and a large number of interrupt lines.

Communications Flow

Figure 3-7 on page 40 illustrates the basic communication flow and the system resources used by USB systems. The USB client initiates a transfer when it calls USB system software and requests a transfer. USB client drivers supply a memory buffer used to store data when transferring data to or from the USB device. Each transfer between a given register (or endpoint) within a USB device and the client driver occurs via a communication pipe that USB system software establishes during device configuration. USB system software splits the client's request into individual transactions that are consistent with the bus bandwidth requirements of the device and the USB protocol mechanisms.

The requests are passed to the USB Host Controller Driver which in turn schedules the transaction to be performed over the USB. The host controller performs the transaction based on the contents of a transfer descriptor that is built by the HCD. The HCD knows all the information necessary to perform the required transaction via the USB. The key information contained within a transfer descriptor includes:

- Address of the target USB device
- Type of transfer to be performed
- Size of the data packet
- Location of the client's memory buffer

The host controller may have registers that are mapped into the processor's IO or memory address space. These registers control the operation of the host controller and must be loaded with values by the HCD to ensure desired operation. For example, a register is loaded with an address pointer that specifies the memory location where the transfer descriptors reside.

The host controller fetches the transfer descriptors that have been built by the host controller driver. Each descriptor defines a given transaction that must be performed to satisfy a client's transfer request. The host controller generates the USB transaction that is specified by each transfer descriptor. Each transaction results in data being transferred either from the client buffer to the USB device or from the device to the buffer depending on the direction of the transfer. When the entire transfer has completed, USB system software notifies the client driver.

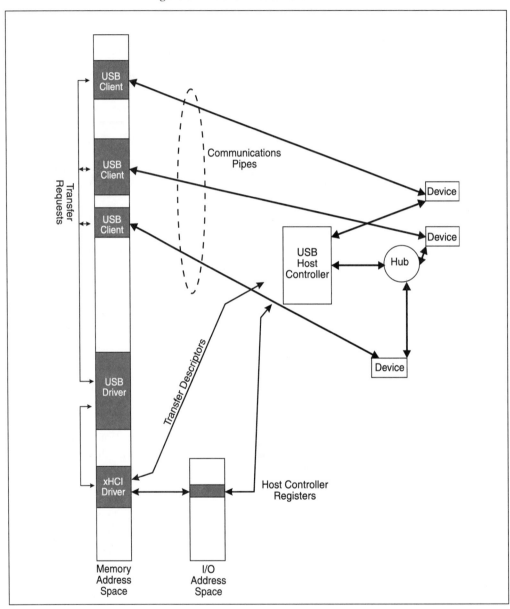

Figure 3-7: The Communications Model

Transfers, IRPs, Frames, and Packets

Figure 3-9 on page 44 illustrates the mechanisms used during the USB communications process and the relationships that exist between each layer of the USB system. Transfers are initiated by the client driver when it issues a transfer request to the USB driver. Ultimately, the transaction is performed via the low-level packetized transactions over the USB. The following sections discuss each layer involved in completing a USB transfer.

Transfers

Each USB function is designed with a collection of registers, or endpoints, used by the client driver when accessing its function. Each endpoint has particular transfer characteristics that is supports. For example, when transferring information to a speaker, the data transfer must continue at a constant data rate to prevent distortion of the audio. Other endpoints may have different characteristics and thus require a different transfer type. The transfer types supported by USB include:

- Isochronous Transfers
- Bulk Transfers
- Interrupt Transfers
- Control Transfers

Client drivers understand the nature of the transfer related to each endpoint associated with its function as does the USB driver. This information is determined by reading descriptors from the device. Chapter 6 describes the unique characteristics of each transfer type.

The USB Driver, IRPs and Frames

When a client driver wishes to perform a transfer to or from a given endpoint, it calls the USB driver to initiate the transfer. The requested transfer is called an IO Request Packet (IRP). Some transfers consist of a large block of data. Since USB is a shared bus (i.e. many device use the same bus at the same time), a single device cannot typically perform an entire block transfer across USB at one time. Rather, a transfer is typically split up and performed in segments (called transactions) over a longer period of time. This ensures that a portion of the USB bandwidth can be allocated for the other USB devices residing on the bus.

USB communication is based on transferring data at regular (1ms) intervals called frames. Each USB device requires a portion of the USB bandwidth be allocated during these 1ms frames. Bandwidth allocation depends on the required throughput of the device (as specified by device descriptors) and the available USB bandwidth not used by other USB devices. As each USB device is attached and configured, system software parses its device descriptors to determine the amount of bus bandwidth it requires. Software checks the remaining bandwidth and if the device's requirements can be satisfied it is configured. If the bandwidth required by the device is not available, due to bus bandwidth already allocated to other devices previously attached, the device will not be configured and the user will be notified.

Figure 3-8 on page 43 illustrates a community of devices attached to the USB and the variety of potential transactions that could be performed during a single 1ms frame. This is a contrived example to illustrate the shared nature of the USB frame. Not every USB device will necessarily transfer data during each frame. For example, host software will poll the keyboard every nth frame to check for keystrokes. Devices are allocated a portion of the overall bus bandwidth that they require during each frame. This will likely result in large bulk transfers, such as print jobs, being split over a fairly large number of 1ms frames. The actual number of frames required depends of the transfer capability of the printer's USB interface, specified limitations placed on bulk transfers, and the amount of bus bandwidth being used by other devices currently installed on the USB.

The Host Controller Driver and Transactions

The host controller driver receives the packet requests from the USB driver and schedules them to be performed during a series of frames. The scheduling order is based on an algorithm defined by the host controller driver. The algorithm is based on USB transfer capabilities and limitations (to be discussed in subsequent chapters).

Scheduling is performed by building a series of data structures (called transfer descriptors) that define each sequential transaction to be performed over the USB. The host controller reads and interprets these transfer descriptors and executes the USB transaction described.

Figure 3-8: USB Devices Performing Transfers during Frame

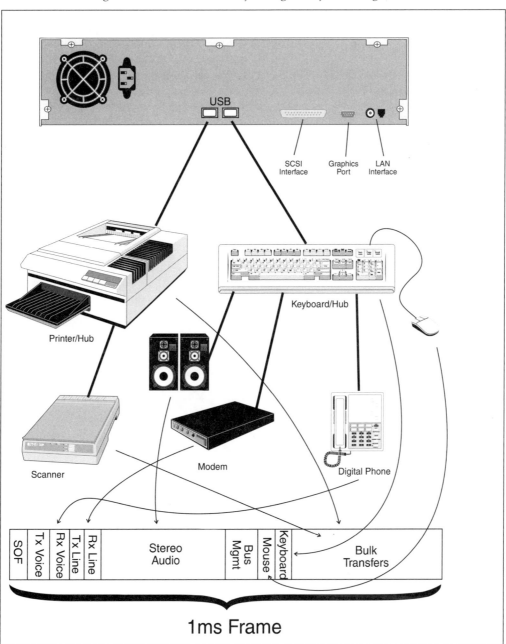

The Host Controller and Packets

The host controller and root hub generates transactions over the USB. Transactions consist of a series of packets that typically include token packets, data packets, and handshake packets. Refer to Chapter 7 for details regarding transactions and packets.

Figure 3-9: Relationship Between IRPs, Transfers, Frames, and Packets

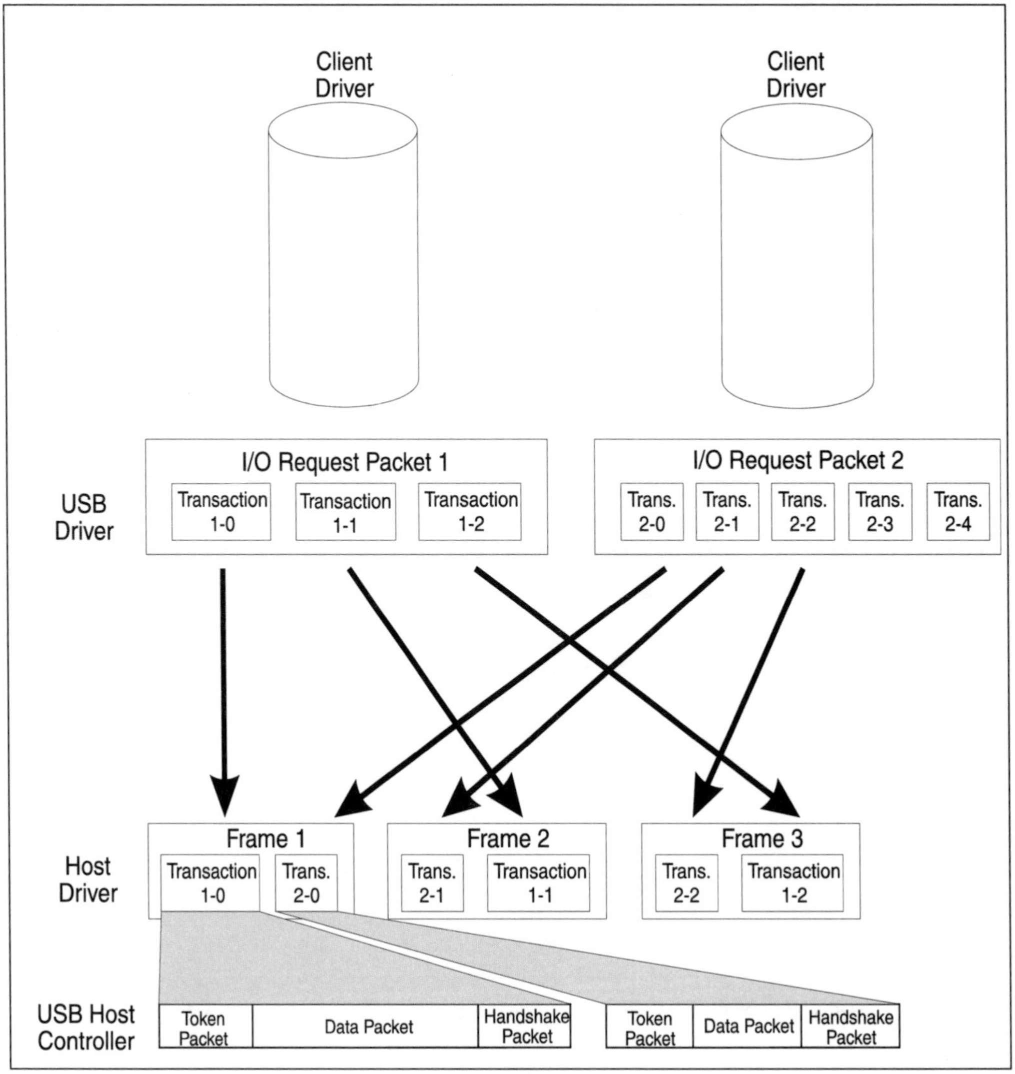

Device Framework (how devices present themselves to software)

USB has been designed to promote class device driver implementations. A set of devices that have similar attributes and services are defined as belonging to a given class of device. These common groupings of devices have a common class driver that can accommodate all devices within the class.

Device Descriptors

A device describes itself to host software via a number of descriptors, illustrated in Figure 3-10 on page 46, These descriptors include:

- Device Descriptor — Each device has a single device descriptor containing information about the default communications pipe that is used to configure the device, along with general information about the device. The device descriptor also identifies the number of possible configurations (one or more) that a device supports.

- Configuration Descriptor — A device has a configuration descriptor for each configuration that it supports. For example, a high-power device may also support a low-power mode, resulting in a configuration descriptor for each power mode. The configuration descriptor includes general information about the configuration and defines the number of interfaces for the device when used in this configuration.

- Interface Descriptor — A given configuration may have one or more interfaces that it supports. An example of a multiple interface device could be a CD-ROM, in which case three device drivers may be used to access the different functional devices. One device driver for the device's mass storage interface (for storing files), one for the audio device (for playing music CDs), and one for the video image driver (for displaying images).

  Interface descriptors provide general information about this interface. It also indicates the class of device supported by this particular interface and specifies the number of endpoint descriptors used when communicating with this interface.

- Endpoint Descriptor — A device interface contains one or more endpoint descriptors, each of which defines a point of communication (e.g., a data register). The endpoint descriptor contains information, such as the transfer type supported by the endpoint (i.e. isochronous, bulk, interrupt, or control), and the maximum transfer rate supported.

- String Descriptors — String descriptors can be defined for the overall device, for a given configuration, and/or for each interface definition. These string descriptors describe the configuration and interfaces in unicode that can be displayed and read by the user.

- Class-specific Descriptors — Some device classes require descriptors beyond the standard descriptors defined by the USB specification. These descriptors are defined by the relevant device class specification.

Figure 3-10 illustrates a set of descriptors. In this example, two separate configurations are defined, each of which include two interface descriptors. This illustration does not show the optional string descriptors, nor does it illustrate any class-specific descriptors that may be required by some device classes.

Figure 3-10: Standard Device Descriptors

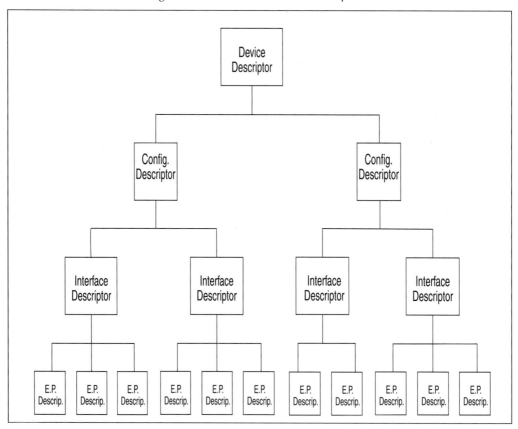

Device Framework

The device framework provides three logical layers that describe the relationship between the host hardware and software, and a corresponding view of each USB device. Figure 3-11 on page 48 illustrates these layers and the relationship between the host and a given USB device. The layered approach helps explain the relationships between each piece of host software and the responsibilities each has in the USB system. The separate layers are provided to ease understanding of the USB communication mechanisms and are discussed in the following sections.

USB Bus Interface Layer

The USB bus interface layer provides the low-level transfer of data over the USB cables. This layer consists of the:

- physical connection
- electrical signaling environment
- packet transfer mechanisms

This layer represents the actual transfer of data across the USB cable between the host system and the USB devices. The host side consists of the USB host controller and root hub, while the USB side consists of the USB interface within the device. Details related to the transfer of data across the USB cable are covered in later chapters.

Figure 3-11: Device Framework — Software's View of Hardware

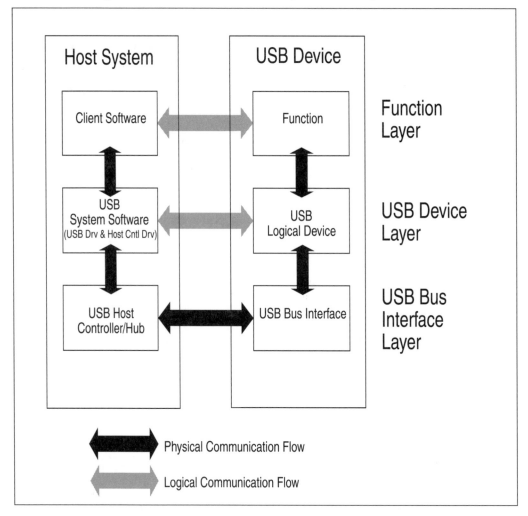

USB Device Layer

The USB device layer represents the portion of USB that comprehends the actual USB communication mechanism and the nature of the transfers required by a USB functional device. This layer consists of USB system software on the host side and a logical view of the USB device on the device side. USB system software views a logical device as a collection of endpoints that comprise a given functional interface.

USB system software provides the services needed to interface client software with its USB function. USB system software has specific knowledge of the USB transfer mechanisms and must allocate bus bandwidth for the community of USB devices. The logical USB device represents the collection of endpoints through which a client communicates with its function. USB system software views these endpoints via the device descriptors, which are parsed by the USB system software to obtain the transfer characteristics of a given device. These characteristics in conjunction with system software's knowledge of the USB transfer mechanisms permit bus bandwidth to be reserved for each functional device as it's configured.

USB System software performs a variety of key functions including:

- Device attachment/detachment detection
- Device configuration
- Bandwidth allocation
- Managing control flow between client and device
- Managing data flow between client and device
- Collecting status and transaction statistics
- Transaction scheduling
- Controlling the electrical interface (e.g. limited cable power management)

Note that one set of USB system software exists in the system to manage accesses to all USB devices attached to the USB bus. USB System software consists of the following entities:

- USB Driver (USBD) — provides interface and services for client software drivers, allocates bus bandwidth, and manages configuration process.
- USB Host Controller Driver — controls operation of the host controller, schedules transactions, and monitors completion status of transactions.

A brief description of the primary jobs that each perform is also provided. A more comprehensive description of these software layers are provided in Chapter 16, entitled "USB Host Software," on page 245.

Function Layer

This layer represents the relationship between client software and a given device's functional interface. Each interface consists of a particular class of device that a matched class driver is designed to manipulate. USB client software cannot access their function directly as is typically done in other environments (e.g. ISA, PCI, and PCMCIA), since they are not mapped directly into memory and IO address space. Instead USB device drivers must use the USBD programming interface to access their devices.

USB clients view their USB devices as consisting of a given interface, which they know how to manipulate. USB system software must report the interface type and other device characteristics to USB clients.

USB Peripheral Connection

As stated in the previous chapters, USB provides a single type of connector for attaching peripheral to a system. USB also supports two different speeds of USB devices:

- low-speed devices — 1.5Mb (megabits)/second
- high-speed devices — 12Mb/second

All USB devices attach via a USB hub that provides one or more ports. Figure 3-12 on page 51 illustrates a variety of devices attached to USB ports provided by the system. Note that a hub port may have either a full-speed or low-speed device attached. Some devices such as keyboards and mice typically operate at low speed, while other devices such as digital telephones must operate at full speed. Each USB port must support the attachment of both low- and full-speed devices, unless the port has a permanently attached device. A device's speed is detected when it is attached to the hub port. (Refer to Chapter 5, entitled "The Signaling Environment," on page 59 for details.)

When a transaction is initiated by the host system, all full-speed devices and all hubs will see the transaction. Each transaction contains an address field that identifies the targeted device or hub. Low-speed devices only see low-speed transactions, which are always preceded by a high speed "preamble" transaction that directs all hubs to enable their low-speed ports.

USB uses differential signaling to perform serial transmission of information between the root hub and the USB devices. Due to related EMI differences the cables used for low-speed versus full-speed devices are subject to different electrical characteristics. See Chapter 4 for details regarding the electrical characteristics of low- and high-speed cables.

Power is supplied to USB devices either via the USB cable or from a local power supply associated with the device. Chapter 9 details USB power issues.

Topology

USB employs a tiered star topology where hubs provide attachment points for USB devices. The host controller contains the root hub which is the origin of all USB ports in the system. As illustrated in Figure 3-12, the root hub provides a number of USB ports (in this example three) to which USB functional devices or additional hubs may be attached.

Figure 3-12: USB's Tiered Star Topology

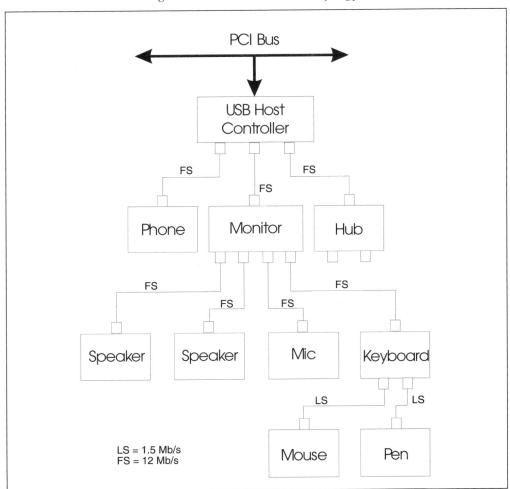

4 *The Physical Environment*

The Previous Chapter

The previous chapter provided an overview of the primary concepts of USB transfers and described the interaction between USB system software, system hardware, and USB devices. The USB communications process was described, including the concept of the device framework. Each hardware and software element in a USB system was introduced and its primary functions were described.

This Chapter

USB defines a single connector type for attaching all USB peripherals to the host system. This chapter describes the physical aspects of USB connectors and cables.

The Next Chapter

USB employs Non-Return to Zero, Inverted (NRZI) encoding along with differential signaling to transfer information across USB cables. The next chapter discusses the differential signaling and NRZI encoding techniques used by the USB.

The Connectors

USB connectors are designed to permit any USB peripheral device to be attached to a hub port. Hub ports will be located at the back of the computer or may be associated with other peripheral devices such as monitors and printers, or are available on stand-alone hub devices.

Many USB peripherals have the USB cable permanently attached, while others have detachable USB cables. If the same connector were used on both ends of a

USB cable, it would be possible to connect the cable between two USB ports. To prevent a detachable cable from being plugged into two USB ports at the same time a separate connector has been designed for the peripheral cable connection. The two connector types are described below:

- Series A connectors — provide the USB port connection to the USB peripheral cable. The series A receptacle is implemented as the hub port connector, while the series A plug is attached to the peripheral cable, permitting attachment of USB peripheral device.
- Series B connectors — provide the cable connection to the USB peripheral device when a detachable cable is implemented. The series B receptacle is implemented at the peripheral and the series B plug is attached to the cable.

Each connector has four contacts: two for carrying differential data and two for powering the USB device. Note that the power contacts are longer than the data contacts to ensure that a USB device receives power prior to the data contacts mating (power pins are 7.41 mm and the data pins are 6.41mm).

The connector contacts are numbered and the cable conductors are color coded for easy identification, as listed in Table 4-1.

Table 4-1: Connector pin designations

Contact Number	Signal Name	Cable Color
1	Vcc	Red
2	-Data	White
3	+Data	Green
4	Ground	Black

Series A Connectors

Series A connectors are used to connect a peripheral cable to a USB hub port. The receptacle comes in four variants and can be obtained in through-hole or Surface Mount Technology (SMT) versions. The four variant are:

- Vertical Mount
- Right Angle Mound

- Stacked Right Angle Mount
- Panel Mount

Series B Connectors

The series B connector is implemented in peripherals that have detachable cables. The specification does not define mounting variations for the series B receptacle; however the author suspects that the same variants defined for the series A receptacle apply to the series B receptacle.

Cables

The USB specification defines both a fully rated USB channel for 12Mb/s signaling (full speed) and a sub-channel for 1.5Mb/s signaling (low speed). The full-speed channel requires a specific cable design for EMI compliance. The low speed cable permits a more economical cable implementation for low speed/ low cost peripherals such as mice and keyboards. The following sections detail the characteristics of each cable type.

Low-Speed Cables

Figure 4-1 illustrates the cross section of a low-speed cable, also referred to a sub-channel cable. These cables are intended only for 1.5Mb/s signaling and are used in a sub-channel application where the wider bandwidth is not required. The maximum cable length shall not exceed three meters for the sub-channel applications.

The differential data signaling pair may be non-twisted 28 AWG stranded conductors. In addition, low speed cables do not require shielding. Except for the differences noted above, the mechanical specification for low speed and full speed cable are identical.

Figure 4-1: Cross Section of a Low Speed Cable Segment

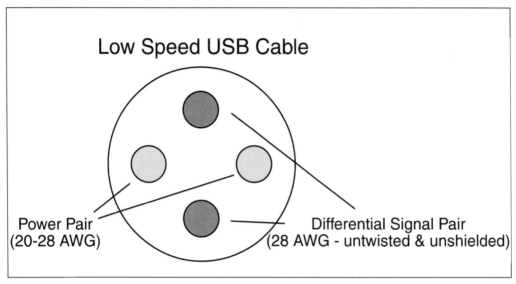

Full-Speed Cables

Full-speed USB devices require cabling that is both shielded and twisted pair for the differential data lines as illustrated in Figure 4-2. The maximum cable length supported for high speed cables is 5.0 meters. The maximum propagation delay must be equal to or less than 30ns over the length of the cable when operating in the frequency range of 1-16MHz. If the cable cannot meet the propagation delay limit of 30ns then the cable must be shortened as shown in Table 4-2.

Table 4-2: Cable Propagation Delay

Cable Propagation Delay	Maximum Cable Length
9.0 ns/m	3.3m
8.0 ns/m	3.7m
7.0 ns/m	4.3m
6.5 ns/m	4.6m

Figure 4-2: Cross Section of High Speed Cable Segment

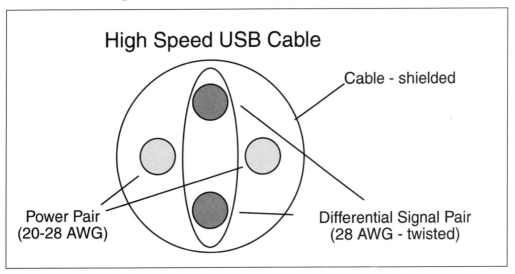

Cable Power

Cable power is 5Vdc and can be used to power the peripheral. Cable power provides up to 500ma or as little as 100ma of current. Some peripherals may include their own local power supply and not use cable power.

Electrical and Mechanical Specifications

The electrical and mechanical specification for the connectors and cables is not included in this text can be found in the USB 1.0 specification. See page 24 for information on obtaining the specification.

5 *The Signaling Environment*

The Previous Chapter

USB defines a single connector type for attaching all USB peripherals to the host system. The previous chapter described the physical aspects of USB connectors and cables.

This Chapter

USB employs NRZI encoding and differential signaling to transfer information across USB cables. This chapter discusses the differential signaling and NRZI encoding techniques used by the USB.

The Next Chapter

USB supports four transfer types; interrupt, bulk, isochronous, and control. These transfer types and the process used to initiate and perform them are described in the next chapter.

Overview

USB serial data is NRZI (Non-Return to Zero, Inverted) encoded before being transferred via the USB cables using differential signaling. Figure 5-1 on page 60 illustrates the steps involved in transferring information across a USB cable segment. NRZI encoding is performed first by the USB agent that is sending information. Next, the encoded data is then driven onto the USB cable by the differential driver. The receiver amplifies the incoming differential data and delivers the NRZI data to the decoder. Encoding and differential signaling are used to help ensure data integrity and eliminate noise problems.

Figure 5-1: Transfer Across USB Cables Employ NRZI Encoding and Differential Signaling

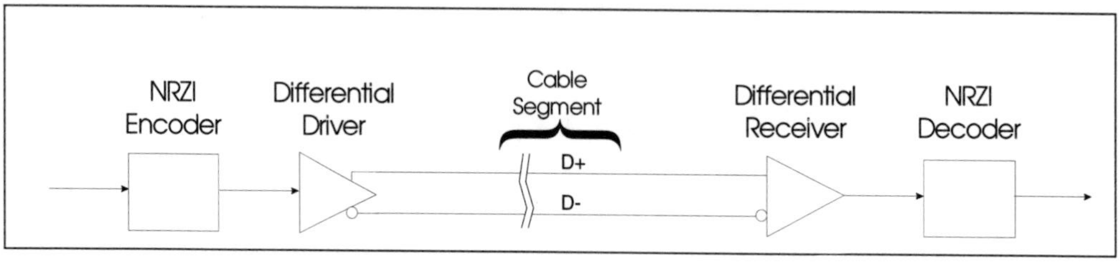

Detecting Device Attachment and Speed

Before transferring information to or from a given USB device, host software must first detect its presence. USB is designed to automatically detect the presence of a device when it is attached to a USB port, as well as its removal. The mechanism employed to detect device attachment also provides a way to determine whether the device is a full-speed or low-speed device.

A USB hub detects that a device has been attached to one of its ports by monitoring the differential data lines, after cable power has been applied to the port. Refer to Figure 5-2. When no device is attached to a USB port, pull-down resistors on the D+ and D- lines ensure that both data lines are near ground. USB devices must include a pull-up resistor on either D+ or D- (depending on its speed) as illustrated in Figure 5-2. When a device is attached current flows across the voltage divider created by the hub's pull-down resistor and the devices pull-up resistor on either D+ or D-. Since the pull-down resistor value is 15KΩ and the device's pull-up resistor is a value of 1.5KΩ, a data line will raise to approximately 90% of Vcc. When the hub detects that one of the data lines approaches Vcc while the other remains near ground, it knows that a device has been attached.

Chapter 5: The Signaling Environment

Figure 5-2: Resistor Connections for Hub and Devices

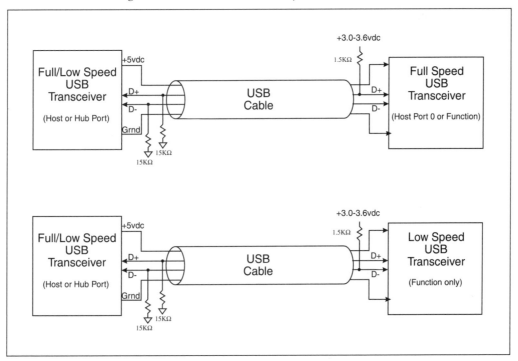

Note that full-speed devices have a pull-up on D+ and low-speed devices have the pull-up on the D-, permitting identification of the device speed. Figure 5-3 on page 62 shows the voltage levels that indicate attachment and detachment of USB devices. When both D+ and D- fall below Vse (min), or 0.8Vdc, for greater than 2.5µs the hub detects device removal. When D+ or D- raises above Vse (max), or 2.0Vdc, for longer that 2.5 µs the hub recognizes device attachment. The hub sets the appropriate status bits in its port status register when detecting device attachment and resets the bit when it detects that the device has been removed. Host software polls each hub periodically to check for device attachment and detachment.

USB devices have two signaling states, which are opposite for low- and full-speed devices:

- J state
- K state

USB System Architecture

When a device is initially attached to the USB one of its data lines is near Vcc and the other is near ground. This state is known as the "J" signaling state and is also the idle state for the device. When a signal transition occurs, the two data lines switch, resulting in a transition to the "K" state.

Figure 5-3: Device Attachment and Detachment

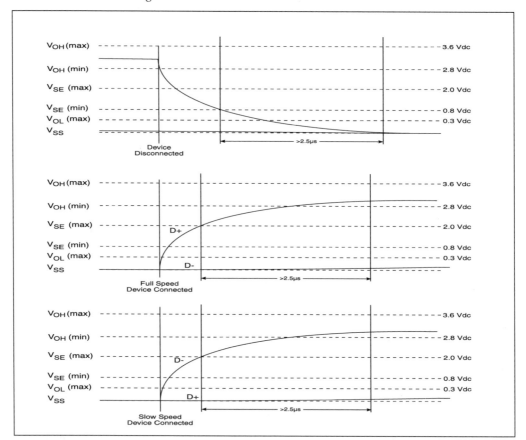

NRZI Encoding

Data transferred via the USB is encoded using NRZI (Non-Return to Zero, Inverted) encoding to help ensure integrity of data delivery, without requiring a separate clock signal be delivered with the data. NRZI is by no means a new encoding scheme. It has been used for decades in a wide variety of applications.

Chapter 5: The Signaling Environment

Figure 5-4 illustrates a serial data stream and the resulting NRZI data. Transitions in the NRZI data stream represent 0s while no transitions represent 1s. The NRZI encoder must maintain synchronization with the incoming data stream to correctly sample the data. The NRZI data stream must be sampled within a data window to detect whether a transition has occurred since the previous bit time. The decoder samples the data stream during each bit time to check for transitions.

Figure 5-4: NRZI Encoded Data

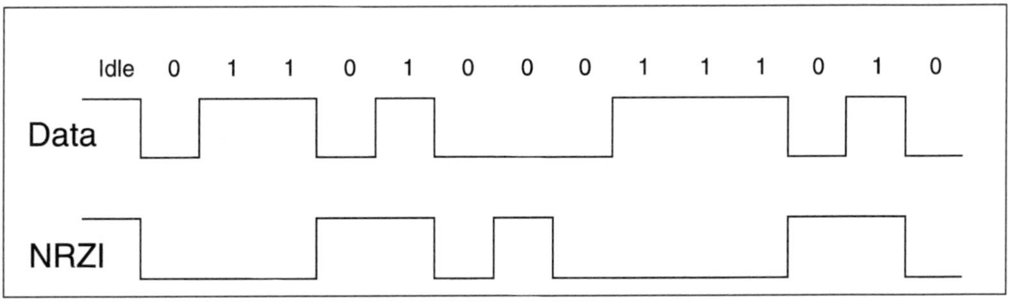

Transitions in the data stream permit the decoder to maintain synchronization with the incoming data, thereby eliminating the need for a separate clock signal. Note however that a long string of consecutive 1s results in no transitions, causing the receiver to eventually lose synchronization. The solution is to employ bit stuffing.

Bit Stuffing

Bit stuffing forces transitions into the NRZI data stream in the event that 6 consecutive ones are transmitted. This ensures that the receiver detects a transition in the NRZI data stream at least every seventh bit time. This enables the receiver to maintain synchronization with the incoming data. The transmitter of NRZI data is responsible for inserting a zero (stuffed bit) into the NRZI stream. The receiver must be designed to expect an automatic transition following six consecutive 1s and discard the 0 bit that immediately follows the sixth consecutive 1.

The top line in Figure 5-5 illustrates raw data being delivered to the receiver. Note that the data stream contains a string of eight consecutive 1s. The second line represents the raw data with the stuffed bits added. A stuffed bit is inserted between the sixth and seventh 1s in the raw data stream. Delivery of the seventh one is delayed by one data time so that the stuffed bit can be inserted. The receiver knows that the bit following the sixth consecutive 1 will be a stuffed bit (0), causing it to be ignored. Note that if the seventh bit in the raw data was a 0, the stuffed bit would still be inserted in the same location, resulting in two consecutive 0s in the stuffed data stream.

Figure 5-5: Stuffed Bit

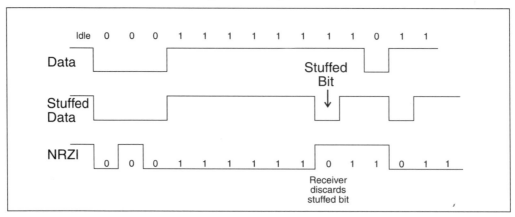

Differential Pair Signaling

USB employs differential pair signaling to reduce signal noise. Differential drivers and receivers are used to help reduce the sources of signal noise listed below:

- Amplifier noise — the noise introduced when a signal is amplified by both the driver and receiver of a signal.
- Cable noise — the noise picked up by the cable due to electromagnetic fields.

Figure 5-6 on page 65 illustrates the data signaling between a USB hub and device. A differential driver places differential data on the D+ and D- lines, which are 180 degrees out of phase. The differential receiver on the other end of the cable amplifies the difference between the incoming data lines. Noise picked up on the cable will be in phase and will not be amplified leaving the original signals unaffected.

Note that the differential signaling is implemented in a half-duplex fashion. That is, the device on either end of the cable can both transmit and receive data, but in only one direction at a time. The half-duplex implementation requires that the drivers be placed into the high impedance state when they are not transmitting data.

Two single-ended receivers are also employed by USB devices to recognize particular bus states. For example, when both differential data lines are driven low for greater than 2.5μs a USB device RESET is signaled.

Figure 5-6: Signaling Interface Between Hub and Device

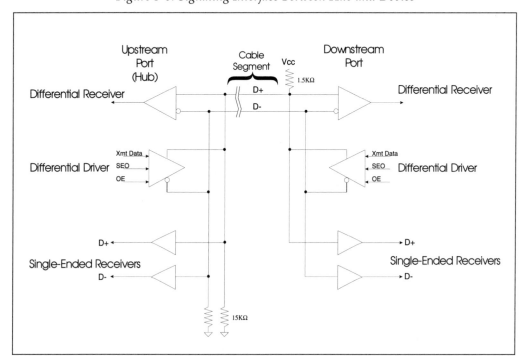

Differential Drivers

USB differential drivers can be designed for low-speed, full-speed, or both low- and full-speed operation. A differential driver employs inverting and non-inverting buffers. The input signal is applied to both buffers, yielding two outputs (D+ and D-). The static output swing of the driver must be below V_{OL} (0.3v) to 3.6Vdc with a 1.5 KΩ load and above V_{OH} (2.8Vdc) to ground with a 15KΩ load. The output swings between the differential high and low state must be well balanced to minimize signal skew. Slew rate control is also required to minimize radiated noise and crosstalk.

Low-Speed Drivers

Low speed buffers drive their signal across an unshielded, untwisted wire cable and must only be used when transmitting information between low-speed hub ports and low speed devices. The rise and fall time of signals (slew rate) on this cable must be greater than 75ns to keep RFI within FCC class B limits, and must be less than 300ns to limit timing delays and signaling skew. Using the slew rate specified, the driver must reach the specified static signal levels with smooth rise and fall times and must exhibit minimal reflections and ringing.

Signaling conventions used by low-speed drivers are based on the D- line being terminated at the device with a 1.5 KΩ resistor. The resulting idle state for a low speed device is a differential "0", or (D+) - (D-) < -200mv and D+ < Vse (min). This is also referred to as the "J" state for a low-speed device, while the "K" state is represented by a differential "1." Cable length is limited to 3.0 meters.

Low-speed buffers are used on all upstream ports of all low-speed devices. All hub ports must also support low-speed driver characteristics (must use low-speed signaling conventions and slew rates) on their downstream side, since a low-speed device may be attached via a low-speed cable segment. Note that these hub ports must also support full-speed driver characteristics to support full-speed device operation.

Full-Speed Drivers

Full-speed drivers signal across the fully rated cable (shielded/twisted pair). A full-speed cable has a characteristic impedance of 90Ω and a maximum length of five meters. Figure 5-7 on page 67 illustrates an implementation of a full-speed differential driver. Note that the equivalent output impedance of the driver must be between 29 and 44Ω As shown in Figure 5-7, series resistors may be required to achieve the required impedance.

Figure 5-7: Example Full-Speed CMOS Differential Driver

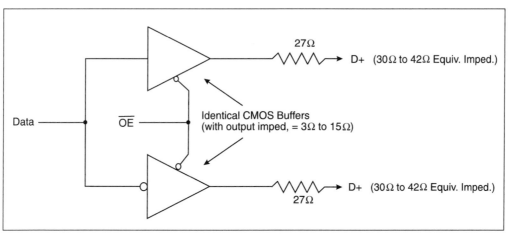

Full-speed driver transmissions must be monotonic in nature and must be matched to control signal skew and RFI, and rise time must be within 4ns to 20ns, measured with a capacitive load of 50 pf. Note however, that the driver and cable impedances are not matched, thus reflections from the receiver end of the cable are expected. Figure 5-8 illustrates the full-speed signal waveform. Note that the reflection at the receiver end causes the receiver to detect the signal transition prior to the driver completing its full output swing.

Signaling conventions used by full-speed drivers are based on the D+ line being terminated at the device with a 1.5 K Ω resistor. The resulting idle state for a full speed device is a differential "1", or (D+) - (D-) > 200mv and D- < Vse (min). This is also referred to as the "J" state for a full-speed device, while the "K" state is represented by a differential "0", which is opposite of the low-speed signaling convention.

A full-speed driver will be designed to send data at both high- and low-speed data rates. Note however that both high- and low-speed signaling use the full-speed signaling conventions and slew rates since it drives data across a fully-rated cable segment to a full-speed receiver.

Figure 5-8: Full-Speed Drive Waveforms

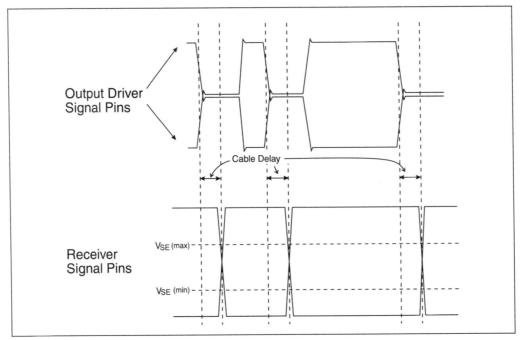

Differential Receivers

USB differential amplifiers must feature an input sensitivity of 200mV when both differential data inputs are in the range of at least 0.8 V to 2.5 V with respect to local ground. This input sensitivity reduces noise generated by the buffers themselves.

Single-Ended Receivers

Single-ended receivers are used to detect various state conditions on the bus. The two single-ended receivers each monitor one of the data lines. Normally, the D+ and D- lines are in opposite states due to the pullup resistor on one of the data lines and the differential signaling. In these conditions, the differential amplifier will amplify the difference between the two data lines. However, in some instances both data lines are driven low to signal a particular condition.

Chapter 5: The Signaling Environment

For example, both data lines are driven low for two bit times after transmitting a packet of information to signify the end of packet, or EOP. The differential amplifiers in this case will have no output, since there is no potential difference at the inputs of the receiver. The single-ended receiver will be able to detect the EOP state when both D+ and D- are low.

Summary of USB Signaling States

Table 5-1 summarizes all of the USB signaling states. The first column identifies the state, column two defines the related signaling condition at the driver, while column three defines the receiver's state.

Table 5-1: USB Bus States

Bus State	Signaling Levels	
	From Originating Driver	**At Receiver**
Differential "1"	(D+) - (D-) > 200mV and D+ or D- < V_{SE} (minimum)	
Differential "0"	(D+) - (D-) < -200mV and D+ or D- < V_{SE} (minimum)	
Data J State: Low Speed Full Speed	Differential "0" Differential "1"	
Data K State: Low Speed Full Speed	Differential "1" Differential "0"	
Idle State: Low Speed Full Speed	Differential "0" and D- > V_{SE} (max.) and D+ < V_{SE} (min.) Differential "1" and D+ > V_{SE} (max.) and D- < V_{SE} (min.)	
Resume State: Low Speed Full Speed	Differential "1" and D+ > V_{SE} (max.) and D- < V_{SE} (min.) Differential "0" and D- > V_{SE} (max.) and D+ < V_{SE} (min.)	
Start of Packet (SOP)	Data lines switch from idle to K State	

Table 5-1: USB Bus States

Bus State	Signaling Levels	
	From Originating Driver	**At Receiver**
End of Packet (EOP)	D+ and D- < V_{SE} (min.) for 2 bit times followed by an idle for 1 bit time	D+ and D- < V_{SE} (min.) for equal to or greater than 1 bit time followed by a J state
Disconnect (Upstream only)	NA	D+ and D- < V_{SE} (min.) for equal to or greater than 2.5μs
Connect (Upstream only)	NA	D+ or D- > V_{SE} (max.) for equal to or greater than 2.5μs
Reset (Downstream only)	D+ and D- < V_{SE} for 10 ms	D+ and D- < V_{SE} (min.) for equal to or greater than 2.5μs (must be recognized within 5.5μs)

Figure 5-9 illustrates the signal levels used for the USB. Note that USB uses 3.3Vdc signaling levels.

Figure 5-9: USB Signaling Levels

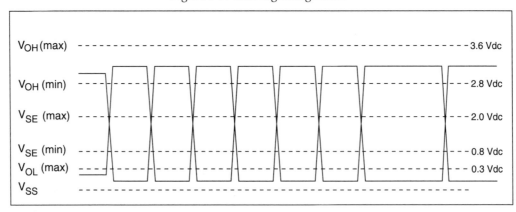

6 *USB Transfers*

The Previous Chapter

USB employs NRZI encoding and differential signaling to transfer information across USB cables. The previous chapter discussed the differential signaling and NRZI encoding techniques used by the USB.

This Chapter

USB supports four transfer types: interrupt, bulk, isochronous, and control. These transfer types and the process used to initiate and perform them are described in this chapter.

The Next Chapter

Every transfer broadcast over the USB consists of a combination of packets. These packets are combined to define individual transactions that are performed as part of a larger transfer. In the next chapter, each transaction type is defined, along with the individual packets that comprise them.

Overview

Each endpoint within a given USB device has particular characteristics that dictate how it must be accessed. The transfer characteristics relate to the requirements of the application. The following four transfer types have been defined by the USB specification, each which reflects the nature of transfers that may be required by a USB device endpoint:

- Interrupt transfer — an interrupt transfer is used for devices that are typically thought of as interrupt driven devices in legacy PC implementations. Since the USB does not support hardware interrupts, USB devices that are interrupt driven must be polled periodically to see if the device has data to transfer. For example, in legacy PC systems a hardware interrupt is generated each time a key is pressed on the keyboard to notify the processor that it must execute a software interrupt routine to service the keyboard, whereas a USB keyboard is polled periodically to determine if keyboard data (e.g. resulting from a key being pressed) is ready to be transferred. The polling rate of course is critical; it must be frequent enough to ensure that data is not lost but not so frequent that bus bandwidth is needlessly reduced.

- Bulk transfer — a bulk transfer is used for transferring large blocks of data that have no periodic or transfer rate requirement. An example of a bulk transfer is a print job being transferred to a USB printer. While transfer speed is important for performance, a print job delivered slowly does not result in lost or corrupted data.

- Isochronous transfer — an isochronous transfer requires a constant delivery rate. Applications that use isochronous transfers must ensure that rate matching between the sender and receiver can be accomplished. For example, a USB microphone and speaker would use isochronous transfers to ensure that no frequency distortion results from transferring data across the USB.

- Control transfers — control transfers are used to transfer specific requests to USB devices and are most commonly used during device configuration. A special transfer sequence is used to pass requests (commands) to a device, sometimes followed by a data transfer, and concluded with completion status.

A given device may have a collection of endpoints, each of which may support a different transfer type. For example, when a file manager program accesses a USB-based CDROM, the data endpoint is defined as a bulk transfer endpoint, whereas, accesses performed by a CD Audio program would require isochronous transfers be performed from a data endpoint.

Client Initiates Transfer

During the configuration process, the USB driver reads the device descriptors to determine the type of endpoints that a given device requires for its function. The USB driver determines if sufficient bus bandwidth is available to accommodate all endpoint transfer requirements. If the bandwidth is available, the USB driver establishes a communications pipe with the bus bandwidth reservation associated with the pipe. The driver also apprises the appropriate USB device driver that the communication pipe exists for its use. Figure 6-1 on page 73 illustrates the concept of the communications pipes that have been established for the client driver to communicate with its function. The communication pipes remain inactive until the client requests a transfer via one of the pipes. Note also that the USB device driver knows only about communication pipes and the endpoints that it must communicate with, and is not aware of the nature of the low-level USB transfer mechanisms.

Figure 6-1: Communication Pipe Between Client Software's Memory Buffer and Device Endpoint

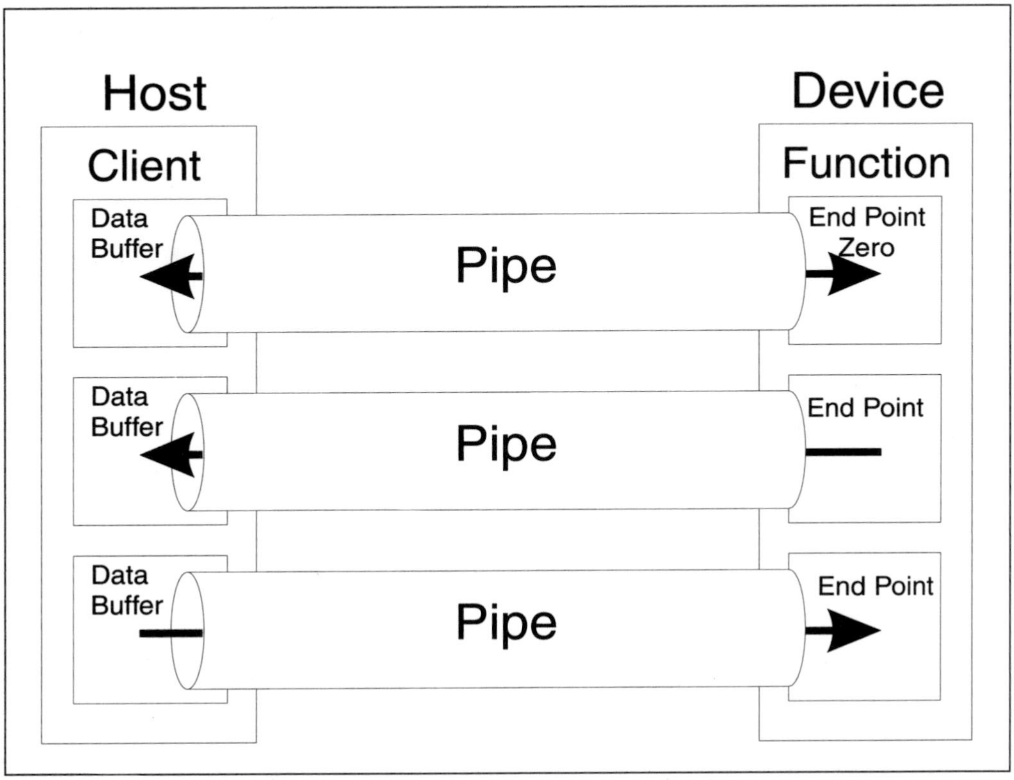

Refer to Figure 6-2 on page 74. A USB device driver calls the USB driver to start a transfer. The client transfer request is referred to as an I/O Request Packet, or IRP. The IRP results in a transfer being performed over the USB. The USB driver allocates the amount of bus bandwidth that is given to this transfer during each frame. The transfer request may take numerous frames to complete.

The host controller driver schedules all IRPs that are presented to it by the USB driver. The host controller then performs the individual transfers that have been scheduled, by performing multiple transactions (reads from or writes to the target USB device) during each frame until the transfer completes.

Figure 6-2: Client Request Converted to USB Transactions.

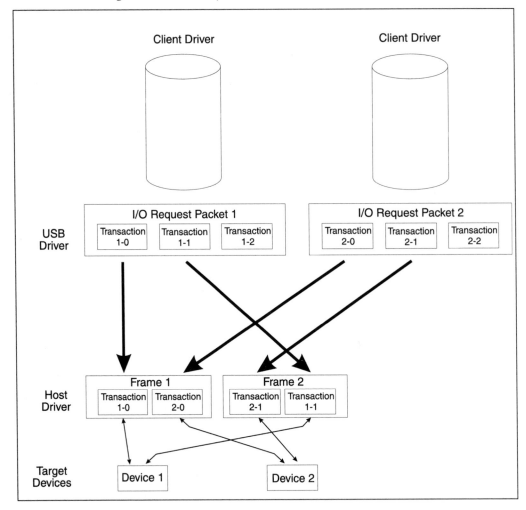

Frame-Based Transfers

Since the USB is shared by a wide variety of devices, a mix of USB transfer types will likely be performed during each 1 ms frame. Since interrupt and isochronous transfers must occur at fixed intervals, they have a special priority during the execution of each frame. The specification states that a maximum of 90% of the USB bandwidth can be devoted to periodic (interrupts and isochronous) transfers, while control transfers have a 10% reservation during each frame. Bulk transfers are allocated the remainder of the available bandwidth.

Transfer Types

The following sections describe the capabilities and limitations of the four transfer types. Each device endpoint has an associated descriptor that defines the transfer type it requires. Table 6-1 on page 75 lists a portion of an endpoint descriptor that includes the transfer type field. The shaded area at offset 03 defines the transfer type associated with a given endpoint.

Table 6-1: Endpoint Descriptor Transfer Type Definition

Offset	Field	Size	Value	Description
0	Length	1	Number	Size of this descriptor in bytes.
1	DescriptorType	1	Constant	ENDPOINT Descriptor Type
2	EndpointAddress	1	Endpoint	The address of the endpoint on the USB device described by this descriptor. The address is encoded as follows: Bit 0..3 Endpoint number Bit 4..6 Reserved, reset to zero Bit 7 Direction (ignored for Control endpoints) 0 = OUT endpoint 1 = IN endpoint
3	Attributes	1	BitMap	This field describes the endpoint's transfer type once the device is configured. Bit 1..0 Transfer Type 00 Control 01 Isochronous 10 Bulk 11 Interrupt All other bits are reserved

Isochronous

Isochronous transfers are typically used by real-time applications that require a constant data transfer rate. This includes applications involved in audio transmission (e.g. CD audio, speakers, and digital telephones). Isochronous data delivery is characterized by the need to provide data on a timely basis and is more important than verifying accurate delivery of data. For this reason valid data delivery is not guaranteed during isochronous transfers.

Figure 6-3 on page 77 illustrates an example isochronous application consisting of a CD-ROM and speaker. An isochronous application must maintain synchronization between the application software and the USB device that is either the sink or source of data. A combination of the data transfer rates between the CD-ROM and memory buffer and the memory buffer and speaker, along with data rate matching ensures that data is transferred between the CD-ROM and speaker synchronously eliminating potential audio distortion.

The specification defines three methods that a USB isochronous device can synchronize it data transfer rate to the host system. These are:

- Asynchronous — Isochronous endpoints using asynchronous synchronization send or receive audio data at a rate that is locked to an external clock or a free running internal clock. The device cannot synchronize the transfer rate to the USB clock (based on the 1ms Start of Frame).
- Synchronous — Devices whose isochronous endpoints have their own notion of timing. The device may be able to synchronize to the 1ms SOF timing provided by USB. If a device cannot synchronize its own clock to the USB clock, its device driver may be required to adjust the USB SOF timing, permitting USB to synchronize with its clock. USB permits one device on USB to become a master device that can adjust the SOF until it is synchronous to its sample clock. (See " Bus Management" on page 253 for details on SOF adjustment.)
- Adaptive — These devices have a specific range of rates at which they can send or receive audio data, permitting them to synchronize to the rate imposed at their interface by SOF timing.

Isochronous transfers are only supported by full-speed devices.

Figure 6-3: Isochronous Application Using USB CD-ROM and Speakers

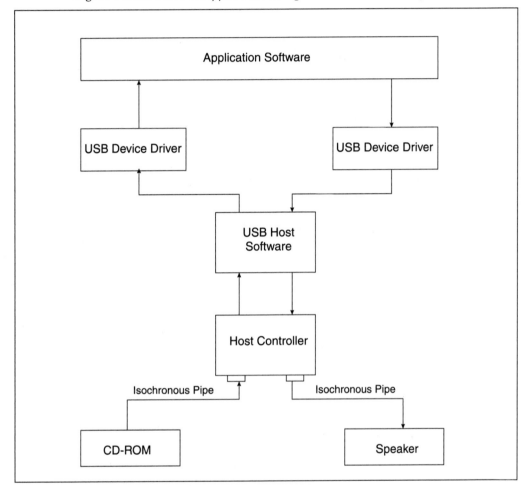

Direction of Transfers

Isochronous transfers are uni-directional. No single endpoint can transfer information in both directions. Isochronous devices that need to both send and receive data must implement two endpoints, one for sending and one for receiving data.

Service Period

An isochronous transfer is scheduled to be performed regularly over the USB during consecutive 1ms frames. This ensures that a constant data rate can be maintained.

Bandwidth Allocation

The data payload during an isochronous transfer is limited to 1023 bytes during each frame. The endpoint descriptor defines the maximum payload supported. If an isochronous endpoint requires more bus bandwidth than is available the device will not be configured, because isochronous pipes require guaranteed data delivery.

Error Recovery

Since a constant data transfer rate is essential for isochronous applications, error detection and recovery are not supported. Recovery involves transferring data again in the event that errors are detected. Attempting retransmission of the data, may result in a loss of synchronization between the data rate coming from the USB device and the application or target device. Therefore, no transfer retries are permitted.

Interrupt Transfers

Interrupt transfers are strictly used to poll devices to determine if they have data that needs to be transferred (i.e. if they have an interrupt request pending). Hence, the direction of interrupt transfers are always from the USB device to the host. If a device does not currently have data to send (i.e. no interrupt is pending), then the device returns no acknowledge indicating that no data is available to send at this time.

Service Period

Interrupt transfers are scheduled periodically based on the requirements of the device so that overrun conditions do not occur. Full-speed interrupt transfers can occur as often as every 1ms frame or as infrequently as every 255th frame. Low speed transfers can occur at a maximum period of every 10ms or as seldom as every 255ms. The polling interval required by a given device is specified within the interrupt endpoint descriptor. Table 6-2 on page 79 shows the portion of an endpoint descriptor, that defines the type and interrupt polling interval. Note that offset six defines the polling interval in 1ms increments.

Table 6-2: Endpoint Descriptor's Interrupt Polling Interval Definition

Offset	Field	Size	Value	Description
3	Attributes	1	BitMap	This field describes the endpoint's attributes when it is configured using the ConfigurationValue.
				Bit 0..1 Transfer Type
				00 Control
				01 Isochronous
				10 Bulk
				11 Interrupt
				All other bits are reserved
4	MaxPacketSize	2	Number	Maximum packet size this endpoint is capable of sending or receiving when this configuration is selected.
				For isochronous endpoints, this value is used to reserve the bus time in the schedule, required for the per frame data payloads. The pipe may, on an ongoing basis, actually use less bandwidth than reserved. The device reports, if necessary, the actual bandwidth used via its normal, non-USB defined mechanisms.
				For interrupt, bulk and control endpoints smaller data payloads may be sent, but will terminate the transfer and may or may not require intervention to restart.
6	Polling Interval	1	Number	Interval for polling endpoint for data transfers. Expressed in milliseconds.
				This field is ignored for Bulk and Control endpoints. For isochronous endpoints, this field must be set to one. For interrupt endpoints, this field may range from 1 to 255.

Bus Bandwidth Allocation

During each frame the maximum data payload supported by interrupt transfers is 64 bytes for full-speed devices. Transfers must always occur at the maximum packet size specified by the endpoint descriptor except for the last transfer. A data packet less than maximum size is viewed as the last transfer.

Like isochronous endpoints, an interrupt pipe requires guaranteed delivery of data within the specified polling interval. Failure to access the endpoint within the polling interval may result in data loss due to buffer overflow. If the available bandwidth cannot support the interrupt pipe the device is not configured.

Error Recovery

Error recovery for interrupt transfers is supported. If an error is detected when performing a transfer, the transfer is attempted again during the next service interval.

Control Transfers

Control transfers provide a way to configure a USB device and control certain aspects of its operation. Each device must implement a default control endpoint (always endpoint zero) used for configuring the device, controlling device states, and other aspects of the device's operation. The control endpoint responds to a variety of USB specific requests that are delivered via control transfers. For example, when a device is detected on the USB, system software must access the device's descriptors to determine the device type and operational characteristics. The USB specification also defines a variety of USB device requests for hubs, as well as other types of USB devices. These requests may be standard requests defined for all USB devices, may be requests defined for a particular device class, or may be vendor-specific requests that only the device driver and device have knowledge of. Chapter 15, entitled "Device Requests," on page 233 for a detailed list of standard commands supported by USB.

A control transfer consists of at least two and perhaps three stages:

- Setup Stage — control transfers always begin with a setup stage that transfers information to a target device, defining the type of request being made to the USB device (e.g. read the device descriptor).
- Data Stage — this stage is defined only for requests that require data transfers. For example, the read descriptor request sends the contents of the descriptor to the system during the data stage. Some requests do not

require data transfers beyond the setup phase.
- Status Stage — this stage is always performed to report the result of the requested operation.

Bus Bandwidth Allocation

Control transfers begin with a setup stage containing an eight byte data packet. This eight bytes defines the amount of the data to be transferred during the data stage of the control transfer. During the data stage, data packets are limited to a maximum data payload of 64 bytes. Control transfers are given a guaranteed 10% bus allocation. If additional bus bandwidth is available then more than 10% can be allocated to control transfers.

Error Recovery

Control transfers participate in error detection and recovery mechanisms to provide a "best effort" delivery. Failure of the recovery mechanism is viewed as a catastrophic failure.

Bulk Transfers

Bulk transfers are used by devices that have no particular transfer rate requirements. A classical example of a bulk transfer device is a printer. No problems will be incurred if the transfer occurs at a slow rate, other than impatience of the user who is waiting for the print job to emerge.

Bus Bandwidth Allocation

Since bulk transfers have no specific needs regarding the rate of data delivery, they are relegated to the lowest priority during each frame. The bandwidth allocation for isochronous and interrupt (90%), and control transfers (10%), leaving no bus bandwidth for bulk transfers in a fully allocated frame. Bulk transfers are scheduled based on bandwidth remaining after all other transfers have been scheduled. If no bandwidth is available for bulk transfers, they are deferred until the bus load diminishes. However, in the absence of other transfer types, a large portion of the bus bandwidth may be allocated to bulk transfers resulting in high performance.

The maximum data packet sizes for bulk transfers are limited to only 8, 16, 32, or 64 bytes. No other packet sizes are permitted. When a bulk transfer is taking place, all packet sizes must be the maximum size specified in the maximum packet size field, except for the last data packet of a transfer. Failure to transmit packets with the expected size results in an error and termination of the transfer.

Bulk transfer endpoints can always be configured by software since there is no requirement to deliver data at any particular rate. If no bus bandwidth is available bulk transfers are deferred until time again become available.

Error Recovery

Bulk transfers support error detection and recovery. Data integrity in bulk transfer applications is far more critical than the rate of transfer. Bulk transfers use all available forms of error detection and recovery.

7 *USB Transactions*

The Previous Chapter

The previous chapter introduced and described the four transfer types supported by USB: Interrupt, Bulk, Control, and Isochronous. The purpose of the transfers and their capabilities and limitations were also discussed.

This Chapter

Every transfer broadcast over the USB consists of a combination of packets. These packets are combined to define individual transactions that are performed as part of a larger transfer. Each transaction type is defined, along with the individual packets that comprise them.

The Next Chapter

The USB supports lossless transfer of data between the host system and the target USB devices. The next chapter details the error detection and handling mechanisms employed by the USB to ensure data delivery.

Overview

The previous chapter discussed the various transfer types used to communicate with endpoints within a device. Transfers are performed across the USB using one or more transactions consisting of a series of packets. Figure 7-1 on page 84 illustrates the relationship between the various layers involved in performing a transfer — from the USB device driver's request to perform a transfer (IRP) to the resulting packets that are transmitted across the USB wire to/from the device. This chapter deals with individual transactions that are initiated by the host to transfer data to or from the target USB device. Each transaction consists of one or more packets that are transmitted over the USB wire.

Figure 7-1: The Layers Involved in USB Transfers

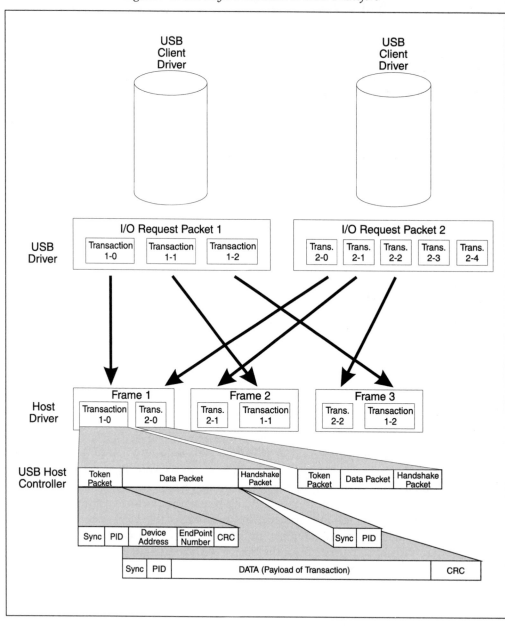

Packets — The Basic Building Blocks of USB transactions

Transactions typically consist of three phases, or packets, as illustrated in Figure 7-2. However, a transaction may consist of one, two, or three phases depending on the type:

- Token Packet phase — each transaction begins with a token phase that defines the type of transaction. A device address is also included in this phase when the transaction targets a specific USB device. Some tokens stand alone and thus are not followed by any additional packets, while others are always followed by either one or two additional packets.
- Data Packet phase — many transaction types include a data phase that carries the payload associated with the transfer. The data phase can carry a maximum payload of 1023 bytes of data during a single transaction, however, the maximum payload permitted depends on the transfer type being performed.
- Handshake Packet phase — all USB transfers are implemented to guarantee data delivery, except isochronous transfers that have no handshake phase. The handshake phase provides feedback to the sender of data whether or not data was received without error. If errors are encountered during a transaction, retries are attempted. (See Chapter 8 for a detailed explanation of the error handling.)

Figure 7-2: Many USB Transactions Consist of Three Phases

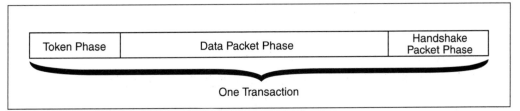

A packet is the mechanism used to perform all USB transactions. Figure 7-3 illustrates the basic format of a USB packet. Immediately preceding each packet is a synchronization sequence that permits USB devices to synchronize to the data rate of the incoming bits within the packet. The type of packet is defined by a bit pattern called a packet ID. Following the ID is packet-specific information (e.g. an address or data) that varies depending on the packet type. Finally, each packet ends with a sequence of Cyclic Redundancy Check (CRC) bits, used to verify correct delivery of the packet-specific information. The end of each packet is identified by an end of packet (EOP) state. Each type of packet is detailed in the following sections.

Figure 7-3: Packet Format

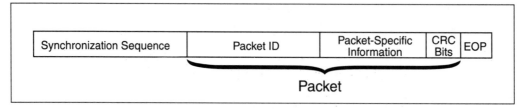

Synchronization Sequence

Figure 7-4 illustrates the synchronization sequence. The synchronization sequence consists of eight bits starting with seven consecutive logic 0s and ending with a logic 1. Since zeros are encoded with transitions of the differential data lines, the seven zeros each create a transition during each bit time, thus providing a clock that can be synchronized to. The synchronization sequence also alerts USB receivers that a packet is being sent, which will immediately follow the 8-bit synchronization sequence.

Figure 7-4: Synchronization Sequence

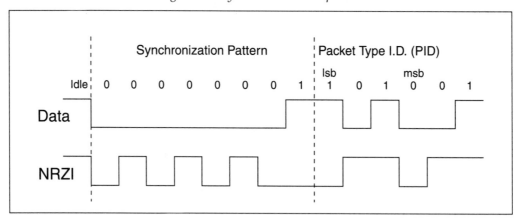

Packets can be broadcast over the USB at either full speed (12Mb/s) or slow speed (1.5Mb/s) and the speed governs the rate at which bits within the packet are transferred. The USB receiver must detect the logic state of each bit value within the packet by sampling the data lines at the correct point during each bit time. The synchronization sequence is transmitted at the transfer speed being used, allowing the receiver to synchronize to either incoming data rate.

Note however, that slow-speed USB devices cannot communicate at full speed. As a result, low-speed cable segment carry only low-speed transactions. USB hubs keep low-speed ports disabled until a low-speed transaction is to be performed. Hubs must be given time to enable their low-speed port prior to the start of the low-speed transfer. This is accomplished with a special packet called a preamble packet and is used specifically to command hubs to enable their low-speed ports. Preamble packets must directly precede each low-speed transaction. Once the low-speed packet has been transferred, bus operation returns to full-speed operation.

Packet Identifier

Packet identifiers define the purpose and thus the content of a given packet. Packets are grouped into three major categories:

- Token Packets - Token packets are sent at the beginning of a USB transaction to define the transfer type. (e.g. transfers to or from a USB device).
- Data Packets — These packets follow token packets during transactions that require data payloads be transferred to or from USB devices.
- Handshake Packets — Handshake packets are typically returned from the receiving agent back to the sender, thus providing feedback relative to the success or failure of the transaction. In some cases, the USB device being requested to send data to the system may send a handshake packet to indicate that it currently has no data to send.
- Special Packets — Currently the only special packet defined is the preamble packet used to enable low speed ports.

The format and length of a packet depends on it type. Token packets are all four bytes in length, but contain different information that describes some aspect of the transaction that it defines. Data packets are variable length depending on the transfer type associated with the transaction. For example, the data payload for bulk transfers is limited to 64 bytes during each transaction, while the data payload limit for isochronous transfers is 1024 bytes.

Refer to Figure 7-5. Packet IDs consist of a four bit identifier field followed by a four bit check field. The check field contains the inverted value (1's complement) of the packet ID value. Immediately following the eight-bit packet ID is the packet-specific information.

Figure 7-5: Packet Identifier Format

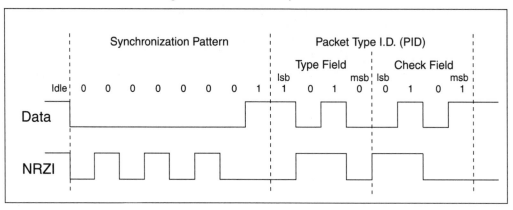

Packet-Specific Information

Each packet contains information that is related to the job it performs. The information may consist of a USB device address, a frame number, data to be transferred to or from a USB device, etc. This information is crucial to the success of a given transaction and is verified at the end of the packet with CRC bits.

Cyclic Redundancy Checking (CRC)

The USB agent that sends a given packet computes either a 5-bit or 16-bit CRC depending on its type. Data packets use a 16-bit CRC, while all other packet types use the 5-bit CRC. The CRC is generated and checked for the packet-specific data only, since the packet ID has its own check bits. See "CRC Errors" on page 111.

End of Packet (EOP)

The end of each packet is signaled by the sending agent by driving both differential data lines low for two bit times followed by an idle for 1-bit time. The agent receiving the packet recognized EOP when it detects the differential data lines both low for one bit time. Figure 7-6 illustrates an EOP being signaled on the USB bus.

Figure 7-6: End of Packet Signalling

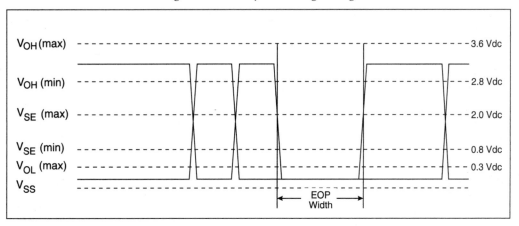

Token Packets

Token packets define the type of transaction that is to be broadcast over the USB. All transactions begin with a token packet. Four types of Token packets are defined by the USB specification:

- SOF (Start of Frame) — indicates start of the next 1ms frame.
- IN — specifies a USB transaction used to transfer data from a target USB device to the system.
- OUT — specifies a USB transaction used to transfer data from the system to a target USB device.
- SETUP — indicates the start of a control transfer. SETUP is the first stage of a control transfer and is used to send a request from the system to the target USB device.

Table 7-1 on page 90 lists the token types supported and describes the token-specific information embedded within the packet and the action specified. Each token is identified by its packet ID, as shown in column three.

Table 7-1: USB Tokens

PID Type	PID Name	PID[3:0]	Description of Token Packet
Token	SOF	0101b	Contains start of Frame (SOF) marker and frame number. The SOF token is used by isochronous endpoints to synchronize its transfers.
Token	SETUP	1101b	Contains USB device address + endpoint number. Transfer is from host to function for setting up a control endpoint (e.g. configuration).
Token	OUT	0001b	Contains the USB device address + endpoint number. The transfer is from host to function.
Token	IN	1001b	Contains the USB device address + endpoint number. The transfer is from function to host.

SOF Packet

SOF provides a way for target devices to recognize the beginning of a frame. As an example, isochronous applications can use SOF to trigger and synchronize the start of a transfer at the beginning of a specified 1ms frame. The SOF packet is broadcast to all full-speed devices (including hubs) at the beginning of each frame. SOF packets are never transferred to low-speed devices since they cannot support isochronous transfers.

Embedded within the SOF packet is an 11-bit frame number as illustrated in Figure 7-7 on page 91. The frame number is verified by the receiver with the five CRC bits. Note that the SOF packet defines a transaction consisting solely of the token packet. No data or handshake packet is associated with an SOF packet; therefore delivery is not guaranteed. However, USB targets must perform the checks and take the appropriate action as follows:

- PID check error — ignore the packet
- Frame CRC error — ignore the frame number

Figure 7-7: Format of a SOF Packet

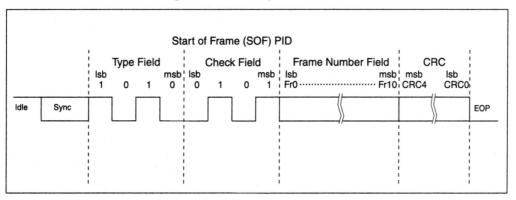

IN Packet

When software wishes to read information from a given device an IN token is used. The IN packet notifies the target USB device that data is being requested by the system. IN transactions may be used in a variety of USB transfers types including:

- Interrupt transfers
- Bulk transfers
- Data phase of control transfers
- Isochronous transfers

As illustrated in Figure 7-8 on page 92, an IN token packet consists of the ID type field, the ID check field, the USB device and endpoints addresses, and five CRC bits. An IN transaction starts with an IN packet broadcast by the root hub, followed by a data packet returned from the target USB device, and in some cases concluded with a handshake packet sent from the root hub back to the target device to confirm receipt of the data. Note that IN transactions used during isochronous transfers do not include a handshake packet.

The amount of data that can be transferred during an IN transfer depends of the transfer type being performed as discussed in Chapter 6.

Figure 7-8: IN Token Packet Format

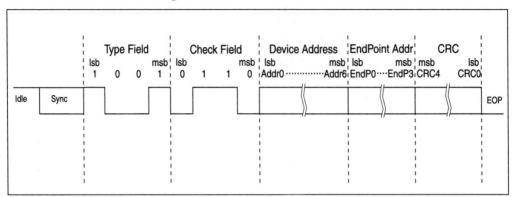

OUT Packet

System software specifies an OUT transaction when data is to be transferred to a target USB device. Three types of transfers employ OUT transactions:

- Bulk transfers
- Data phase of control transfers
- Isochronous transfers

Figure 7-9 on page 93 illustrates the contents of an   OUT token packet. An out packet consists of the packet ID or type field, the type check field, the USB target device and endpoint ID, and a 5-bit CRC. The OUT token packet is followed by a data packet, and a handshake (for bulk transfers only). The data payload size is governed by the transfer employing the OUT transaction.

Figure 7-9: OUT Token Packet Format

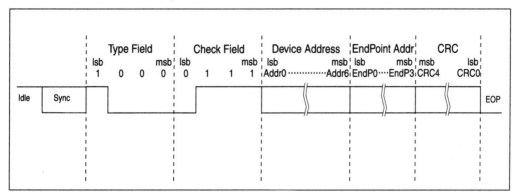

SETUP Packet

Setup packets are used only during the setup stage of control transfers. The SETUP transaction starts a control transfer, and is defined as the setup stage. A setup transaction is similar in format to an OUT transaction: the setup packet is followed by a data0 packet, and an acknowledge packet. The setup packet transfers a request to be performed by the target device. A variety of requests are supported by hubs and other USB devices and are defined in Chapter 13 and Chapter 15. Depending on the request, the SETUP transaction may be followed by one or more IN or OUT transactions (data stage), or may be followed only by a status stage consisting of a final data packet transferred from the endpoint to the host system.

Figure 7-10 illustrates the format of a SETUP packet.

Figure 7-10: SETUP Token Packet Format

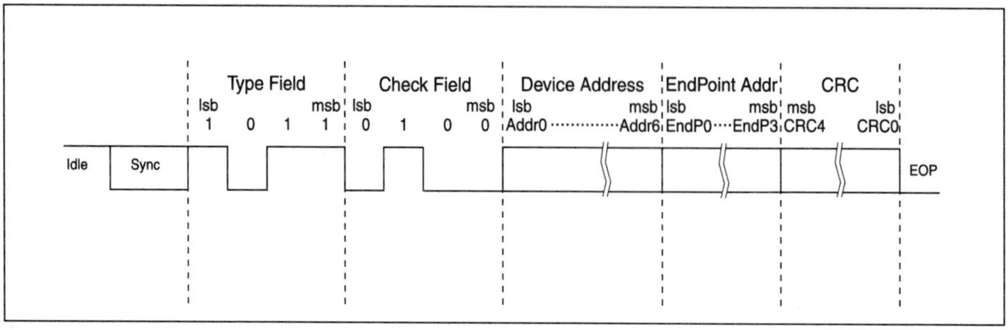

Data Packets — Data0 and Data1

Data packets carry the data payload associated with a given transaction. Direction of a data packet transfer is specified by the transaction type and may be used to transfers data either to or from a target USB device as listed in Table 7-2 below.

Table 7-2: Direction of Data Packets

Transaction Type	Direction of Data Packet
IN transaction	from USB device
OUT transaction	to USB device
Setup transaction	to USB device

Two types of data packets (data0 and data1) are defined to support synchronization of long transfers between the sender and receiver. For example, if a long transfer is being sent from the host to a printer, the transfer will be performed in small blocks via a relatively large number of frames. To verify that a data transaction is not missed during a long transfer, a technique called data toggle can be employed. For a detailed discussion of Data toggle see "Data Toggle Errors" on page 116.

The format of Data0 packets is illustrated in Figure 7-11, and the format for Data1 is illustrated in Figure 7-12.

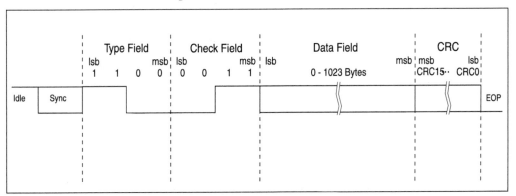

Figure 7-11: Data0 Packet Format

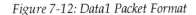

Figure 7-12: Data1 Packet Format

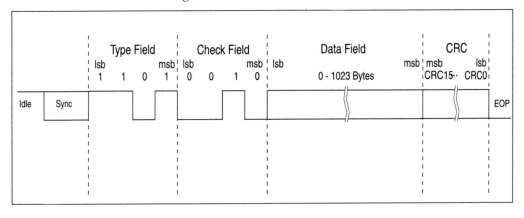

Handshake Packets

USB devices use handshake packets to report the completion status of a given transaction. The receiver of the data payload (either the target device or the root hub) is responsible for sending a handshake packet back to the sender. Three possible results can be reported via different handshake packets:

- Acknowledge packet (ACK) — this acknowledges error-free receipt of the data packet.

USB System Architecture

- No Acknowledge packet (NAK) — reports to the host that the target is temporarily unable to accept or return data. During interrupt transactions NAK signifies that no data is currently available to return to the host (i.e. no interrupt request is currently pending).
- Stall packet (STALL) — used by the target to report that it is unable to complete the transfer and that software intervention will be required for the device to recover from the stall condition.

The handshake packets are illustrated in Figure 7-13.

Figure 7-13: Handshake Packet Formats

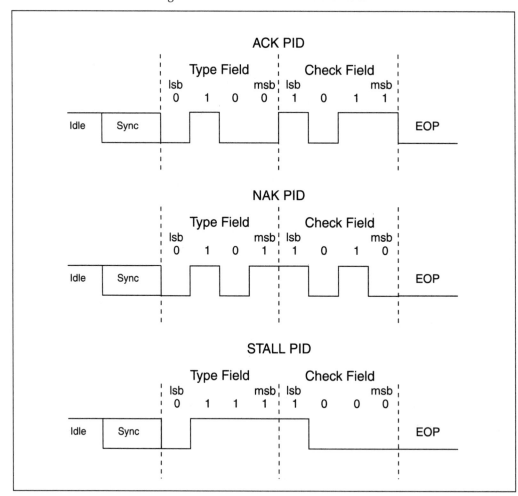

Preamble Packet

Hubs disable low-speed ports to block all high-speed transactions from occurring over low-speed cable segments. Prior to broadcasting a low-speed packet, a preamble packet must be broadcast to notify all hubs that a low-speed transaction will follow. Hubs must respond to a preamble packet by enabling their low-speed ports, while all other devices must ignore the preamble packet. The host guarantees that the packet transfered immediately after the preamble packet will be sent at low speed. All low-speed packets are broadcast across all cable segments, requiring high-speed hub ports to transmit both low and full speed in the downstream direction. Upsteam connectivity is not affected by whether a packet is sent at low or full speed. That is, the hub receivers and upstream transmitters are designed to handle both low and full speed packets.

Figure 7-14 illustrates the format of the preamble packet. The preamble packet consists of a synchronization sequence and a packet ID that are transferred at full speed. Following the PID the host must delay the beginning of the low-speed packet transfer by inserting four full speed bit times. This delay gives hubs time to enable their low-speed ports and configure their repeater to accept low-speed signaling. During this delay hubs drive their ports (low and full speed) to the idle state. Note that the preamble packet differs from all other packets in that it does not end with an EOP.

Once the preamble packet and four bit-time delay have completed, a low-speed token packet is sent by the host over the USB, specifying the type of transaction to be performed. The hub once again disables it's low-speed ports when it detects the low-speed EOP.

In the event of an IN transaction, the target device returns data at low speed to the host controller. Data returned upstream to hub receiver ports can be either low- or full-speed transactions. In the event of an OUT transaction, the data packet must also be transferred at low speed to the USB device, requiring another preamble packet be send directly preceding the data packet.

Low-speed devices can support control and interrupt transfers only and the data payload size is limited to eight bytes during a transaction.

Figure 7-14: Preamble Packet Format

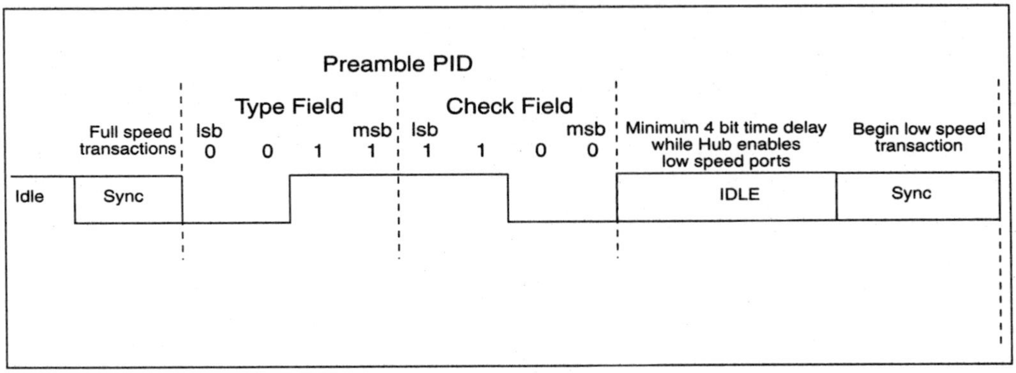

Transactions

The following sections describe each type of transaction and specifies the possible forms that each may take.

IN Transactions

A typical IN transaction, consists of the token phase, data phase, and handshake phase. However, in some instances an IN transaction may not consist of all three phases. IN transactions are employed when performing all four types of transfers. Several conditions may occur when performed an IN transaction:

- data is received without errors.
- data is received with errors.
- the target is temporarily unable to return data.
- the target is unable to return data without an existing error condition being cleared.
- an isochronous transfer is taking place, thus, data is returned by the target, but no handshake follows the data phase.

IN Transaction without Errors

In Figure 7-15, the IN transaction could occur when performing an interrupt transfer, bulk transfer, isochronous transfer, or control transfer. In this example, data returned by the target device to the root hub is received without error, and an ACK handshake is returned to the target device. Note that the data packet is defined as a data0 packet, which is the data packet used for single data phase transfers, interrupt transfers, and is always used during the first transaction of a transfer requiring multiple IN transactions (e.g. bulk or control transfers from a USB device). In multiple transaction transfers, consecutive transactions will alternate between data0 and data1 transactions.

Figure 7-15: IN Transaction without Errors

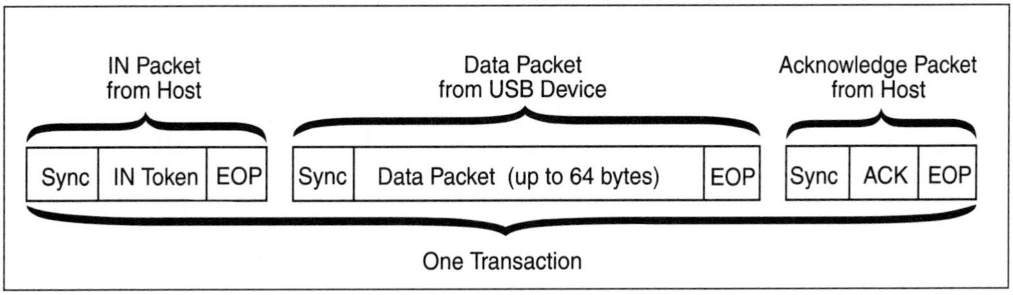

IN Transaction with Errors

In Figure 7-16, the IN transaction consists of two phases: the IN token phase and the data phase. The handshake is not returned from the host controller to the target device because an error was detected by the host when it received the data packet. The target device will detect a time-out condition since the acknowledge is not returned by the host. The host is responsible for retrying the IN transaction at a later time.

Figure 7-16: IN Transaction with Data Phase Errors

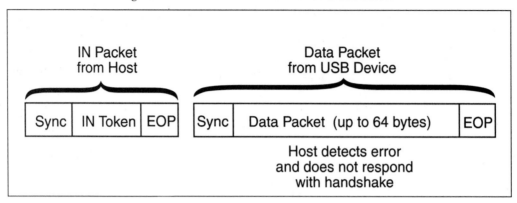

IN Transaction with No Interrupt Pending/Target Busy

Figure 7-17 illustrates a condition in which the target device is temporarily unable to return data. Since the device is unable to return data during the data phase of the transaction, it returns a NAK during the data phase. This informs the root hub and host controller that the device is temporarily unable to return data. This form of IN transaction can occur during interrupt transfers if no interrupt is currently pending within the device, or during bulk or control transfers if a busy condition exists within the device, preventing it from returning data.

Figure 7-17: IN Transaction with Target Temporarily Unable to Return Data

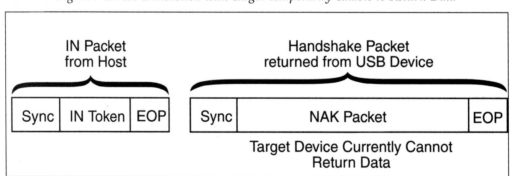

IN Transaction with Target Stalled

Figure 7-18 illustrates a condition in which the target device has incurred an error condition that prevents it from returning data. The target device returns a STALL handshake to the root hub to inform system software that the error condition must be cleared before data can be returned. Note that this error may be part of normal operation, rather than a serious USB device problem. For example, a scanner that inadvertently loses power during a scan, would not be able to return data via the USB interface. Once power is restored the transfer can continue.

Figure 7-18: IN Transaction with Target Stalled

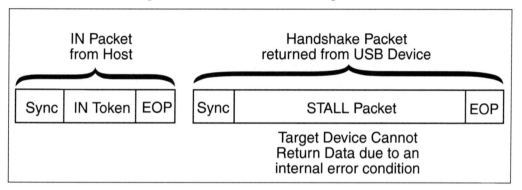

IN Transaction during Isochronous Transfer

In Figure 7-19 the IN transaction results from an isochronous transfer. Both the host controller and the target device are aware that the transaction is part of an isochronous transfer. The target device has this knowledge because the endpoint address selects one of its isochronous endpoints. The host controller has knowledge that the transaction is isochronous because system software specifies the transfer type in the transfer descriptor that the host controller executes. The IN transaction consists of the token phase and the data phase only and does not include a handshake since data delivery is not guaranteed with isochronous transfers.

Figure 7-19: IN Transaction during Isochronous Transfer

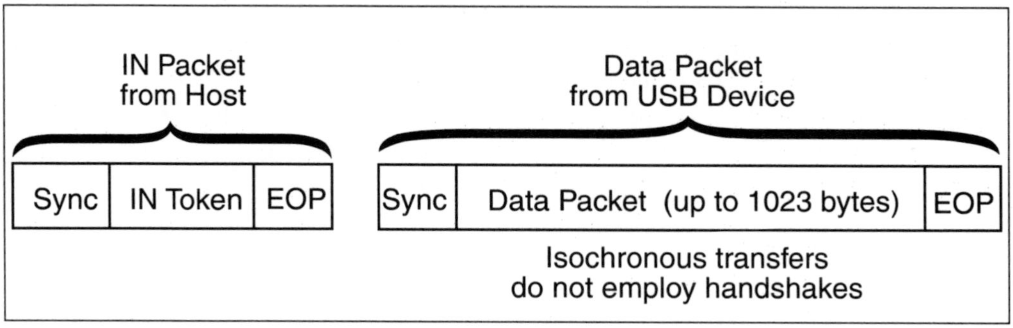

```
         IN Packet                        Data Packet
         from Host                       from USB Device

 ┌──────┬──────────┬──────┐  ┌──────┬──────────────────────────────┬──────┐
 │ Sync │ IN Token │ EOP  │  │ Sync │ Data Packet (up to 1023 bytes)│ EOP  │
 └──────┴──────────┴──────┘  └──────┴──────────────────────────────┴──────┘
                                        Isochronous transfers
                                        do not employ handshakes
```

OUT Transactions

A typical OUT transaction, consists of the token phase, data phase, and hand-shake phase. However, in some instances an OUT transaction may not consist of all three phases. OUT transactions can be employed when performing bulk, control, and isochronous transfers. Several conditions may occur when performed an OUT transaction:

- data is sent without errors.
- data is sent with errors.
- the target is temporarily unable to accept data.
- the target is unable to accept data without an existing error condition being cleared.
- an isochronous transfer is taking place, thus, data is sent to the target, but no handshake follows the data phase.

Each of these conditions are discussed and illustrated in the following paragraphs.

OUT Transaction without Data Packet Errors

Figure 7-20 illustrates a normal OUT transaction in which data is successfully sent to the target device without error. The target device, having received the data without error returns a ACK handshake to the root hub. Such OUT transactions can take place during bulk and control transfers.

Figure 7-20: OUT Transactions without Errors

OUT Packet from Host			Data Packet to USB Device			Acknowledge Packet from Target Device		
Sync	OUT Token	EOP	Sync	Data Packet (up to 64 bytes)	EOP	Sync	ACK	EOP

OUT Transaction with Errors/Target Busy

Figure 7-22 assumes that the same transaction described in the preceding paragraph is performed except that in this instance, the target device detects errors when receiving the data. The target device discards the data and does not respond with a handshake. The host will detect a bus time-out since the expected handshake packet does not appear. The host must retry the OUT transaction at a later time.

Figure 7-21: OUT Transaction with Data Packet Errors

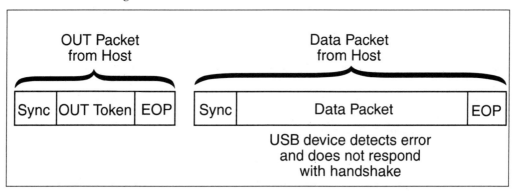

OUT Transaction — Target Unable to Accept Data

The transaction illustrated in Figure 7-22 results if the target device is temporarily unable to accept data. The target receives the data without error, but cannot accept it (e.g. due to a busy or buffer full condition). In response, the target returns NAK during the handshake phase of the transaction. This informs the host that the target did not accept the data and that the transaction must be retried later.

Figure 7-22: OUT Transaction to Target That is Unable to Accept Data

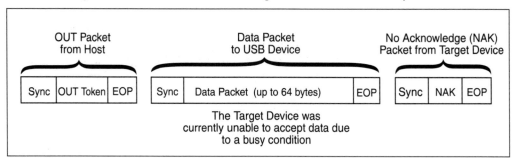

OUT Transaction with Target Stalled

Figure 7-23 illustrates a transaction that results from the target device being unable to receive data due to an internal error condition. The target receives the OUT token recognizing that it is addressed, however when the host sends the data packet, the target device is unable to accept the data and returns a STALL to the host during the handshake phase of the transaction. The stall condition is reported to the host software, which must clear the error condition within the target.

Figure 7-23: OUT Transaction to Stalled Endpoint

```
┌─────────────────────────────────────────────────────────────────────────────────┐
│                                                                                   │
│      OUT Packet              Data Packet               STALL handshake Packet     │
│      from Host               to USB Device             from Target Device         │
│                                                                                   │
│  ┌────┬─────────┬───┐   ┌────┬──────────────────┬───┐   ┌────┬──────┬───┐         │
│  │Sync│OUT Token│EOP│   │Sync│Data Packet (up to│EOP│   │Sync│STALL │EOP│         │
│  │    │         │   │   │    │  64 bytes)       │   │   │    │      │   │         │
│  └────┴─────────┴───┘   └────┴──────────────────┴───┘   └────┴──────┴───┘         │
│                          The Target Device is unable to accept                    │
│                            data due to a device stall condition                   │
│                                                                                   │
└─────────────────────────────────────────────────────────────────────────────────┘
```

OUT Transaction during Isochronous Transfer

Figure 7-24 illustrates an OUT transaction performed during an isochronous transfer. Whether data is received with or without errors by the target device, no handshake phase is performed.

Figure 7-24: OUT Transaction during Isochronous Transfer

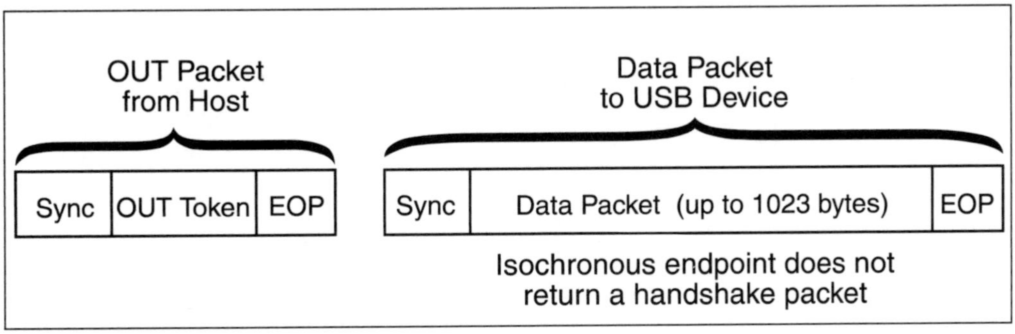

OUT Packet from Host			Data Packet to USB Device		
Sync	OUT Token	EOP	Sync	Data Packet (up to 1023 bytes)	EOP

Isochronous endpoint does not
return a handshake packet

Setup Transactions/Control Transfers

Control transfers provide a mechanism for supporting configuration, to issue commands, or request status to or from the device. Control transfers always begin with a setup transaction, called the setup stage. The setup stage defines the nature of the control transfer. Some control transfers include a data stage consisting of one or more IN or OUT transactions that are used to deliver the payload of the control transfer. Whether data is sent to or received from the device is defined by setup stage. The final stage of a control transfer is the status stage. This stage confirms that the requested operation has been completed successfully. Control transfers exist in two basic forms:

- Transfers consisting of a setup stage and status stage.
- Transfers consisting of a setup stage, data stage, and status stage.

The data phase of a setup transaction contains 8 bytes of information as defined in Table 7-3. The information specifies a variety of information that defines the device request to be performed.

Table 7-3: Format of Setup Transaction Data Phase

Offset	Field	Size	Value	Description
0	Request-Type	1	Bit-map	Characteristics of Request D7 Data xfer direction 0 = Host to device 1 = Device to host D6..5 Type 0 = Standard 1 = Class 2 = Vendor 3 = Reserved D4..0 Recipient 0 = Device 1 = Interface 2 = Endpoint 3 = Other 4..31 = Reserved
1	Request	1	Value	Specific Request.
2	Value	2	Value	Word-sized field that varies according to request.
4	Index	2	Index or Offset	Word-sized field that varies according to request. Typically used to pass an index or offset.
6	Length	2	Count	Number of bytes to transfer if there is a data stage required for this transfer.

Two Stage Control Transfer

A two-stage control transfer consists solely of the setup and status stages as illustrated in Figure 7-25. In this instance the 8 bytes delivered during the setup transaction contains all the information needed to perform the specified request (e.g. remote wake-up request). The status stage consists of an IN transaction to verify that the request has been successfully processed.

Figure 7-25: Format of a Two-Stage Control Transfer

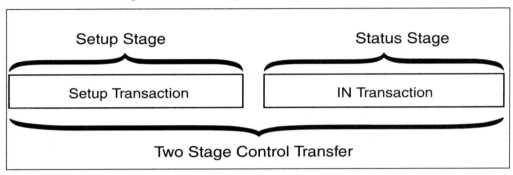

Three Stage Control Transfer with IN Data Stage

Figure 7-26 illustrates a control transfer that requires data be returned from the target device back to the host. As an example, a control transfer may performed when the host system issues a request to read a device descriptor. The first stage of the transfer consists of the setup transaction that defines the nature of the control transfer. The setup transaction consists of the setup token, data packet, and handshake. During setup transactions data is always sent to the target device to specify the type of request. Following the setup phase, the host initiates one or more IN transactions, prompting the target to return the requested data. The host completes the control transfer by using an OUT transaction to request verification that the device endpoint has successfully returned the contents of the descriptor. Note that the target device indicates successful completion of the request by issuing an ACK handshake during the OUT transaction. The OUT data packet issued by the host has a length of zero.

Figure 7-26: Control Transfer Requesting Data from Target

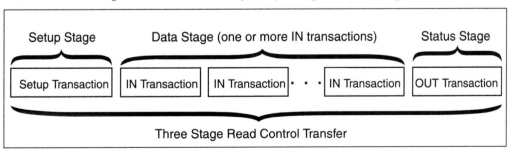

Three Stage Control Transfer with OUT Data Stage

Figure 7-27 illustrates the format of a control transfer in which a command is issued to a control endpoint. The setup transaction defines the request being issued and is followed by the data stage (one or more OUT transactions). The host then issues an IN token to the control endpoint to obtain completion status. The target returns a data packet with a length of zero to indicate that it has successful processed the initial control request.

Figure 7-27: Control Transfer Issuing a Command to a Target's Control Endpoint

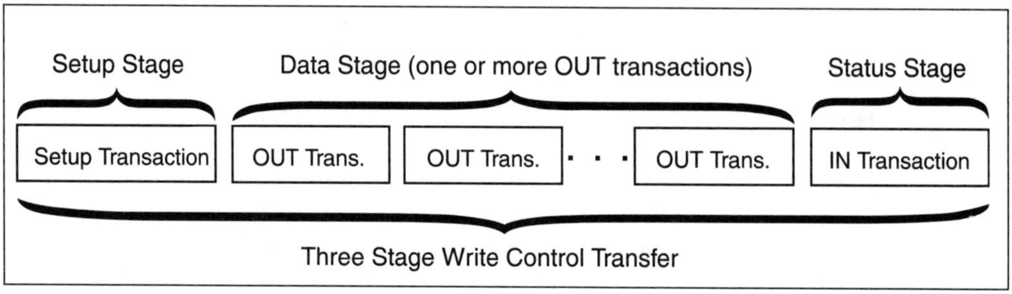

Setup Stage	Data Stage (one or more OUT transactions)			Status Stage
Setup Transaction	OUT Trans.	OUT Trans. • • •	OUT Trans.	IN Transaction

Three Stage Write Control Transfer

Control Transfers with Errors

The host system attempts retries to ensure that a control transfer completes successfully. The action taken by the target and host depends on the nature of the error condition and when the error occurs during the transfer. See Chapter 8 for further details.

8 *Error Recovery*

The Previous Chapter

The previous chapter introduced transaction and packet types and explained how they are used with each transfer type. Various forms of transactions were described for each transfer type.

This Chapter

All transfer types except isochronous are designed to complete over the USB even when error conditions are detected. This chapter discusses error types, the mechanisms used to detect them, and explains the error recovery mechanisms.

The Next Chapter

Next power distribution via the USB is discussed, along with issues related to bus-powered devices and the operation of self-powered devices. The chapter also discusses the role of host software in detecting and reporting power-related problems.

Overview

A variety of error conditions are detectable by hardware during transfer of data across the USB. The previous chapter introduced the handshake packet that has been designed into the USB transaction protocol to verify that a packet has been successfully received. This chapter details all the USB error checking mechanisms and describes the related error recovery procedures. Error checking mechanisms supported by the USB include:

- Packet error checks
- False EOP
- Bus time-out (no response)
- Data toggle error checks
- Babble — transactions occurring beyond end of frame
- LOA — Loss Of Activity on bus

Packet Errors

The USB devices detect three types of packet errors:

- Packet ID (PID) checks
- Cyclic Redundancy Checks (CRC)
- Bit stuff errors

If any of these error conditions exist, the receiver of the packet must ignore the packet and not respond to it in any manner. The receiver consequently never sends a packet back to the transmitter if the packet just received contains an error. Note that the type of packet error detected is not significant to the USB devices or Host as it relates to error recovery. However, the host system may capture statistics regarding the nature of packet failures. The following sections discuss each form of packet-related error.

PID Checks

Each packet broadcast over the USB starts with a Packet ID (PID) consisting of four bits and is followed by a PID check field as illustrated in Figure 8-1. The check field is the PID inverted (1's complement). All potential USB target devices must perform the PID check and ignore the packet if an error is detected, since the definition of the packet is unknown.

Figure 8-1: PID Check

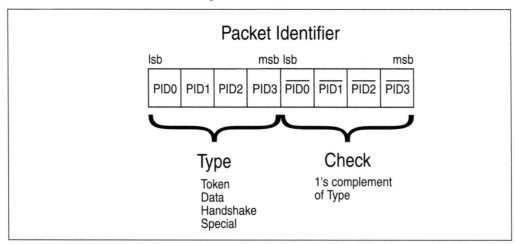

CRC Errors

Each packet contains CRC bits used to validate the information send following the Packet ID field. The nature of this information varies depending on the packet type. Each packet contains either 5 or 16 CRC bits determined by the packet's potential size. Furthermore, the packet type the fields covered by the CRC vary according to packet type. Refer to Table 8-1.

Table 8-1: Packet Type and CRC

Packet Type	Fields	Max. Size of Fields	Number of CRC bits
Start of Frame	frame number	11-bits	5
IN	device and endpoint address	11-bits	5
OUT	device and endpoint address	11-bits	5
SETUP	device and endpoint address	11-bits	5
DATA0	data payload	1023 bytes	16
DATA1	data payload	1023 bytes	16
ACK	NA — packet ID only	NA	NA
NAK	NA — packet ID only	NA	NA
STALL	NA — packet ID only	NA	NA
PREAMBLE	NA — packet ID only	NA	NA

The 5-bit CRC field for the token packets is based on a generator polynomial:

$$G(X) = X^5 + X^2 + 1$$

The bit pattern representing this polynomial is 00101b. The five bit residual at the receiver will be 01100b is all bits are received correctly.

The 16-bit CRC field for the data packets is based on the generating polynomial:

$$G(X) = X^{16} + X^{15} + X^2 + 1$$

The bit pattern representing this polynomial is 1000000000000101b. If the data is received without errors then the 16-bit residual will be 1000000000001101.

Note that the CRC bit stream will contain stuffed bits if the CRC contains six consecutive ones.

Bit Stuff Errors

Bit stuffing ensures that the sender and receiver of NRZI data maintain synchronization by forcing a transition into the data stream after detecting six consecutive 1s. See the heading entitled, "Bit Stuffing" on page 63 for details.

USB receivers expect to see a guaranteed transition (stuffed bit) in the data stream after six consecutive 1s. If a stuffed bit is not present, this indicates that the packet has been corrupted or that the sender is not properly generating stuffed bits, or that the receiver is not decoding the NRZI data correctly.

Packet-Related Error Handling

Any one of the packet-related errors cause the same reporting a error handling to occur. In every instance, the receiver of a corrupted packet must ignore the packet and not respond. The error handling issues however, vary depending on the transaction and which packet of a given the transaction is corrupted.

Token Packet Errors

IN Packet Errors. Consider an IN packet during which some form of packet error occurs. Since an error is detected in the token packet, it is ignored by the target device and no response is returned to the host. The host expects either a data or handshake packet to be returned in response to the IN token. However, since the target does not respond, the host will detect a bus time-out and the transaction fails. The host is then responsible for retrying the failed transaction.

OUT or Setup Packet Errors. If an OUT or SETUP packet is being broadcast by the host when a packet error is detected, the host will follow the token packet with a data packet. The target may decode the data packet without error, but may not be able to verify that it is the intended recipient (due to an address CRC error), or may not be able to detect the meaning of the data packet (due to a PID check error). Since the target does not respond to the OUT token nor the following data packet, the host detects a bus time-out and knows and that the transaction has failed. The host then reschedules the transaction.

Data Packet Errors

During OUT or Setup Transactions. Errors occurring during data packets cause the receiving device to discard the data and not respond to the sender. During an OUT transaction, the target having detected a data packet error will not respond with a handshake. The resulting time-out tells the host of the failed write. The host then retries the transaction later.

During IN Transactions. During IN transactions, valid data is returned by the target but the host receives a corrupted data packet. Since the host does not response with an ACK handshake, the target is informed that the host did not receive the data. The host then must retry the transaction.

Handshake Packet Errors

Handshake packet errors leave the target and host in disagreement about whether the transaction has completed successfully or has failed. The following paragraphs explain the problem.

During OUT Transactions. During OUT transaction the token and data packets may be received without errors. The target indicates receipt of the data by returning an ACK handshake packet to the host. If errors are detected when the ACK packet is received, the packet will be ignored by the host and the handshake will fail. The target has in fact received the data, but the corrupted handshake misinforms the host of the completion status. The host and target now disagree on whether the transaction has completed successfully or not.

The host believing that an error has occurred attempts to send the packet again. The target recognizing that the packet has been received expects the next consecutive data item. This causes the same data to be accepted twice as valid data, due to the synchronization problem between the host and target.

During IN Transactions. Note that a similar circumstance can occur during an IN transaction where data has successfully transferred between the target and host. The host returns ACK to the target, but an ACK packet error is detected by the target. The target fails to get confirmation of the transfer, but the host has successfully received the data.

The host, recognizing that the transfer has completed successfully, requests the next data item in the transfer. However, the target believes that the transaction has failed and therefore sends the same data again.

This type of disagreement between the target and host must be handled through the use of the data toggle mechanism. Refer to the section entitled, "Data Toggle Errors" on page 116.

Bus Time-Out

The transmitter and receiver involved in a transaction, must know how long they must wait for a response. For example, transmitters expect responses from targets devices after sending token and data packets. Similarly, a target device expects a response from the host after it transmits data to the host. However, if the response is not returned within the specified bus turn-around time an error is detected.

No response from a target is defined by the specification as the method of notifying the sender of a packet that was not received correctly. That is, if errors are detected within the packet being received, no response is sent as expected. Since no response is sent, the transmitter of the packet will detect a bus time-out, thereby recognizing that some error has occurred during the packet transfer.

The bus time-out defines the maximum number of cable segments supported downstream from the host. The delays associated with transferring data from the host to a downstream port include:

- Cable delay=30ns maximum
- Hub delay=40ns maximum

The total delay from the downstream port of the root hub to the downstream port of the first hub is a maximum value of 70ns. The worst case timing occurs when six cable segments are supported via a single downstream path as illustrated in Figure 8-2. The total round-trip delay between the host port to the upstream end of the device's cable is 700ns. Additional delays occur as the signal propagates over the target device cable. The target then decodes the token packet, accesses the selected endpoint, and initiates the return packet back to the upstream end of the cable. This 7.5 bit time delay is specifically defined as the time from the end of packet (EOP to idle transition) seen on the upstream end of the functions cable until the SOP transition from the device is returned to the upstream end of the target cable.

Figure 8-2: Total Trip Delay

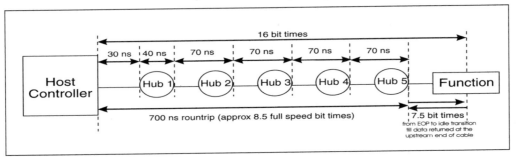

Figure 8-2: Total Trip Delay

The transmitter of the transaction must not time-out before 16-bit times but must time-out by 18-bit times. This is true of both slow- and full-speed transactions.

False EOPs

Problems can occur if the receiver detects the end of packet (EOP) prior to the transmitter having actually completed it transfer. This condition is known as a false EOP. If the receiver were to respond to the premature EOP by returning either a data or a handshake packet, a collision would occur on the bus. This would have the effect to corrupting two consecutive packets. Fortunately, false EOPs can be detected and the collision avoided. The false EOP having truncated the packet will very likely result in a CRC error. It is highly unlikely that the CRC will be correct for a truncated packet. The following sections describe the detection and response.

False EOP during Host Transmission

USB target devices that detect any form of packet error simply ignore the packet and do not respond to the host. Therefore, if a false EOP occurs, the resulting CRC error forces the target to simply wait for the host to deliver the next packet. This passive behavior by the target device prevents a collision from occurring. Furthermore, when the host fails to receive a response from the target, it recognizes that the packet transfer has failed and performs a retry.

Since the error condition described above results from a false EOP, the host may continue to transmit data after the target has incorrectly detected the EOP. The target device will not likely recognize the remainder of the packet as being valid and will ultimately detect the real EOP at the end of the packet. The target then waits for the next packet to be sent by the host.

False EOP during Target Transmission

If the target is transmitting data and the host receives a false EOP, the CRC error dictates that the host ignore the packet by not responding to the target. This prevents a collision since no response is sent to the target. Since the target fails to get the handshake, it knows that the packet was not received by the host and waits for the next transaction to be initiated.

The host in this case needs to know when it's safe to transmit the next packet. Since the EOP detection was premature, the target may continue to transmit data. If the host detects no additional bus transitions, within the bus time-out period of 16-bit times, it can safely assume that no more data will be sent by the target. The host can then safely transmit the next packet and be assured of no collisions on the bus. If however, bus transitions continue the host must wait for the EOP, and then wait for 16-bit times before transmitting the next packet. Note that the 16-bit time delay is required to ensure that the target detects that the host has not responded (i.e. the target time-out counter expires). This ensures that the target recognizes that the packet transfer has failed.

Data Toggle Errors

Data toggle is a mechanism used to ensure that the transmitter and receiver of a transfer remain synchronized, throughout a long transfer requiring a large number of individual transactions. Data toggle solves the problem associated with corrupted handshake packets as described in the section entitled, "Handshake Packet Errors" on page 113.

Data Toggle Procedure without Errors

Data toggle is supported for interrupt, bulk, and control transfers only. The transmitter and receiver involved in a transfer that supports the data toggle mechanism must implement toggle bits. The transmitting device and receiving device both transition their toggle bit to the opposite state when they both agree that the transaction has occurred without error. The two data packet types (DATA0 and DATA1), are transmitted alternately and compared by the receiver of the packet to verify that the correct packet has been received. The transmitter uses the data packet type that matches the current state of its toggle bit. (e.g., if the toggle bit = 0, then DATA0 is used). To explain the concept of the data toggle mechanism consider the following transactions that are described and illustrated in the following sections.

Data Toggle during OUT Transactions

Figure 8-3 on page 118 illustrates the packet sequence and toggle bit transitions for bulk data transfer from the host to a target device. Assume that the toggle bits in the transmitter and receiver toggle bits are initially cleared (zero). The transfer proceeds as follows:

Transaction 1

1. The host transmits an OUT token to the target device.
2. The target device receives the token without any packet errors.
3. The host then transmits a DATA0 packet (consistent with its toggle bit) to the target device.
4. The target receives data packet zero, which matches the toggle bit.
5. Having successfully received the DATA0 packet, the toggle bit transitions to one.
6. The target transmits an ACK handshake packet to inform the host that data was received without error.
7. The host receives the ACK packet without error.
8. Having successfully received the ACK packet, the host transitions the toggle bit to a one.

Transaction 2

1. The next transaction to the target begins with the OUT token transmitted to the target.
2. The target device receives the OUT token without errors.
3. The host transmits a DATA1 packet (consistent with its toggle bit).
4. The target receives the packet without error and DATA1 matches the state of its toggle bit.
5. Having successfully received the DATA1 packet, the receiver toggles the bit to zero.
6. The target transmits an ACK handshake packet to inform the host that data was received without error.
7. The host receives the ACK packet without error.
8. Having successfully received the ACK packet, the host transitions the toggle bit to a zero.

This procedure is performed for each transaction until the entire transfer completes. As long as the data packet received matches the toggle bit and the transmitter receives the ACK without error, the transmitter and receiver remain in synchronization.

Figure 8-3: OUT Transaction with Data Toggle Sequence and No Error

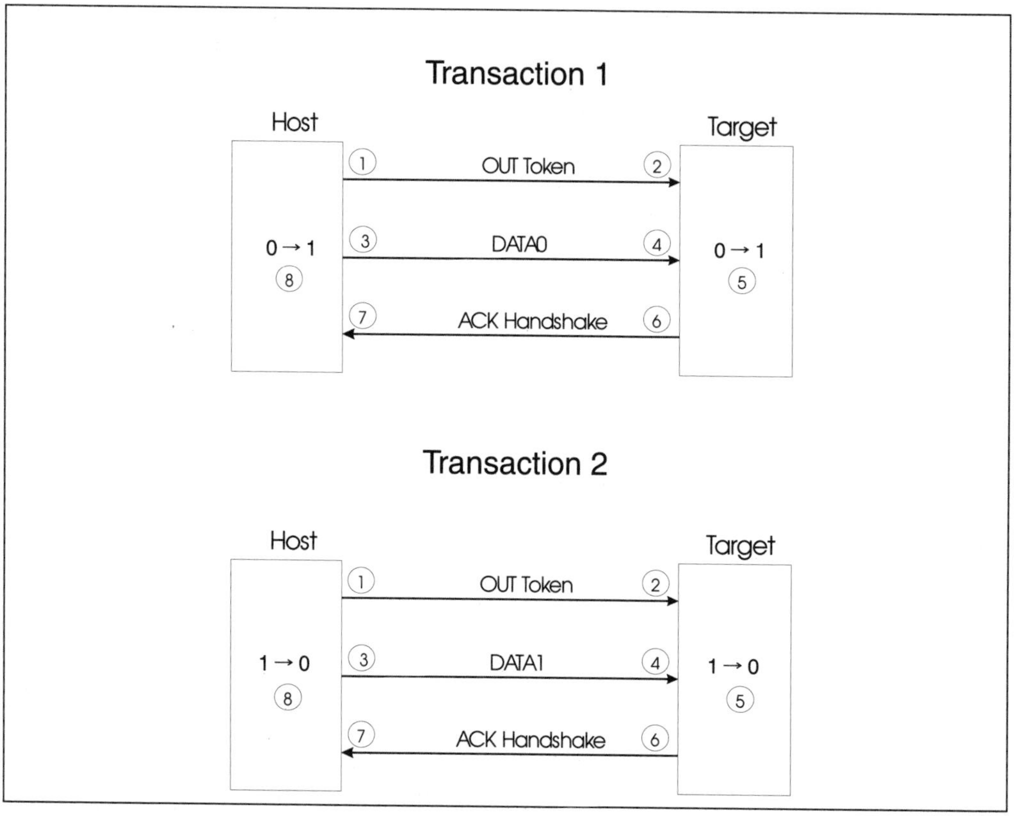

Data Toggle during IN Transactions

Figure 8-4 illustrates the sequence of two IN transactions and the transitions that would take place during an error free transfer. The sequence occurs as follows:

Transaction 1

1. The host transmits an IN token to the target device.
2. The target device receives the token without errors.

3. The receiver then returns a DATA0 packet (consistent with the state of the toggle bit) to the host.
4. The host receives data packet zero, which matches its toggle bit.
5. Having successfully received the DATA0 packet, the toggle bit transitions to one.
6. The host transmits an ACK handshake packet to inform the target that it received the data packet without error.
7. The target receives the ACK packet without error.
8. Having successfully received the ACK packet, the target transitions its toggle bit to a one.

Transaction 2

1. The next transaction to the target begins with an IN token transmitted to the target.
2. The target device receives the IN token without errors.
3. The target returns a DATA1 packet (consistent with the state of its toggle bit).
4. The host receives the DATA1 packet without error and it correctly matches the host's toggle bit.
5. Having successfully received the DATA1 packet, the host toggles the bit to zero.
6. The host transmits an ACK handshake packet to inform the target that it has received the data packet without errors.
7. The host receives the ACK packet without errors.
8. Having successfully received the ACK packet, the host transitions the toggle bit to a zero.

This procedure is performed for each transaction until the entire transfer completes. As long as the data packet received matches the toggle bit and the transmitter receives the ACK without error, the transmitter and receiver remain in synchronization.

Figure 8-4: IN Transactions with Data Toggle Sequence and No Errors

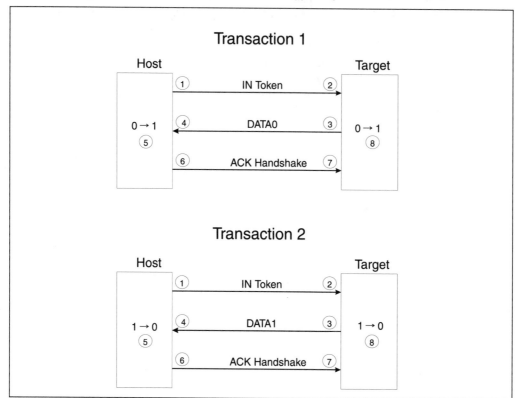

Data Toggle Procedure with Data Packet Errors

If data packet errors occur during a transfer, the toggle bits are not incremented by either the host or target devices. The following sections describe the operation of data toggle when data packet errors occur.

Data Toggle and Data Packet Errors — OUT Transactions

Figure 8-5 on page 121 illustrates a sequence of packet transfers during consecutive OUT transactions. During the first transaction a data packet error occurs.

Figure 8-5: OUT Transaction with Data Toggle and Data Packet Errors

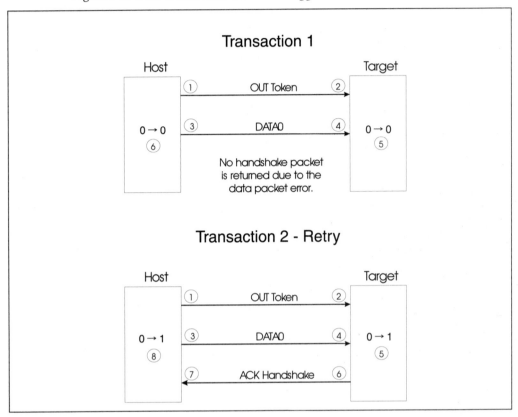

The actions taken by the host and target are as follows:

Transaction 1

1. An OUT packet is transmitted by the host.
2. The target receives the packet without errors.
3. The host transmits data via the DATA0 packet (consistent with it toggle bit).
4. Packet errors are encountered when the target receives the DATA0 packet.
5. Having detected errors in the data packet the target device ignores the packet. Data is discarded and no handshake packet is sent to the host. Since the data packet was not received correctly, the toggle bit remains unchanged.
6. The host awaits the return of the handshake packet but gets no reply. After the bus time-out period (16 bit times), the host detects no response and rec-

ognizes that the data packet transfer was not successful. The toggle bit remains unchanged and the host must retry the transaction later.

Transaction 2 — the retry

1. The host transmits an OUT token to the target device.
2. The target device receives the token without any packet errors.
3. The host then retransmits the DATA0 packet (consistent with its toggle bit) that failed during the previous transaction.
4. The target successfully receives data packet zero, which matches the toggle bit.
5. This time having received DATA0 without errors, the target toggles the bit to one.
6. The target then transmits an ACK handshake packet to inform the host that data was received without error.
7. The host receives the ACK packet without error.
8. Having successfully received the ACK packet, the host transitions its toggle bit to a one.

The host and the target remain synchronized even though the data transfer was corrupted.

Data Toggle and Data Packet Errors — IN Transactions

Figure 8-6 on page 123 illustrates a sequence of packet transfers during consecutive IN transactions. In this example the IN transaction incurs a data packet error.

Figure 8-6: IN Transactions with Data Toggle and Data Packet Errors

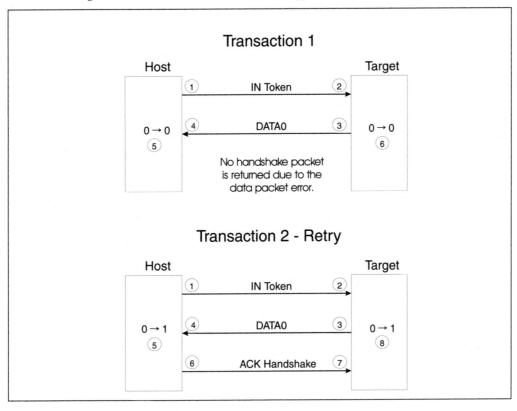

The actions taken by the host and target are as follows:

Transaction 1

1. An IN packet is transmitted by the host.
2. The target receives the packet without errors.
3. The target returns data via the DATA0 packet (consistent with it toggle bit).
4. Packet errors are encountered by the host when it receives the DATA0 packet.
5. Having detected errors in the data packet, the host ignores the packet. Data is discarded and no handshake packet is returned to the target. Since the data packet was received with errors, the toggle bit remains unchanged.
6. The target awaits the return of the handshake packet but gets no reply from the host. After the bus time-out period (16 bit times), the target detects no

response and recognizes that the data packet transfer was not successful. The target's toggle bit remains unchanged and the host must retry the transaction later.

Transaction 2 — the retry

1. The host once again transmits the OUT token to the target device.
2. The target device receives the token without any packet errors.
3. The target then retransmits the DATA0 packet (consistent with its toggle bit) knowing that data was not received by the host during the previous transaction.
4. This time the host successfully receives data packet zero, which matches the toggle bit.
5. Having received DATA0 without errors, the host toggles the bit to one.
6. The Host then transmits an ACK handshake packet to inform the target that data was received without error.
7. The target receives the ACK packet without error.
8. Having successfully received the ACK packet, the target transitions its toggle bit to a one.

The host and the target maintain their synchronization and the retry ensured that not data is lost.

Data Toggle with Handshake Packet Errors

The previous discussions of data toggle describe the actions taken by the host and target when either no packet errors occur or when data packet errors occur. While its important that the host and target toggle bits remain synchronized, the error recovery mechanism does not require the use of the data toggle bits. However, when errors occur during the handshake phase, the host and target become de-synchronized, and data loss would occur without the use of the data toggle mechanism.

Data Toggle and Handshake Errors — OUT Transactions

Figure 8-7 on page 126 illustrates an OUT transaction that fails due to an ACK packet error. The sequence of events that occur in detecting and recovering from the error is enumerated below:

Transaction 1

1. The host transmits an OUT token to the target device.
2. The target device receives the token without any packet errors.
3. The host then transmits a DATA0 packet (consistent with its toggle bit) to the target device.
4. The target receives data packet zero, which matches the toggle bit.
5. Having successfully received the DATA0 packet, the toggle bit transitions to one.
6. The target transmits an ACK handshake packet to inform the host that data was received without error.
7. The host receives the ACK packet with errors.
8. Since errors are detected by the host, it cannot verify that the target has successfully received the data. Thus, the host leaves the toggle bit unchanged (zero). The host presumes that the target did receive the data and therefore, initiates a retry.

Transaction 2 — the retry

1. The host transmits the OUT token to the target.
2. The target device receives the packet without errors.
3. The host re-transmits the DATA0 packet (consistent with the state of its toggle bit).
4. The target receives the packet without error but DATA0 does not match the state of its toggle bit.
5. The target recognizes that it is out of sync with the host and therefore discards the data, and leaves the toggle bit unchanged (one).
6. The target transmits an ACK handshake packet to inform the host that data was received without error. This is because the host apparently did not receive the previous ACK handshake.
7. The host receives the ACK packet without error.
8. Having successfully received the ACK packet, the host transitions the toggle bit to a one. The host and target are now ready to proceed to the next transaction.

The host and target temporarily disagreed on whether the data had actually been completed. However, the data toggle mechanism ensures that the de-synchronization is detected and permits re-synchronization.

Figure 8-7: OUT Transaction with Data Toggle and Handshake Errors

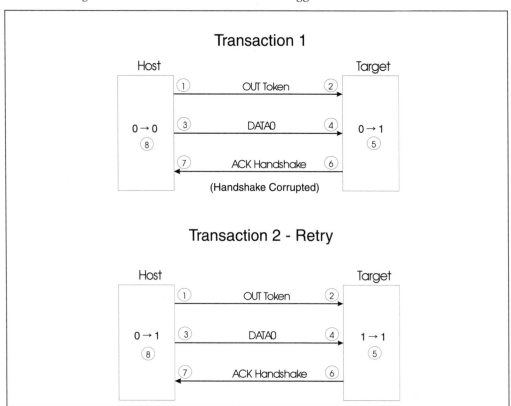

Data Toggle with Handshake Packet Error — IN Transaction

Figure 8-8 on page 128 illustrates an IN transaction that fails due to an ACK packet error. The sequence of events that occur when detecting and recovering from this error is enumerated below:

Transaction 1

1. The host transmits an IN token to the target device.
2. The target device receives the token without any packet errors.
3. The target then transmits a DATA0 packet to the host.
4. The host receives data packet zero without error and the toggle bit matches DATA0.

5. Having successfully received the DATA0 packet, the host transitions the toggle bit to one.
6. The host then transmits an ACK handshake packet to inform the target that data was received without error.
7. The target receives the ACK packet with errors.
8. Since errors are detected by the target, it cannot verify that the host has successfully received the data. Thus, the host leaves the toggle bit unchanged (zero). The target presumes that the host did not receive the data and therefore will attempt a perform this transaction again. The target then will return the same data again during the next transaction.

Transaction 2

1. The host transmits the IN token to the target to get the next consecutive data.
2. The target device receives the packet without errors.
3. The target re-transmits the DATA0 packet (consistent with the state of its toggle bit), since it believes that the host failed to receive the data during the last transaction.
4. The host receives the packet without error but DATA0 does not match the state of its toggle bit.
5. The host recognizes that it is out of sync with the target and therefore discards the data, knowing that it correctly received this same data during the previous transaction. The host also leaves the toggle bit unchanged (one).
6. The host transmits an ACK handshake packet to inform the target that data was received without error. This is done because the target apparently did not receive the previous ACK handshake.
7. The target receives the ACK packet without error.
8. Having successfully received the ACK packet, the target transitions its toggle bit to a one. The host and target toggle bits now agree.

The host and target temporarily disagreed on whether the data had actually been completed. However, the data toggle mechanism ensures that the de-synchronization is detected and permits re-synchronization.

Figure 8-8: IN Transaction with Data Toggle and Handshake Errors

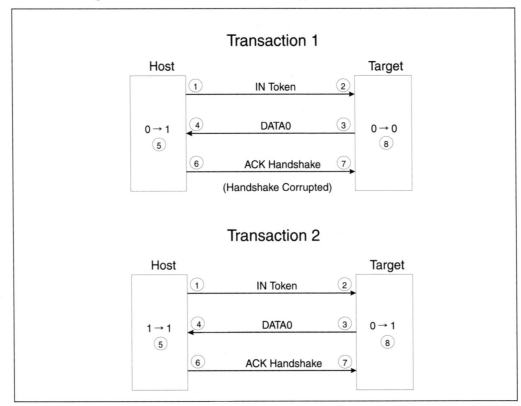

Special Case: Data Toggle During Control Transfer

During control transfers the data toggle sequence is used to ensure that the host and target remain synchronized during the entire control sequence. The Setup transaction begins with a DATA0 data phase and each subsequent data phase will alternate between DATA1 and DATA0 as illustrated in Figure 8-9.

A problem arises when a data toggle error occurs on the last data transaction of the data stage during a control read. If the last IN transaction of the data stage results in a failed handshake, the target believes that the root hub did not receive the last IN transaction successfully and expects a retry. The target does not transition its toggle bit and is prepared to resend the IN data. The root hub having receive the last IN transaction of the data stage without error transitions its toggle bit and proceeds to the SETUP stage by sending an OUT transaction. In this case the data toggle procedure fails since the target is expecting a retry and the root hub has moved on to the OUT status stage.

Figure 8-9: Data Toggle During Control Transfers

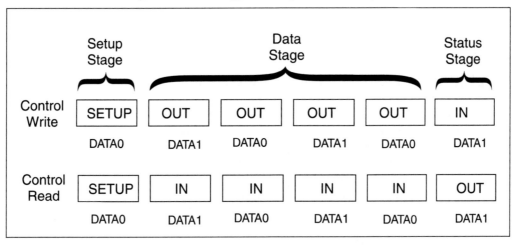

This problem is avoided by a special protocol that requires the host to issue an OUT setup token upon successfully receiving the last IN transaction of the data stage. The target recognizing that the token direction specifies an OUT data stage, interprets the hosts action as verification that the last IN transaction completed successfully. The target transitions it toggle bit and advances to the status phase, along with the root hub.

Babble

Bus failures can occur if a device on the bus fails to end its transaction (i.e. it continues to babble on and on). This type of endless babbling has the potential of deadlocking the entire bus, and therefore, must be prevented. Babble is detected at the end of a frame, and therefore is characterized by a SOP followed by bus activity that continues past the end of the frame. If the bus is not in the idle state at the end of the frame due to a babbling device, it must be isolated by disabling the hub port to which it attaches.

Loss of Activity (LOA)

Another form of potential bus failure is loss of activity, or LOA. LOA is characterized by a device starting a packet transfer followed by a constant J or K state on the bus and no EOP. LOA, like babble, has the potential to deadlock the bus and must be prevented. Also, like a babble error, the LOA error is detected at the end of a frame by hubs.

Babble/LOA Detection and Recovery

Hubs are responsible for detecting and recovering from babble and LOA errors. These errors are characterized by expected conditions at the end of frame. The host discontinues transactions prior to the end of packet to ensure that no bus activity occurs by the end of frame. In a normal condition, the last transaction ends with an EOP followed by idle. An error condition exists if the bus is in any state other than idle at the end of frame.

Frame Timer

Hubs are responsible for tracking each frame and sampling bus activity near the end of each frame. A frame timer within each hub is synchronized by the SOF packet that is broadcast at the beginning of each frame. These timers must be able to maintain synchronization in the absence of two consecutive SOF tokens.

Figure 8-10 illustrates two sample windows near the end of frame (EOF). If the hub detects bus activity (babble) or the bus stuck in a non-idle state after EOF1, it must terminate upstream traffic and float the bus. All hubs in the upstream direction will detect a bus idle condition. If however, a hub detects a non-idle state after EOF2, it must disable the port to which the offending device is attached. In this way, hubs assure that the bus will be in the idle state when the next frame begins.

Figure 8-10: Hub EOF Points

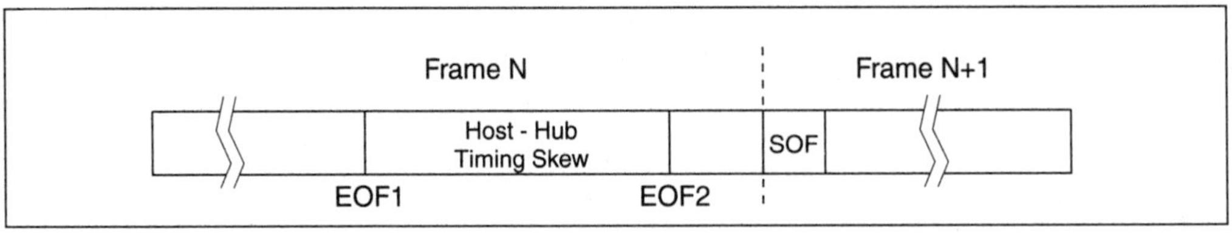

Host to Hub Skew

Timing skew exists between the host generated frame and the hub frame timer. Sources of skew include:

- The hub may miss up to two consecutive SOFs from the host for a maximum timing wander of ± 3 clocks.
- The host clock can be adjusted by up to one bit time per frame, resulting in a wander of 1+2+3=6 clocks.

This results in a maximum host-hub skew of ± 9 clocks.

To support the detection and recovery of babble and LOA, the second EOF point must be separated from the next SOF point. All hub EOF2 points must occur at least one bit time before the host issues SOF. If due to skew problems an EOP from downstream fails to reach a hub before it detects its EOF2 point, a inadvertant error will be detected by the hub.

Figure 8-11 illustrates the EOF1 and EOF2 ranges that relate to the lastest EOP that can be issued by a hub. The specification defines the EOF1 point to occur at 32 bit times before the next SOF. The earliest that a hub might start sending EOP is 9 bit times before the first EOF point, or at bit time 41 and at the latest at bit time 23. The EOP must complete at least 19 bit times before the next SOF, or 9 bit times prior to the median EOF2 point (10 bit times before SOF). EOF2 must occur no later than one bit time before SOF.

Figure 8-11: EOF Timing Ranges

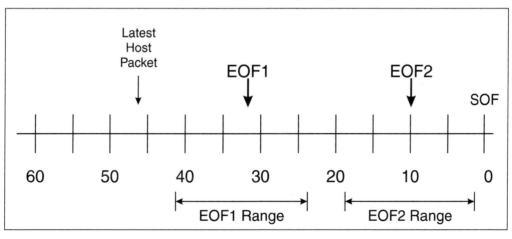

Hub Repeater State Machine

Figure 8-12 illustrate the state machine for the hub's repeater. Note that this figure is based on the state machine descriptions from the 1.1 USB specification. The state diagram in the 1.0 hub specification differs from the state machine described in the 1.1 specification.

The behavior of the hub near the end of packet is crucial for LOA and babble detection. The hub repeater is in its Wait For Start Of Packet (WFSOP) state during bus idle. When a SOP is detected, the repeater transitions to its Wait For End Of Packet (WFEOP) state. When EOP occurs the repeater returns to WFSOP.

Normally, a packet ends prior to EOF1 sample point. In this instance, the hub repeater will be in its WFSOP state when EOF1 occurs, causing it to transition to its Wait for downstream start of packet (WFDSOP) state. However, if EOP has not occurred prior to the EOF1 sample point the repeater will be in its WFEOP state when the EOF1 point occurs, resulting is an error. Note that EOP and EOF1 can occur simultaneously resulting in a transition to the WFDSOP state, without incurring an error.

When upstream connectivity is occurring near the end of frame, the hub repeater will be in its WFEOP state. If the EOF1 sample point occurs before the packet ends (i.e., EOP), the hub transitions to its Wait For End Of Frame 2 (WFEOF2) state. The hub leaves the WFEOF2 state under two conditions:

- an EOP occurs after EOF1 but before EOF2, the hub ten transitions to WFSOF and awaits the next SOP (which is presumed to be the SOF).
- the EOF2 sample point occurs before an EOP is detected. The hub transitions to the WFSOF state and disables the port that initiated the upstream packet, thereby isolating the port that is encountering LOA or babble.

Once the repeater is in the WFSOF state, it remains there until the hub detects the beginning of the next frame, i.e. next downstream start of packet (DSOP), causing it to transition to the WFEOP state.

Figure 8-12: Hub Repeater State Diagram

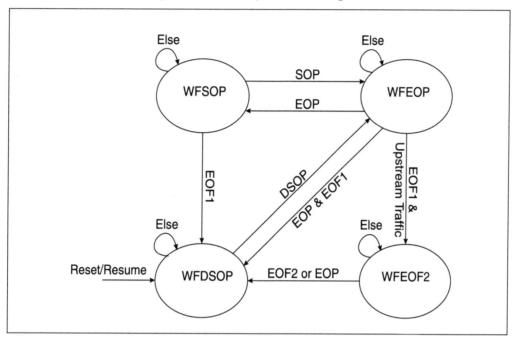

Isochronous Transfers (Delivery Not Guaranteed)

The nature of isochronous transfers requires that data be delivered at a constant rate, therefore retries are not supported and no handshake packets are delivered when performing isochronous-related transactions.

Interrupt Transfer Error Recovery

Interrupt transfers use the handshake phase along with the data toggle mechanism to verify correct delivery of data. If a given interrupt transfers fails, it will be retried at the next regularly scheduled service interval.

Bulk Transfer Error Recovery

Bulk transfers support handshakes and data toggle checks to verify correct delivery of the data. If a transaction fails, it will be scheduled for retry at a later time.

Control Transfer Error Recovery

Because control transfers can consist of three stages, they present some special problems associated with error recovery. The handshake phase is supported during all three stages and the data toggle sequence is also used to verify delivery of the data. Data toggle begins with the setup stage and continues through the status stage.

9 *USB Cable Power Distribution*

The Previous Chapter

All transfer types except isochronous are designed to complete over the USB even when error conditions are detected. The previous chapter discussed error types, the mechanisms used to detect them, and the error recovery mechanisms.

This Chapter

This chapter discusses USB power distribution, along with issues related to bus powered devices and the operation of self-powered devices. The chapter also discusses the role of host software in detecting and reporting power related problems.

The Next Chapter

USB devices support power conservation by entering their suspend state. The next chapter discusses the USB implementation of power management.

USB Power

All USB ports supply power for devices that are attached. Peripheral devices and hubs can be attached to a given port and use the available cable power or can implement their own power supply. This chapter details both cable and self-powered hubs and devices.

Hubs

A major function associated with a hub is the distribution and control of cable power. Hubs may derive all power from the upstream cable or may include their own power supply for powering downstream ports. Hubs must also provide voltage regulation and ensure current is limited to downstream ports for safety considerations.

Hubs like all USB devices must include descriptors to specify its capabilities. A major portion of a hub's descriptor definition relates to power related issues.

Current Budget

A fully rated port must be able to provide five units of current (500ma) to the attached device. Self-powered hubs (including the root hub) having their own local power supply can provide the maximum rated power to each port. However, bus-powered hubs have only the bus power that they receive from the upstream cable to distribute to all of their USB ports. This can severely limit the amount of current that is available for USB devices that attach to bus-powered hub ports. The minimum current available at a port is 100ma.

Hubs specify whether they are bus- or self-powered as part of their configuration descriptor as shown in Table 9-1. The shaded area shows a bit-mapped field that defines whether the hub uses bus power, local power, or both.

Table 9-1: Source of Hub Power Defined in Configuration Descriptor

Offset	Field	Size	Value	Description
0	Length	1	Number	Size of this descriptor in bytes.
1	DescriptorType	1	Constant	CONFIGURATION
2	TotalLength	2	Number	Total length of data returned for this configuration. Includes the combined length of all descriptors (configuration, interface, endpoint, and class or vendor specific) returned for this configuration.
4	NumInterfaces	1	Number	Number of interfaces supported by this configuration.
5	Configuration-Value	1	Number	Value to use as an argument to Set Configuration to select this configuration.
6	Configuration	1	Index	Index of string descriptor describing this configuration.

Table 9-1: Source of Hub Power Defined in Configuration Descriptor

Offset	Field	Size	Value	Description
7	Attributes	1	Bitmap	Configuration characteristics D7 Bus Powered D6 Self Powered D5 Remote Wakeup D4..0 Reserved (reset to 0) A device configuration that uses power from the bus and a local source at runtime may be determined using the Get Status device request. If a device configuration supports remote wakeup, D5 is set to one (1).
8	MaxPower	1	ma	Maximum amount of bus power this hub will consume in this configuration. (value based on 2ma increments)

Over-Current Protection

USB ports must be current limited due to safety regulations. No more than five amps of current can be supplied to a single port due to personal safety concerns. Current protection can be ganged to multiple ports or done on a per port basis as long as the current protection satisfies the 5a limit. Note also that a bus-powered hub has only the power it receives from the cable to distribute to USB ports. In this instance, no current limiting is needed.

Voltage Drop Budget

Power may supplied to USB peripheral devices via the cable. Voltage at a powered hub port can be no less than 4.75Vdc, while voltage at a bus-powered hub may be no lower than 4.40Vdc as illustrated in Figure 9-1. Consequently USB devices must operate properly with as little as 4.40 volts at the upstream end of their cable.

Figure 9-1: Minimum Cable Voltage and Voltage Drop Budget

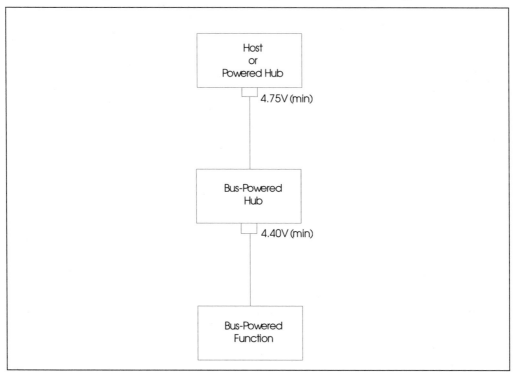

Power Switching

Hubs apply power to ports in one of the following ways:

- Direct power — not switched
- Ganged switching to all port in common
- Individual port switching

The power switching supported by a given hub is specified within the hub's endpoint zero descriptor. Table 9-2 on page 139 shows a portion of the hub's endpoint descriptor. Note that data bits D0 and D1 at offset 3 define the power switching mode supported by the hub.

Table 9-2: Power Switching Mode Supported is Defined by the Hub Class Descriptor

Offset	Field	Size	Description
0	DescLength	1	Number of bytes in the descriptor, including this byte.
1	Descriptor-Type	1	Descriptor Type
2	NbrPorts	1	Number of downstream ports that this hub supports.
3	HubCharac-teristics	2	D1..D0 Power Switching Mode 00 Ganged power switching (all ports powered at once) 01 Individual port power switching 1X No power switching (ports always powered on when hub in on, and off when hub is off). D15..D2 Defines other hub characteristics

Bus-Powered Hubs

Bus-powered hubs obtain all of their power from the bus. Therefore, they can only distribute some portion of the total current they get from the upstream port to all functions, including; the hub controller, embedded function (if included) and all downstream ports. This dictates that to guarantee full hub functionality a bus powered hub must connect to an upstream port that has the full 500ma of current available.

Power During Hub Configuration

Prior to supplying power to attached devices the hub must first be configured. Host software must be able to access the hub controller to read the hub descriptors that define it capabilities (e.g. number of ports, bus-powered, or self-powered). Prior to being configured, USB devices (including hubs) must not draw more than 100ma of current. This is required because devices attached to bus-powered hubs may supply a maximum of only 100ma of current. Not until the hub is configured can it draw more than 100ma for powering embedded devices or ports.

Bus-Powered Hub Attached to 500ma Port

Since the maximum current available to a bus-powered hub is 500ma, the maximum number of ports that can be supported is four. Figure 9-2 on page 141 is a block diagram of a bus-powered hub, showing power distribution to an embedded function and four ports. Since each port must be able to supply a minimum of 100ma (one unit) of current, the hub controller and embedded function combined must draw less than 100ma.

Bus-Powered Hub Attached to 100ma Port

If a bus-powered hub attaches to another bus-powered hub port that only supplies a maximum of 100ma, then the available current must be used to power the hub controller. This permits configuration software to access the descriptors to determine the power requirements of the device. If the bus-powered hub contains an embedded function (i.e. a compound device), it may be powered along with the hub controller. This is permissible when the total current drawn by the hub controller and the embedded device does not exceed 100ma.

If the current draw is greater than 100ma, the embedded function must be power-switched. In this way, configuration software can evaluate the power requirements of all devices by reading the device descriptors and enable only those functions that can be supported based on the available current. In this case, configuration software would not configure the hub since the available current is insufficient to power any one function.

Bus-Powered Hub Attached to Port with >100ma but <500ma

Bus powered hubs must provide power switching to the downstream ports, as well as the embedded function if $I_{embedded\ function} + I_{hub\ controller} > 100ma$. Since the embedded function and hub controller combined draw more than 100ma of current, they cannot both be powered during configuration. Therefore, the embedded function must be power switched. This requirement also provides flexibility when the port to which the hub attaches can supply only supply enough current to power the hub controller and embedded function. In this case, the ports must remain powered off since insufficient power is not available for devices attached to the ports.

For bus-powered hubs, the specification states that "power to downstream ports must be switched," but does not specify that the ports be switched individually. The advantage of individually power-switched ports is that ports can be selectively powered based on the amount of current available.

Current Limiting

Since the only source of power is the USB cable, bus-powered hubs can only have 500ma of current available and therefore cannot exceed the 5.0a limit per port. If total current draw from the upstream USB bus cable, exceeds 5.0a, then current limiting in the upstream hub would prevent an over-current condition.

Figure 9-2: Bus-Powered Hub with Embedded Function and Four Ports

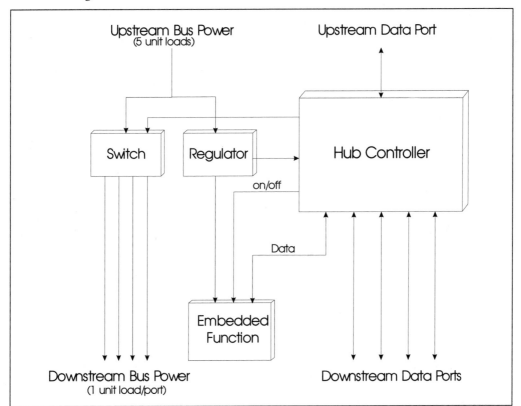

Bus-Powered Devices

Bus powered devices may attach to either a fully rated port or to a bus powered hub port that may supply only 100ma of maximum current. Depending on whether a USB device is a low- or high-powered and whether it attaches to a bus- or self-powered hub, the configuration may fail due to insufficient power.

Low-Power Devices

A low-power device consume less than one unit load of power. The USB specification dictates that when power is first applied to a USB device, it must consume less than 100ma of current. Since low-power devices never consume more that 100ma no special design considerations apply. Also, since the minimum current that a hub port can supply matches or exceeds the current requirements of low-power devices, no restrictions exist.

Figure 9-3: Low-Power USB Function

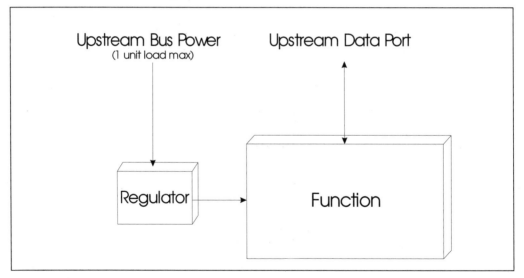

High-Power Devices

High-power devices consume more than 100ma but cannot draw more than 500ma of current from the bus. High-power devices can be designed with their own local power supply to eliminate illegal configurations.

Power During Configuration

Figure 9-4 illustrates a bus-powered device connected to a fully rated port. When bus power is initially applied to a USB device it must not consume more than a single unit of power, or 100ma until the device is configured. Consequently, the application of power is staged such that power is applied only to the function controller until the device has been configured. Once configured, maximum current can be drawn by the device.

Insufficient Port Power

If a high-power device that is powered solely by the bus, is connected to a bus-powered hub, there may not be sufficient current for the device to work properly. Host software must detect the amount of current that the high power function requires by reading its configuration descriptor. If the current requirements of the device exceed the current available at the port, the device should not be configured, and the deficiency should be reported to the user. Table 9-3 on page 145 shows a portion of the configuration descriptor definition that defines the maximum bus power consumed by a device once it's configured (shaded area).

Note that a high-power device may provide an alternate configuration that reduces the total power consumed to 100ma, thereby ensuring compatibility with any USB port. The low power configuration may however, lead to reduced performance and/or functionality when compared with the full power configuration.

Figure 9-4: High-Power/Bus Powered Function

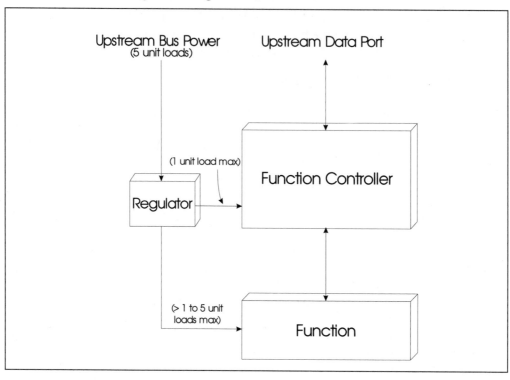

Table 9-3: Maximum Power Defined in Device's Configuration Descriptor

Offset	Field	Size	Value	Description
7	Attributes	1	Bitmap	Configuration characteristics D7 Bus Powered D6 Self Powered D5 Remote Wakeup D4..0 Reserved (reset to 0) A device configuration that uses power from the bus and a local source at runtime may be determined using the Get Status device request. If a device configuration supports remote wakeup, D5 is set to one (1).
8	Max-Power	1	ma	Maximum power consumption of USB device from the bus in this specific configuration when the device is fully operational. Expressed in 2 ma units (i.e. 50 = 100 ma). Note: A device configuration reports whether the configuration is bus-powered or self-powered. Device status reports whether the device is currently self-powered. If a device is disconnected from its external power source, it updates device status to indicate the device is no longer self-powered. A device may not increase its power draw from the bus when it loses its external power source beyond the amount reported by its configuration.

Self-Powered Hubs

Hubs may be incorporated into other USB devices that have their own power supplies, such as monitors, or be designed as stand-alone hubs with their own supplies. The obvious advantage to powered hubs is that they can supply the full 500ma of current to each of their downstream USB ports. The obvious disadvantages include added complexity and cost when compared to bus powered versions. Self-powered hubs may also require current limiting (5.0a/port) to meet the safety requirements defined by the specification.

Self-powered hubs may also incorporate optional features, such as LEDs for each port to indicate which ports are powered and/or enabled.

Power During Configuration

Figure 9-5 on page 147 illustrates a basic block diagram of a self-powered hub. The hub must include a 1.5KΩ pullup resistor on its D+ data lines to identify itself as a full speed device. The system, having detected the device's attachment must access its descriptors to determine the device type. This requires access to the hub controller's control endpoint so that the hub's descriptors can be read.

Locally Powered Bus Interface

A self-powered hub may power its host controller solely from its local supply. Consequently, if the hub is not plugged into AC, the 1.5KΩ resistor on the D+ line may not have Vcc available and device (hub) when attached will not be detected by the system. This could be highly confusing to the end user who fully expects all USB devices to work automatically when attached.

It is also possible that the pullup resistor is powered by the bus, but that the hub controller is powered by the local supply. In this instance device attachment would be detected, but host attempts to read the device descriptors would fail. Specifically, host generated accesses to the default endpoint would result in no response from the hub. The host would detect the error condition but have no idea what caused the failure.

The dotted line in Figure 9-5 on page 147, running between the local supply and the hub controller electronics, illustrates the option of powering the bus interface using the local power supply.

Hybrid-Powered Device

A self-powered hub may power the entire bus interface and hub controller function via the USB cable, making it possible to detect the hub's attachment and read its descriptors. Power for embedded functions and each port however, would be obtained from the local supply. This is termed a "hybrid" powered hub. Hybrid powered hubs, like any USB device must draw no more than 100ma of current from the cable during configuration.

The advantage of a hybrid implementation is that it is possible to differentiate between an un-powered hub and a disconnected hub or connected but apparently broken hub.

In Figure 9-5, the dotted line labeled upstream power illustrates the option of powering the hub controller electronics with bus power.

Current Limiting

Figure 9-5 also illustrates current limiting implemented in a ganged fashion. Since the current limit is 5.0a per port, the current limiter must trip when the current draw reaches the 5.0a limit. If for example, a self-powered hub supports ten ports in conjunction with one current limiter, the total legal current draw on each of the ten ports (500ma) would exceed the maximum current. As a result, a ten port hub might be implemented with two current limiters, each providing protection for a group of five ports.

Figure 9-5: Self-Powered Hub with Embedded Function

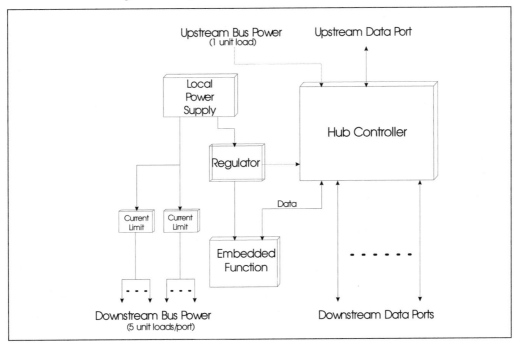

Self-Powered Devices

Self-powered devices must provide the 1.5KΩ on its D+ line, indicating that it's a full-speed device. Note that a self-powered device can be a low-speed device, however, the author seriously doubts that any will be built.

Power During Configuration

A device's bus interface may be powered from bus power or solely from its local supply. This impacts whether a device will be detected when it is attached and whether its descriptors can be read. The following sections describe each case.

Locally Powered Bus Interface

A self-powered hub may power its host controller solely from its local supply. Consequently, if the hub is not plugged into AC, the 1.5KΩ resistor on the D+ line may not have Vcc available and device, when attached, will not be detected by the system.

It is also possible that the pullup resistor be powered by the bus, but that the device controller be powered by the local supply. In this instance, device attachment is detectable, but attempts by the host to read the device descriptors will fail. Specifically, host generated accesses to the default endpoint will result in no response from the device. The host detects the error condition but has no idea what caused the failure.

The dotted line in Figure 9-6 on page 149, running between the local supply and the device controller electronics, illustrates the option of powering the bus interface using the local power supply.

Hybrid Powered Device

A self-powered device may use bus power for its function controller, but must limit current draw to 100ma. The dotted line illustrating the bus power lines in Figure 9-6 indicates that bus power use is optional. Obtaining power from the bus makes it possible to detect the hub's attachment and read its descriptors. Power for the function however, is obtained from the local supply. This is termed a "hybrid" powered device.

Chapter 9: USB Cable Power Distribution

The advantage of a hybrid implementation is that it is possible to differentiate between an un-powered device and a disconnected device or connected but apparently broken device.

Figure 9-6: Self-Powered Device

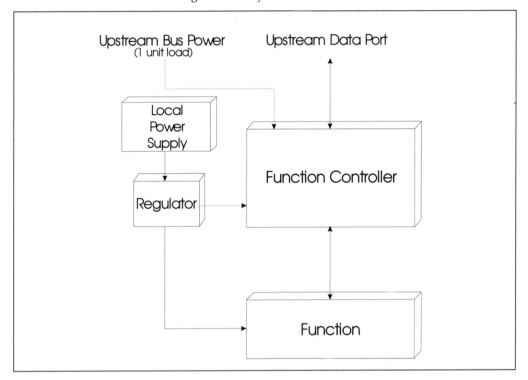

10 *USB Power Conservation*

The Previous Chapter

The previous chapter discussed USB power distribution, along with issues related to bus powered devices and the operation of self-powered devices. The chapter also discussed the role of host software in detecting and reporting power related problems.

This Chapter

USB devices support power conservation by entering their suspend state. The next chapter discusses the USB implementation of power management.

The Next Chapter

The next chapter provides an overview of the configuration process. Each of the major steps are defined and discussed.

Power Conservation-Suspend

Suspend is designed to reduce overall power consumption under software control. USB supports two types of suspend:

- Global suspend — all USB devices are placed into a suspended state
- Selective suspend — selected devices are placed into a suspend state

When a device enters its suspend state it must consume no more than 500µa of current. Devices enter suspend after 3ms of no bus activity. Normally devices are kept from entering the suspend state because they receive a SOF token at the beginning of every 1ms frame, even if no other USB traffic is occurring.

Low speed devices however, see only low-speed traffic, meaning that they do not see the SOF packet nor any full-speed transactions. Consequently, hubs must signal an idle to K state transition on all low speed ports at intervals of less than 3.0ms to prevent low-speed devices from inadvertently entering the suspend state.

Device Response to Suspend

When devices enter the suspend state, they must preserve their state and consume no more than 500μa of current. This limit includes the current draw associated with the pull-up and pull-down resistors on the D- and D+ lines.

Some devices may need to wake the system up in response to an external event. For example, a modem function could be designed to wake the system up from its suspend state. If the modem receives a ring indicate from an external line, it would be necessary to notify system software that the modem requires attention.

Hub Response to Suspend

When a hub detects greater than 3ms of inactivity on its upstream port it must also enter the suspend state. Since the hub has detected no bus activity for 3.0ms, by definition no activity will have been broadcast to any of the hub's downstream ports for 3.0ms. All downstream ports, along with the hub itself, will detect the suspend state at approximately the same time.

Upon detecting suspend, hubs take the following actions:

- place their repeaters into the wait for start of packet (WFSOP) state
- float all output drivers
- maintain static values of all control and status bits
- preserve current state info for all downstream ports

All internal clocks are stopped and power consumption from the hub function is reduced to a minimum.

Since each device attached downstream also enters the suspend state, they can each draw up to 500μa each. This means that the hub itself may draw more than 500μa from its upstream port during suspend. Further, when in the suspend state, hubs must be able to supply the maximum current defined for their downstream ports to support remote wakeup. That is, a device may drive the bus during suspend to wake up the system as discussed later in this chapter.

Chapter 10: USB Power Conservation

Global Suspend

Global suspend places the entire USB network of devices into the suspend state from the top down. This provides for minimum power consumption from the USB. The host initiates global suspend typically in response to a prolonged period of activity over the USB.

Initiating Global Suspend

Global suspend is initiated when all downstream traffic from the root hub is terminated. This is done under software control by issuing a global suspend request to the root hub's control endpoint. All USB devices (hubs and functions) automatically enter the suspend state when they encounter 3.0ms of inactivity.

Resume from Global Suspend

Devices awaken from their suspend state when they detect resume signaling on the bus. Resume is signaled by a non-idle state (K state).

Resume can be initiated in the following ways:

- by the root hub, causing the resume signaling to occur on all downstream cable segments.
- by a device on any downstream cable segment attached to an enabled port, causing the hub to reflect the resume signaling back to that port, to all other enabled ports downstream, and upstream to its root port.
- by device attachment.
- by device detachment.
- by reset, causing all devices to be reconfigured.

The following sections detail the operation of the hubs and devices for each type of resume.

Resume Initiated By Host

Host software may initiate USB wakeup by issuing a resume request to the root hub. The root hub responds by signaling resume to all downstream ports that are enabled as illustrated in Figure 10-1 on page 154. The resume signalling must be maintained for 20ms to given each attached device sufficient time to recover from suspend and be ready to receive transactions. The root hub ends resume signaling by driving an EOP for two low speed bit times.

Downstream hubs that receive the 20ms of resume signaling must also propagate the resume signaling to all of its enabled downstream ports as illustrated in Figure 10-1.

Figure 10-1: Host Initiated Resume

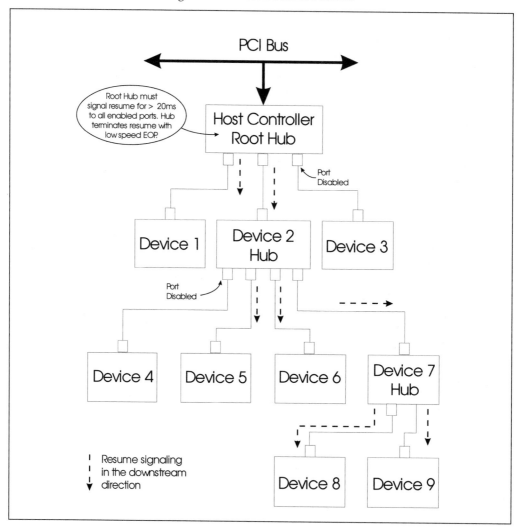

Remote Wakeup from Device

A device in the suspend state may respond to an external event by signaling a wakeup to the system via the USB. Resume signaling is initiated by the device by driving a k state (non-idle) onto the bus. The actions taken by the hub are:

- signal resume to upstream port
- signal resume to all enabled downstream ports
- reflect resume signaling back to the originating device

Figure 10-2 illustrates the sequence of events and describes the timing associated with device initiated resume. The following steps and timing applies:

1. A K state is signaled by the device to the hub port.
2. The port detects the resume signaling (t_0).
3. Resume signaling is broadcast by hub 7 to its upstream port and to all enabled downstream ports within 100µs of receiving the resume (t_1).
4. Hub 2 signals resume to all of its enabled ports within 100µs of receiving the resume from hub 7.
5. Hub 7 ceases driving resume in the upstream direction within 1-15ms of t_0 but not earlier than 100µs and reverses connectivity. This is referred to as t_2.
6. Hub 2 ceases driving resume in the upstream direction within 10ms of receiving resume from hub 7 but not earlier than 50µs and reverses connectivity.
7. When the root hub detects the resume signaling, it initiates 20ms of resume signaling downstream on all ports, including on the originating port.
8. The root hub terminates resume signaling by driving two low speed EOPs.

Note that during the interval between t_0 and t_2, the host may have started driving resume signaling from the upstream direction, while the downstream hub is still driving resume signaling. Since it is acceptable to drive both ends of a bus segment to the same state, no problem is encountered.

Figure 10-2: Global Resume Signaling Due to Wakeup from Target Device

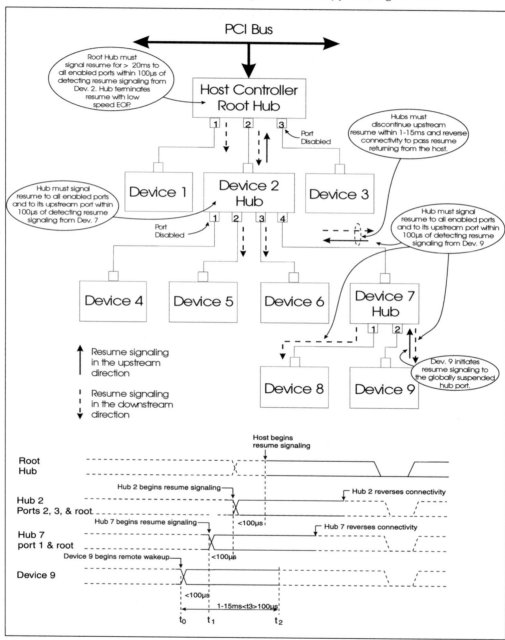

Remote Wakeup via Device Attachment and Detachment

When a hub detects that a device has been either attached or detached, it signals wakeup to the system in the same fashion as described for remote wakeup.

Selective Suspend

Permits software to suspend individual devices or particular segments of the bus. Selective suspend is initiated by software when a given hub port is placed into the suspend state. Ports in the suspend state block all downstream traffic, allowing devices downstream to detect 3.0ms of inactivity and thereby enter their low power states.

Initiating Selective Suspend

Host software can suspend an individual device or a group of devices residing on a particular bus segment. Selective suspend is accomplished via a control transfer that issues a *SetPortFeature* (PORT_SUSPEND) request. (See page "Set/Clear Port Feature" on page 211.) A hub receiving this request will place the specified port in the suspended state. Note that the hub will not suspend a port during a packet transfer. At the conclusion of the packet transfer, the port is suspended.

When suspended, a port will not propagate downstream bus traffic to the device attached, except for the *port reset* request. The hub similarly will not pass activity on the downstream port in the upstream direction. Since bus traffic is stopped, any and all devices residing on the bus segment downstream from the suspended port will no longer detect bus activity, and after 3ms will enter their suspended state.

Resume from Selective Suspend

Selective resume may be initiated by the host system or by a suspended device via remote wakeup. These two forms of selective suspend are discussed below.

Host Initiated Selective Resume

The host initiates selective resume via a *ClearPortFeature* (PORT_SUSPEND) request to the suspended hub port. This causes the port to signal resume to the device attached to the port to wake the device up. Suspend must be signaled for at least 20ms, followed by a low speed EOP. A status bit is set within the hub to indicate that resume has completed and the device is now ready to be accessed. The status bit must not be set until 3ms after the low speed EOP is signaled. This delay ensures that devices have time to synchronize their frame counters prior to being addressed as the target of a transaction. Resumed devices will however, see bus activity within this 3ms period.

Selective Wakeup from Device

Remote wakeup is supported for selective suspend as it is for global suspend. However, in the selective suspend environment, it is likely that other devices are awake and receiving bus traffic. The actual difference between global and selective suspend is at the hub. The device knows only that it has detected 3ms of inactivity on the bus and has transitioned to its suspended state. The hub recognizes that one of its ports is in the suspended state, however the hub itself and other hub ports are not suspended and are receiving bus traffic. As a result, when the selectively suspended device signals resume, the hub must not forward the resume signaling upstream or to any other port. In essence, the remote wakeup is a private matter between the selectively suspended device and the suspended hub port.

When the selectively suspended hub port detects remote resume signaling from the device (idle to K transition), it responds as follows (see Figure 10-3):

1. Return resume signaling to the device within 100μs of receiving resume from the device.
2. Continue signaling resume for a minimum of 20ms.
3. Terminate resume signaling with a low speed EOP.
4. 3ms after EOP the hub sets the resume completed status bit.

Figure 10-3: Selective Resume Signaled by Target Device

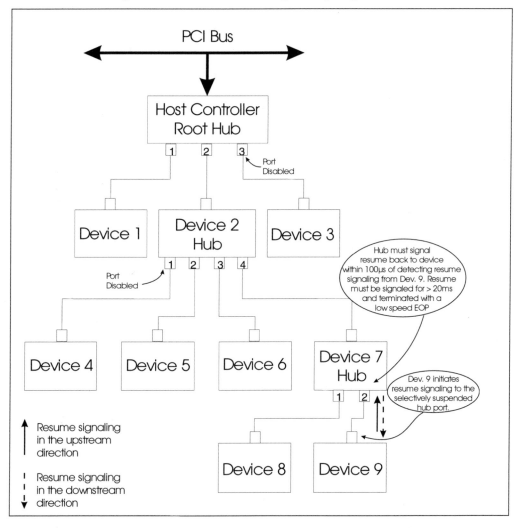

In summary, selective resume exclusively involves the suspended hub port and target device attached to the port. No other devices are notified of the wakeup since they may be involved in transactions currently being broadcast over the USB. Neither should resume signaling be sent to devices that have been selectively suspended.

Since selective suspend in this case has not been initiated by the host, the host must check status on a regular basis (poll the hub) to determine if resume has occurred. (The sections entitled " Get Port Status Request " on page 206 defines the mechanism used to check port status).

If wakeup at the port is due to device attachment or detachment, the same actions are taken by the hub, except that resume signaling is not sent back to the initiating port. Instead, the port's output buffers are placed into the high impedance state, and port status bits are changed to reflect the device attachment or detachment.

Selective Suspend When Hub is Suspended

After an individual hub port has been suspended, host software could subsequently suspend the entire hub (via either global or selective suspend). Three conditions may occur that requires the hub to take action:

- device currently attached to suspended port signals resume
- device is connected to selectively suspended port
- device is disconnected from selectively suspended port

Device Signals Resume

If the device attached to the suspended port signals resume (wakeup), the suspended hub takes the following action as illustrated in Figure 10-4:

1. Resume is signaled to all downstream ports that are enabled and back to the suspended port. (Resume must be signaled within 100µs of receiving resume from the device and must continue resume signaling for a minimum of 20ms.) Note that selectively suspended ports are left alone and remain in their selectively suspended state.
2. Resume is signaled upstream on its root port, also within 100µs of receiving resume from the device. However, resume must be released and connectivity reversed within 10ms.
3. The upstream port will signal resume back to the hub for a minimum of 20ms. This resume signaling is reflected to all enabled downstream ports, including the device that initiated wakeup.
4. The root port drives a low speed EOP at the end of resume signaling and the hub enters the wait for start of frame (WFSOF) state.
5. Status is set by the hub to indicate that the selectively suspended port is now awake. The bit must be set no earlier that 3ms to give time for the hubs frame timer to synchronize with the host.

Note that the upstream port may either be suspended due to global suspend, or may have been selectively suspended. In the event of global suspend, resume signaling will be reflected upstream to the root hub. If the upstream port is selectively suspended, as illustrated in Figure 10-4 then resume signaling will be reflected back to the downstream hub, but not propagated to other ports. The hub labeled Device 2 has not been suspended, but its port number four has been selectively suspended. When resume is detected at port 4, the hub returns resume to device 7 and takes no further action.

Figure 10-4: Device Initiated Selective Resume to Suspended Hub

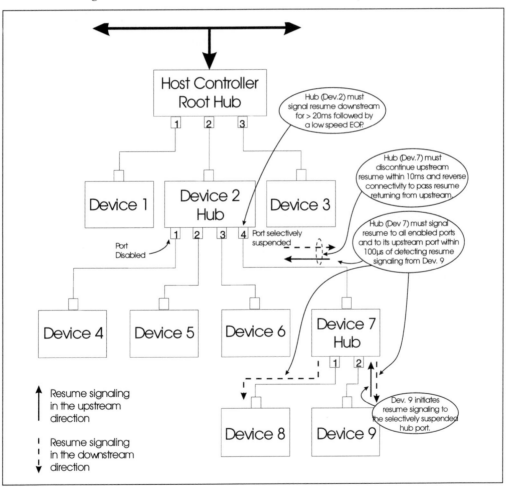

Port Receives Connect or Disconnect

If the selectively suspended port receives either a single-ended zero (SE0) to idle transition (device connect) or an idle to SE0 transition (device disconnect), resume signaling is not sent back to the selectively suspended port, rather the port's output buffers are placed in the high impedance state. Status bits will be set by the hub to indicate the connect or disconnect event and that the port is no longer is the suspend state.

Selective Suspend Followed by Global Suspend

Consider the situation in which several devices have been selectively suspended prior to a global suspend occurring. Figure 10-5 illustrates such an example. Port 1 on the root hub, port 1 on the device 2, and port 2 on the device 7 are selectively suspended. All other devices are in their suspended states due to the global suspend. In this example, when a remote wakeup is signaled by device 9, the hub (device 7) forwards resume signaling to its other port and to its root port. Device 2 recognizes the resume signaling and forwards resume to all ports except port 1 since it has been selectively suspended. The root hub detects resume signaling on its port 2 and reflects resume back to device 2, but not to port 1 since it is selectively suspended nor to port 3 since it is disabled.

Once the system completes global resume processing, the host may then selectively awaken the devices that were selectively suspended prior to the global suspend.

Resume Via Reset

When a suspended hub detects a reset on its upstream port (>2.5µs of SE0), it must initiate it wakeup sequence. The hub must be awake and have completed reset no later than 10ms from the completion of reset signaling. After reset has been completed the hub controller must be in the following state:

- Default address is zero
- Control bits set to default values
- Hub repeater in the WFSOP state
- All downstream ports in Powered Off state (power-switched hub)
- All downstream ports in Disconnected state (no power switching)

A bus containing power switched ports, cannot guarantee that host initiated reset will propagate all the way downstream. This is because an upstream hub that supports power switching goes to the Powered Off state, after reset. Consequently, power downstream might be removed from bus powered hubs and devices before reset processing has completed. However, a powered off device will effectively be reset if power is removed long enough. Note that once reset has been performed all devices must be reconfigured.

Figure 10-5: Resume with Selective and Global Suspend

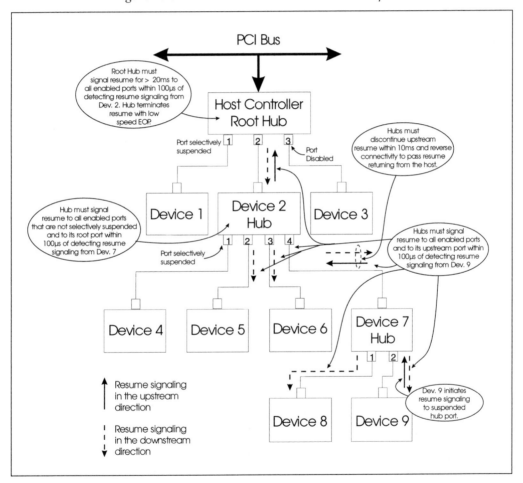

Hub Frame Timer after Wakeup

While in the suspend state hubs shut their frame timers off to reduce power consumption. When a resume occurs the frame timer must be restarted and given time to synchronize to the host by receiving a SOF packet. The time interval between the hub returning to the awake state and the first SOF packet leaves the hub unable to detect babbling devices and loss of activity (LOA). Normally, the hub checks the state of the bus near the end of frame to determine if a device is babbling or hung in a non-idle state. However, immediately after leaving suspend, the hub has no concept of frame timing and cannot detect these forms of bus errors.

To prevent babbling devices or LOA from hanging the bus, a hub must not propagate bus activity in the upstream direction until it has received a SOF packet. Upstream sub traffic is blocked by a hub when it enters its wait for start of frame (WFSOF) state. Hubs leave the suspend state and enter the WFSOF, thereby blocking upstream bus traffic. Hubs transition from WFSOF to WFSOP when they receive the first SOF packet after being awakened. See "Hub Repeater State Machine" on page 132.

Note that downstream traffic is propagated downstream even when the hub is in the WFSOF state. If devices downstream are addressed, they will likely respond by sending packets back to the host. Since the packet transmission is blocked by the hub, a time-out will be detected by the host, due to no response from the device. Consequently, the specification recommends that the host not address any device residing on a bus segment that has been just resumed, thus avoiding needless bus time-outs.

Part III

USB Configuration

11 *Configuration Process*

The Previous Chapter

USB devices support power conservation by entering their suspend state. The previous chapter discussed the USB implementation of power management.

This Chapter

This chapter provides an overview of the configuration process. Each of the major steps involved in USB device enumeration are defined and discussed.

The Next Chapter

The next chapter details the process of configuring USB hubs.

Overview

Host software is responsible for detecting and configuring all devices attached to the root hub. The process of identifying and configuring a USB device is commonly referred to as USB device enumeration. Device enumeration begins at the root hub. Each hub port must be powered in turn. When powered, the hub determines if a low- or full-speed device is attached or no device at all. If a device is present, status bits within the root hub are set to reflect device attachment. Software recognizes that a device is attached, enables the port, resets the USB device, assigns a unique address, and completes the configuration. This operation is performed for each port until all devices attached to the root hub have been configured.

The discussion in this chapter presumes that software has already initialized the USB host controller and that it is capable of generating USB transactions.

Different operating systems will define different software components involved in USB device configuration and will perform configuration in their own particular sequence. The following discussions identify the primary steps involved in the configuration process, but should not be interpreted as the specific sequence that is followed by a given host software solution. The following list specifies actions taken by host software and the root hub when configuring a device that is connected to a root hub port:

- Host configures root hub.
- Host requests power be applied to the ports.
- Hub detects device attachment.
- Hub sets status change.
- Host polls hub and identifies that a device is attached.
- Host issues port enable to hub.
- Host issues reset to port/USB device (minimum of 10ms).
- Port now enabled and 100ma of power is available.
- USB device now answers to default address (zero).
- Host queries device's control endpoint (zero) at address zero to determine max payload supported by the default pipe.
- Host assigns unique address to USB device.
- Host reads and evaluates configuration information from the device descriptors.
- Host verifies that the USB resources needed by the device are available.
- Host issues a configuration value to the USB device specifying how it's to be used. When the configuration value is received, the device assumes its described characteristics. The device is now ready to be accessed by client software and can draw the amount of bus power described in the configuration.

The operations performed above are primarily accomplished via control transactions. Software uses the control endpoint (endpoint zero) within the hub and each device to access their descriptors and for controlling other features supported by the device. (The hub and device requests are detailed in Chapter 13 and Chapter 15, respectively.)

The following sections provide an overview of the configuration process. More detail regarding hub and device configuration can be found in the following chapters.

The Configuration Model

Figure 11-1 illustrates the model that configuration is based upon and identifies the conceptual software elements involved.

Figure 11-1: The Configuration Software Model

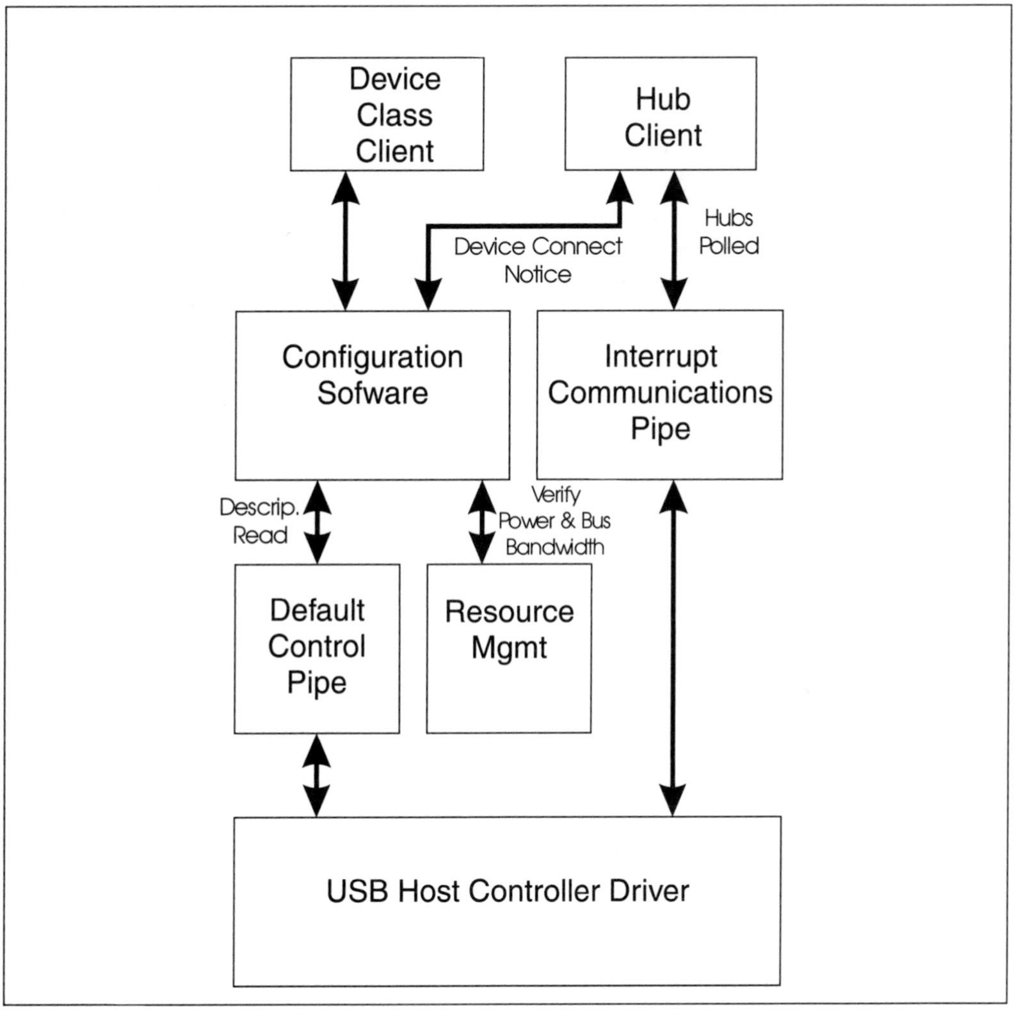

During system boot and initialization, all USB hub and devices will be detected and configured. Following initialization device may be detached or new devices may be connected. The hub client periodically polls all USB hubs to detect device attachment or detachment. If a status change results from a new device having been attached, the configuration process is triggered.

The hub client must notify configuration software that a new device has been attached. In response, configuration software must identify the newly attached device by reading its standard descriptors, using the default control pipe. Information read from the descriptors specify the USB resources that are required by the device (e.g. bus bandwidth and power requirements). These descriptors must be interpreted by configuration software.

A device can support more than one configuration, requiring software to select the configuration of choice. Each configuration provides alternatives for configuring the device. For example a device may support both high-power and low-power configurations. That is, if the hub port cannot support a high-power function, then configuration software could select the low-power configuration. Note that the client driver may also be involved in selecting the configuration.

Configuration software must ensure that the available USB resources can support the device configuration that is selected. Resource management software must track the bus bandwidth consumed by all USB devices as they are configured. If the USB can provide the bus power needed and can support the bandwidth requirements of all endpoints specified by a device configuration, then a communications pipe is established for each endpoint and the device is completed. If the USB cannot support the requested configuration, the device is not configured and the user is notified.

Root Hub Configuration

Host software begins USB device enumeration by configuring the root hub. Two hub designs have been defined: the Universal Host Controller (UHC) and the Open Host Controller (OHC). Each provides the same basic functionality and accomplish the same jobs, but do so in different ways. These host controllers are discussed in Chapter 18 and Chapter 19 respectively.

The root hub must implement a status change endpoint (see Figure 11-2) that can be used by the hub client to detect status changes pertaining to each ports. Once the hub is configured, software can poll the status change endpoint to detect which ports currently have devices attached to them.

Figure 11-2: Root Hub's Control and Status Change Endpoints

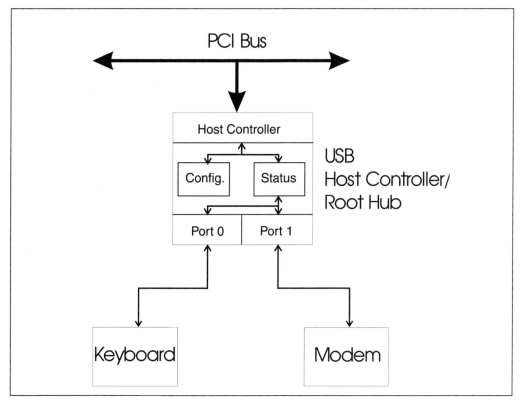

Each Device is Isolated for Configuration

Each device is initially isolated from the USB since all hub ports are initially disabled. Host software detects the presence of a device when power is applied to the port by reading the Status Change endpoint. One at a time, host software must enable each port that has a device attached. Software uses the *Set Port Enable Feature* request to enable a port. Each device is reset and configured as each port is enabled in turn.

Reset Forces Device to Default Address (zero)

Prior to accessing a device it must be reset, forcing it to respond to its default device address (zero). Host software uses the *Set Port Reset Feature* request causing the hub to reset the selected port. Every USB device after reset responds to address zero. In this way, one device at a time, configuration software can read every device's descriptor at the same default address.

Host Assigns a Unique Device Address

During the configuration process, each device is assigned a unique address that it will respond to thereafter. No contention occurs since each device is assigned a unique address prior to enabling the next port. The standard *Set Address* request is used by software to assign the device address.

Host Software Verifies Configuration

Host software must probe each device that it detects to determine if the endpoints associated with the device can be accommodated based on the bandwidth that remains free. It must also ensure that the bus power required by the device can be satisfied by the hub port to which it is attached.

Devices may have one or more configurations that can be selected. Each configuration descriptor represents a different set of resources that can be chosen for the device. Host software ensures that the USB resources (bus power and bandwidth) required by the device can be satisfied. If a given configuration cannot be satisfied, then the next configuration is evaluated. If after evaluating all configurations, the USB cannot provide the necessary resources, the device is not configured.

Power Requirements

Host software must verify that the bus power required by the device can be supplied by the hub port. During configuration a device is specified to consume no more than 100mA of bus current. Only after the device is configured can it then consume the maximum power defined by the configuration selected. The maximum bus power needed is defined in the configuration descriptor. Similarly, a hub also reports the amount of power that it can supply via its descriptors. If every configuration specifies more bus power than the hub can supply, then the device is not configured.

Bus Bandwidth

Host software must also verify that the bus bandwidth required by the USB device can be satisfied. Each configuration defines the set of endpoints that must be accessible by client software. Each endpoint descriptor specifies the maximum amount of USB bandwidth it requires. If sufficient bandwidth is available for all endpoints, a communications pipe is setup by software, reserving the specified bus bandwidth for each device endpoint. After successfully allocating bandwidth to all endpoints within the device, the device can be configured.

If the bus bandwidth needed is not available, then other configurations are checked. If every configuration exceeds the bus bandwidth available, the device is not configured.

Configuration Value is Assigned

Once a configuration is selected, host software configures the device by assigning a configuration value that corresponds to the chosen configuration. The configuration value is obtained from the selected configuration descriptor and written to the device via the *Set Configuration* request. The device can now be accessed by client software and can consume the maximum amount of current specified in its configuration.

Client Software is Notified

When a device has successfully been configured, USB system software must locate the appropriate class driver or drivers designed to access the device. These USB class drivers must be notified that the device has been installed and must be provided information regarding the characteristics and capabilities of the device. The exact procedure that USB system software uses to identify the a USB device driver and communicates with it is operating system dependent.

12 *Hub Configuration*

The Previous Chapter

The previous chapter provided an overview of the configuration process. Each of the major steps involved in USB device enumeration were defined and discussed.

This Chapter

The hub is the linchpin of USB device enumeration. This chapter focuses on the hub characteristics and features involved in device configuration.

The Next Chapter

The next chapter discusses the control transfer requests defined for USB hubs. Hubs like all USB devices support standard requests and also must support hub class specific requests.

Configuring the Hub

Hubs must be configured like any other device, but also involves identifying other devices that may be attached to the port. The steps taken by configuration software include:

- Reading the standard device descriptors to obtain a variety of information needed to configure the device.
- Assigning a unique address to the hub.
- Powering the ports
- Checking the hub status change endpoint to detect port events.
- Reading status information to determine the nature of the event.
- Enabling the port to provide access to the attached device.

As indicated above, a hub must implement a status change port in addition to the default port. Figure 12-1 illustrates the required hub endpoints. The default control port provides access to the descriptors that define the type of device requiring configuration. A hub may also be implemented as part of a compound device, hence the descriptors may describe additional functions beyond the minimum required of the hub alone.

The Default Pipe

All devices including hubs have a default control pipe at endpoint zero. Host software owns the default control pipe that is used to configure hubs and USB devices. This communications pipe is established during initialization so that USB devices can be accessed based on established defaults. The configuration process requires numerous default pipe accesses for configuring and controlling hub features, including: reading the device descriptors, powering hub ports, resetting ports, reading port status, and enabling ports.

The Status Change Pipe

Hubs must implement a status change endpoint that can be polled to detect status changes that have occurred at the hub ports (e.g. device attachment and detachment). Note that the status endpoint provides status information for all hub ports. Configuration software determines the characteristics and the endpoint number of the status change register by reading the endpoint descriptor.

Reading the Hub's Descriptors

Hubs have a class specific descriptor called the hub descriptor. This descriptor contains information about the hub implementation. The hub class descriptor is read via the class specific *Get Descriptor* request.

Figure 12-1: Required Hub Endpoints

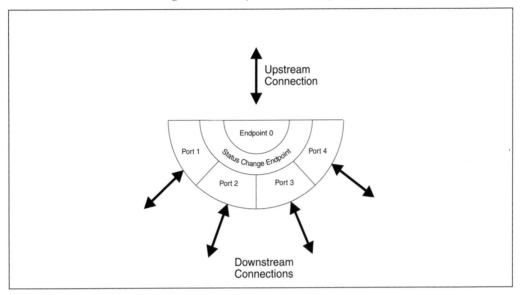

Hubs, like other devices, also contain standard descriptors that must be read to determine how to configure the hub. Standard descriptors are read via the standard request, *Get Descriptor.* Hubs contains the following standard descriptors as illustrated in Figure 12-2:

- Each USB device contains a single device descriptor that describes the number of configurations supported by the device.
- Each device contains one or more configuration descriptors that describe one or more interfaces.
- Each interface descriptor defines the number of endpoints related to the interface.
- Endpoint descriptors specify the attributes associated with a given endpoint along with information needed by host software to determine how the endpoint should be accessed.
- String descriptors are optional and consist of a UNICODE string that provides human-readable information that can be displayed.

Figure 12-2: Standard Hub Descriptors

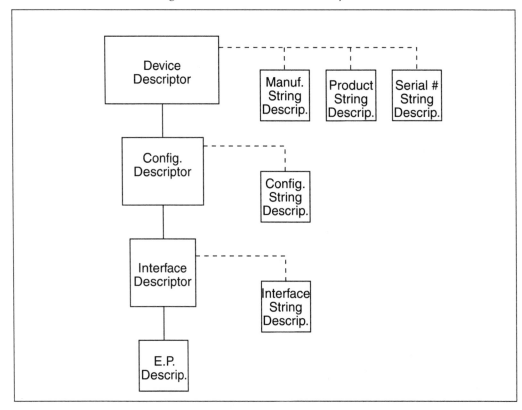

Hub Device Descriptor

Hubs implement the standard device descriptor just like other USB devices. However, hubs contain some pre-defined descriptor fields as indicated below:

- DeviceClass field = HubClass
- DeviceSubClass field = HubSubClass
- MaxPacketSize0 field = 8 bytes

Refer to Table 12-1. The first access made by configuration software is to the device descriptor to determine the maximum payload supported by the default pipe (offset 7 within the device descriptor). In this case, the packet size is pre-defined for hubs to 8 bytes. Software may also detect the device class type by reading the device descriptor. However, if the hub is a composite device, the class field will be zeros and the interface descriptors will define the device class (one interface for the hub function and one interface for each embedded function).

Table 12-1: Hub's Device Descriptor

Offset	Field	Size	Value	Description
0	Length	1	Number	Size of this descriptor in bytes
1	DescriptorType	1	01h	DEVICE Descriptor Type
2	USB	2	BCD	USB Specification Release Number in Binary-Coded Decimal (i.e. 1.00 is 0x100). This field identifies the release of the USB Specification that the device and its descriptors are compliant with.
4	DeviceClass	1	Hub-Class-Code	Hub Class code (assigned by USB). If this field is reset to zero, each interface within a configuration specifies its own class information and the various interfaces operate independently. If this field is set to 0xFFh, the device class is vendor specific.
5	DeviceSubClass	1	0	Hub Subclass code (assigned by USB) These codes are qualified by the value of the DeviceClass field. If the DeviceClass field is reset to zero, this field must also be reset to zero.
6	DeviceProtocol	1	0	Protocol code (assigned by USB) These codes are qualified by the value of the DeviceClass and the DeviceSubClass fields. If a device supports class-specific protocols on a device basis as opposed to an interface basis, this code identifies the protocols that the device uses as defined by the specification of the device class. If this field is reset to zero, the device does not use class-specific protocols on a device basis. However, it my use class -specific protocols on an interface basis. If this field is set to 0xFF, the device uses a vendor-specific protocol on a device basis.

Table 12-1: Hub's Device Descriptor

Offset	Field	Size	Value	Description
7	MaxPacketSize0	1	08h	Maximum packet size for endpoint zero.
8	Vendor	2	ID	Vendor ID (assigned by USB).
10	Product	2	ID	Product ID (assigned by manufacturer).
12	Device	2	BCD	Device release number in Binary-Coded Decimal.
14	Manufacturer	1	Index	Index of string descriptor describing manufacturer.
15	Product	1	Index	Index of string descriptor describing product.
16	SerialNumber	1	Index	Index of string descriptor describing the device's serial number.
17	NumConfigurations	1	Number	Number of possible configurations.

Hub Configuration Descriptor

A typical hub has a single configuration descriptor. This descriptor has the same definition as it does for standard USB devices. Configuration software accesses this descriptor to obtain the following information:

- number of interfaces supported by this configuration
- the configuration value used to configure the hub
- whether hub is bus powered or self powered
- maximum amount of bus powered consumed by hub in this configuration

Table 12-2 defines the standard configuration descriptor fields implemented by a hub device. Refer to Table 12-2 during the following discussions.

Number of Interfaces

The number of interfaces defined at offset 4 depends on whether the hub is a compound device or not. If the hub is a single function device (no embedded devices) then the hub will contain only one interface. However, composite devices that contain hubs contain one or more embedded devices each of which require one or more interfaces.

Configuration Value

The configuration value at offset 5 is used by the USB enumerator to assign the selected configuration for the hub. The configuration value is assigned using the *Set Configuration* request. This also enable access to the hubs status change port, which the enumerator reads to determine the number of devices attached to the hub's ports.

Setting the configuration also allows power to be applied to the hub ports if the hub does not implement power switching. If power switching is supported, additional accesses must be made to apply power to the ports. Note that the status change port cannot report device attachment until power is applied to the ports.

Bus- or Self-Powered Hub

Offset 7 within the configuration descriptor is defined as device attributes. These attributes specify whether the hub uses bus power, is self-powered, or both. If both bit fields are set, then the hub is a hybrid powered device. If the hub is bus-powered, the maximum bus power field can used by configuration software to determine the amount of power available at each port. See Chapter 9 for details regarding issues related to bus- and self-powered hubs.

Maximum Bus Power Consumed

This field is only valid to hubs that are bus- or hybrid-powered. It specifies the maximum amount of current this hub will draw from the USB bus. Configuration software can use this value to deduce the maximum amount of current available at each port. This value includes power consumed by pull-up and pull-down resistors, the hub controller, all embedded devices, and all ports.

Table 12-2: Hub Configuration Descriptor

Offset	Field	Size	Value	Description
0	Length	1	Number	Size of this descriptor in bytes.
1	Descriptor-Type	1	02h	CONFIGURATION

Table 12-2: Hub Configuration Descriptor

Offset	Field	Size	Value	Description
2	TotalLength	2	Number	Total length of data returned for this configuration. Includes the combined length of all descriptors (configuration, interface, endpoint, and class or vendor specific) returned for this configuration.
4	NumInterfaces	1	Number	Number of interfaces supported by this configuration.
5	ConfigurationValue	1	Number	Value to use as an argument to Set Configuration to select this configuration.
6	Configuration	1	Index	Index of string descriptor describing this configuration.
7	Attributes	1	Bitmap	Configuration characteristics D7 Bus Powered D6 Self Powered D5 Remote Wakeup (not used by hub) D4..0 Reserved (reset to 0) A device configuration that uses power from the bus and a local source at runtime may be determined using the Get Status device request.
8	MaxPower	1	ma	Maximum amount of bus power this hub will consume in this configuration. This value includes the hub controller, all embedded devices, at all ports (value based on 2ma increments).

Hub Interface Descriptor

An interface descriptor is included for each function. The first interface descriptor will define the hub function and subsequent interfaces will be included for embedded devices (i.e. compound hub). The specification pre-defines values for two fields within a hub's interface descriptor:

- **Number of endpoints** (offset 4 in Table 12-3 on page 183) — The hub function must contain at least one endpoint descriptor to define the status change endpoint, thus the number of endpoints in pre-defined as 01h. However, additional endpoints can be defined by a hub class device. Note that the default endpoint is pre-defined by the specification and does not require a descriptor. The enumerator is aware that every device implements the default control endpoint to permit access to the device; therefore, a descriptor for the default endpoint is not needed. Note that when reading this descriptor, the USB enumerator will not know that the interface being described is a hub function, if the hub is a compound device.

- **Interface** (offset 8 in Table 12-3 on page 183) — The interface value of 01h identifies the offset of the string descriptor that describes this interface.

Table 12-3: Hub Interface Descriptor

Offset	Field	Size	Value	Description
0	Length	1	Number	Size of this descriptor in bytes.
1	Descriptor-Type	1	Constant	INTERFACE Descriptor Type.
2	Interface-Number	1	Number	Number of interface. Zero-based value identifying the index in the array of concurrent interfaces supported by this configuration.
3	Alternate-Setting	1	Number	Value used to select alternate setting for the interface identified in the prior field.
4	NumEnd-points	1	Number	Number of endpoints used by this interface (excluding endpoint zero). Hub must implement a status change endpoint. (Hubs must implement a status change endpoint, but may also include additional endpoints.)
5	Interface-Class	1	Class	Class code (assigned by USB). If this field is reset to zero, the interface does not belong to any USB specified device class.

Table 12-3: Hub Interface Descriptor

Offset	Field	Size	Value	Description
6	Interface-SubClass	1	SubClass	SubClass code (assigned by USB). These codes are qualified by the value of the InterfaceClass field.
7	Inter-faceProto-col	1	Protocol	Protocol code (assigned by USB). If this field is reset to zero, the device does not use a class-specific protocol on this interface. If this field is set to 0xFF, the device uses a vendor-specific protocol for this interface.
8	Interface	1	01h	Index of string descriptor.

Status Endpoint Descriptor

The hub function defines only the status change endpoint. Table 12-4 shows the definition of the status endpoint descriptor. Enumerator software obtains the following information from the endpoint descriptor:

- Status change endpoint address
- Direction of transfer
- Transfer type supported by this endpoint
- Maximum data packet size supported
- Interval at which the endpoint should be polled

Note that the specification requires that the status change endpoint be the first endpoint descriptor read from the hub when the standard *Get Descriptor* device request is made.

Status Change Endpoint Address/Transfer Direction

The status change endpoint number is specified within the field at offset 2 of the endpoint descriptor. This field specifies the endpoint number (bits 0..3) which is determined at design time and hardwired into the device's address decoder and is implementation dependent. Bit 7 within the same field specifies the direction of the data transfers associated with the endpoint. This bit must be set to indicate that transfers are from the status change endpoint to the host (i.e. IN transactions).

Transfer Type

The transfer type required by this endpoint is defined in the attribute field (offset 3). The status change endpoint is accessed based on the interrupt transfer type and is pre-defined by the specification. Host software will poll the status register at regular intervals to determine if a status change has occurred. Section "Detecting Hub Status Changes" on page 191 describes the information read from the status change port during an interrupt transfer.

Maximum Data Packet Size

The maximum packet size field (offset 4) specifies the maximum data payload that can be supported by this endpoint during a single transaction. The options for an interrupt transfer are 8, 16, 32, or 64 bytes, and relates to the data buffer size for this endpoint and is implementation dependent.

Polling Interval

Since the status change endpoint is defined for interrupt transfers, the polling interval (offset 6) defines how often the endpoint should be polled. The specification pre-defines the polling interval for the status change endpoint to the maximum allowable value of FFh. As a result, configuration software polls this endpoint every 255ms to check for port events (e.g. device connect or disconnect).

Table 12-4: Hub Status Endpoint Descriptor

Offset	Field	Size	Value	Description
0	Length	1	Number	Size of this descriptor in bytes.
1	DescriptorType	1	Constant	ENDPOINT Descriptor Type
2	EndpointAddress	1	Endpoint	The address of the endpoint on the USB device described by this descriptor. The address is encoded as follows: Bit 0..3 the endpoint number Bit 4..6 reserved, reset to zero Bit 7 must be "1" — IN endpoint

Table 12-4: Hub Status Endpoint Descriptor

Offset	Field	Size	Value	Description
3	Attributes	1	BitMap	This field describes the endpoint's attributes when it is configured using the ConfigurationValue: Bit 0..1 Transfer Type: 11 Interrupt only All other bits are reserved
4	MaxPacketSize	2	Number	Maximum packet size this endpoint is capable of sending or receiving when this configuration is selected. For interrupt endpoints smaller data payloads may be sent, but will terminate the transfer and may or may not require intervention to restart.
6	Interval	1	FF	Interval for polling endpoint for data transfers. Expressed in milliseconds. For interrupt endpoints, this field may range from 1 to 255.

Hub Class Descriptor

A class-specific descriptor is defined for hub devices as defined in Table 12-5 on page 188. This descriptor is read via the class-specific *Get Descriptor* request. Note that this descriptor is pre-defined by the specification with an index of zero. The USB enumerator reads the hub-class descriptor to determine the following information:

- Power switching mode implemented
- Whether hub is part of compound device or not
- Whether device implements global, individual port, or no over-current protection.
- The time delay from software requesting power be applied to a port until power is valid.
- Maximum bus current required by the hub controller (compare offset 8 of Table 12-2 on page 181).
- Whether the device attached to a port is removable or not.

- Whether a port is powered in gang-mode or individually.

Refer to Table 12-5 on page 188 during the following discussions.

Power Switching Mode Implemented

A hub may control power to ports in three ways. Offset 3, bits 1..0, within the hub class descriptor defines which method is employed by this hub:

- Ganged power switching — power is switched to all ports at the same time.
- Individual port power switching — power is applied to each port separately. The *Set Port Power Feature* request is used to apply power to the individual port selected.
- No power switching — power is applied to all ports when the hub is configured (i.e. when the *Set Configuration* request is made).

Note that if ganged power mode switching is defined, some ports may be un affected by the ganged power switching. Refer to the section entitled, "Port Power Mask" on page 188 for more information.

Compound Device or Hub Only

Whether a hub is part of a compound device implementation or not is defined at offset 3, bit 2, within the hub class descriptor.

Over-current Protection Mode

A hub may choose to implement over-current protection in different ways, so long as it conforms to the safely requirement of allowing no more than 5a of current to be drawn by a given port. Offset 3, bits 4..3, specify which overcurrent protection mode is implemented for this hub as described in Table 12-5 on page 188.

Power On to Power Good Delay

Configuration software must know how long the device requires to apply power to the device. Once system software requests that powered by applied to the hub, there will be a delay until power is good at the port. Software must wait until it knows that power is good before accessing the port. Offset 5 defines the delay between the power-on request and power good. The value is defined in 2ms intervals.

Maximum Bus Current for Hub Controller

Offset 6 within the hub class descriptor specifies the maximum amount of current that the hub controller consumes. Note that this value is different from the maximum current field in the configuration descriptor, which specifies total power that the device consumes (See the section entitled, "Maximum Bus Power Consumed " on page 181

Device Removable/Non-removable

The DeviceRemovable field at offset 7 provides a bit map of all ports supported by this hub. Each bit position corresponds to a given hub (i.e. bit 1 specifies port 1). If the bit field corresponding to a port is cleared the device is removable and if the bit is set the device is permanently attached (e.g. an embedded device). The field size is one byte for hubs that support from one to seven ports. Another byte must be added for 8 to 15 ports, etc.

Port Power Mask

The offset within the hub class descriptor depends on the size of the Device Removable field. The Port Power Control Mask consists of a bit map of ports just as the DeviceRemovable field does. Each bit position corresponds to a given port and defines whether the port is power via ganged power mode or if the port must be powered individually. If ganged power is masked the bit field is set and power must be applied via the *Set Port Power Feature* request.

Table 12-5: Hub Class Descriptor

Offset	Field	Size	Description
0	DescLength	1	Number of bytes in the descriptor, including this byte.
1	DescriptorType	1	Descriptor Type = 29h (hub class descriptor)
2	NbrPorts	1	Number of downstream ports that this hub supports.

Table 12-5: Hub Class Descriptor

Offset	Field	Size	Description
3	HubCharacteristics	2	D1..D0 Power Switching Mode 00 Ganged power switching (all ports' power at once) 01 Individual port power switching 1X No power switching (ports always powered on when hub in on, and off when hub is off). D2 Identifies a Compound Device 0 Hub is not part of a compound device 1 Hub is part of a compound device D4..D3 Over-current Protection Mode 00 Global Over-current Protection. The hub reports over-current as a summation of all ports' current draw, without a breakdown of individual port over-current status. 01 Individual Port Over-current Protection. The hub reports over-current on a per port basis. Each port has an over-current indicator. 1X No Over-current Protection. This option is only allowed for bus-powered hubs that don't implement over-current protection. D15..D5 Reserved
5	PwrOn2PwrGood	1	Time (in 2ms intervals) from the time power on sequence begins on a port until power is good on that port. System software uses this value to determine how long to wait before accessing a powered-on port.
6	HubContrCurrent	1	Maximum current requirements of the hub controller electronics, in 2 mA increments.

Table 12-5: Hub Class Descriptor

Offset	Field	Size	Description
7	DeviceRemovable	Depends on num of ports	Indicates if a port has a removable device attached. If a non-removable device is attached to a port, that port will never receive an insertion change notification. This field is reported on byte-granularity. Within a byte, if no port exists for a given location, then the field representing the port characteristics returns to 0. Bit definition: 0 Device is removable 1 Device is not removable This is a bitmap corresponding to the individual ports on the hub: Bit 0 Reserved Bit 1 Port 1 Bit 2 Port 2 : Bit n Port n (implementation dependent)
Vari-able	PortPwrCtrlMask	Depends on num of ports	Indicates if a port is not affected by a gang-mode power control request. Ports that have this field set always require a manual SetPortFeature (PORT_POWER) request to control the port's power state. Bit definition 0 Port does not mask the gang-mode power control capability. 1 Port is not affected by gang-mode power commands. Manual commands must be sent to this port to turn power on and off. This is a bitmap corresponding to the individual ports on the hub Bit 0 Reserved for future use. Bit 1 Port 1 Bit 2 Port 2 : Bit n Port n (implementation dependent)

Powering the Hub

Once a hub has been configured, power may need to be applied to the ports. Configuration software detects the port power mode when reading the hub class descriptor. If power must be manually applied, then the software issues a *Set Port Power Feature* request. Once power is applied to a port, the hub port will be able to detect that a device is connected to the port and set status bits to indicate the connect event. The hub port also transitions from it powered-off state to it powered-on state. This status change event will be detected by software when status is checked.

Checking Hub Status

Configuration software polls the status change endpoint to detect which ports have incurred a status change event. The status change endpoint merely reports whether the hub or a hub port has incurred a status change but does not identify the nature of the change. Specific requests must be made to the hub or port to determine the:

1. specific event(s) that has occurred.
2. current state of the item causing the event.

Detecting Hub Status Changes

Figure 12-3 illustrates the hub and port status change bitmap that is returned when the status change endpoint is polled. All status changes are sampled at the end of frame (EOP2 sample point), and are available to be read during the next frame. Configuration software is aware of the number of ports and therefore the size of the bit map returned when the hubs status change endpoint is polled. Status is reported in byte-sized fields and zeros are returned in the bit field corresponding to ports that are not implemented. For most implementations a byte will be returned, because hubs will rarely implement more than 7 ports.

When software polls the status change endpoint, the bitmap illustrated in Figure 12-3 on page 192 is returned, providing a status change has occurred. If none of the bits are set, then no changes need be reported. In this case, the status change endpoint returns NAK during the IN transaction, indicating that no change has occurred.

If a specific port change is detected, then software can perform the *Get Port Status* request. Hub requests are defined in Chapter 13.

Figure 12-3: Hub and Port Status Change Bitmap

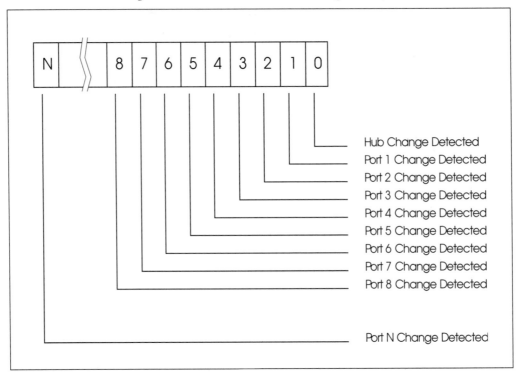

Reading the Hub Status Field

If a hub status change is detected, software can perform the *Get Hub Status* request to obtain the source of the change. Hub status changes consist of:

- Local power change
- Over-current change

Chapter 13 details the hub status fields. Refer to the section entitled, "Hub Status Fields" on page 203 for details. Once the specific hub status item that has changed is detected, software can take the appropriate action (e.g., by notifying the user of the event). Software must also acknowledge and clear the hub status change field by using the related *Clear Hub Feature* request. For example, if a local power change has occurred, software uses the *Clear Hub Local Power Feature* request.

Reading Port Status Field

When a port status change occurs, software uses the *Get Port Status* request to determine the which port feature or features have experienced a change. The hub returns the port status field which is discussed in the section entitled, "Reading Port Status Field" on page 193. The possible sources of port changes are:

- **Connect Status Change** — device either connected or disconnected from port
- **Port Enable/Disable Change** — change caused by hardware event
- **Suspend Change** — changed indicated when resume has completed
- **Over-Current Indicator Change** — used only by hubs that report over-current on a per port basis.
- **Reset Change** — change set when reset processing is completed.

Consider the following example. A Connect Status Change is indicated when power is applied to a port that currently has a device attached. The port status change field will be set and the current status field will indicate that a device is currently attached. Configuration software recognizes that a device has been connect and acknowledges the change by performing a *Clear Port Feature* request.

Enabling the Device

Having detected a device attached to the port, configuration software will enable the port and attempt to configure the device. A port is enabled by software via the *Set Port Enable Feature*. Once the port is enabled it transitions to its enabled state, permitting it to receive bus traffic.

USB System Architecture

Summary of Hub Port States

The following table lists the hub port states and the transitions that take place for given signaling events or control requests.

Table 12-6: Hub Port States

Signaling/State	Powered off	Disconnected	Disabled	Enabled	Suspended
Reset on root port (hub with power switching)	Stay in powered off	Go to powered off	Go to powered off	Go to powered off	Go to powered off
Reset on root port (hub without power switching)	N.A.	Go to disconnected	Go to disconnected	Go to disconnected	Go to disconnected
ClearPortFeature PORT_POWER (power switching)	Stay in powered off	Go to powered off	Go to powered off	Go to powered off	Go to powered off
SetPortFeature PORT_POWER (power switching)	Go to disconnected	N.A.	N.A.	N.A.	N.A.
SetPortFeature PORT_RESET	Stay in powered off	Go to enabled	Go to enabled	Stay in Enabled	Go to enabled
SetPort Feature PORT_ENABLE	ignore	ignore	Go to enabled	Stay in Enabled	ignore
ClearPort Feature PORT_ENABLE	ignore	ignore	Stay at disabled	Go to disabled	ignore
Downstream packet traffic (hub awake)	Do not propagate	Do not propagate	Do not propagate	Propagate traffic	Do not propagate
Upstream packet traffic (hub awake)	Do not propagate	Do not propagate	Do not propagate	Propagate traffic	Set status field, do not prop.
SetPortFeature PORT_SUSPEND	ignore	ignore	ignore	Go to suspend	ignore
ClearPortFeature PORT_SUSPEND	ignore	ignore	ignore	ignore	Go to resume

Table 12-6: Hub Port States

Signaling/State	Powered off	Disconnected	Disabled	Enabled	Suspended
Disconnect detect	ignore	ignore	Go to disconnected	Go to disconnected	Go to disconnected
Connect detect	ignore	Go to disabled	N.A.	N.A.	N.A.

$\boldsymbol{13}$ *Hub Requests*

The Previous Chapter

The hub is the linchpin of USB device enumeration. The previous chapter focused on the hub characteristics and features involved in device configuration.

This Chapter

This chapter discusses the control transfer requests defined for USB hubs. Hubs, like all USB devices, support standard requests and also must support hub class specific requests.

The Next Chapter

The next chapter discusses configuration of non-hub devices that are attached to the USB. Device descriptors and other characteristics and features that relate to configuring the device are discussed.

Overview

Hubs must respond to a variety of USB device requests or commands. Standard requests are used for configuring the hub, for controlling the state of its USB interface, as well as other miscellaneous features. Hubs must also support class-specific requests that are used to control specific hub and port features. All requests are issued by the host using the control transfer mechanism. Prior to configuration a device responds to its default address of zero. This permits configuration software to request the contents of any device's descriptors (from endpoint zero) using device address zero during configuration.

Control transfers, used to transmit device requests, consist minimally of a setup stage and a status stage, but may also include a data stage, depending on the type of request being performed. The setup stage consists of setup transactions as illustrated in Figure 13-1. The eight byte data payload of a setup transaction defines the type of request being issued by the host.

Figure 13-1: Format of Setup Transaction that Specifies the Device Request Being Performed

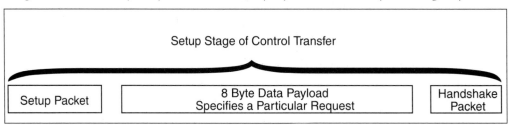

Hub Request Types

The eight byte data packet that defines the type of request being made is illustrated in Table 13-1. Byte zero of the data packet contains a bit-map that defines:

- Direction of data transfer
- Type of request
- Recipient of request

Byte zero of the data packet consists of a bit-mapped value that identifies the packet type for a standard request. That is, if bits 5 and 6 are both zero, then the request is one of the standard requests listed in Table 13-2, and a value of 01b specifies that the request is hub-specific. The hub-specific requests are listed in Table 13-4.

Table 13-1: Format of Setup Transaction Data Phase

Offset	Field	Size	Value	Description

0	Request-Type	1	Bit-map	Characteristics of Request
				
				D7 Data xfer direction
				     0 = Host to device
				     1 = Device to host
				
				D6..5 Type
				     0 = Standard
				     1 = Class
				     2 = Vendor
				     3 = Reserved
				
				D4..0 Recipient
				     0 = Device
				     1 = Interface
				     2 = Endpoint
				     3 = Other
				     4..31 = Reserved

1	Request	1	Value	Specific Request
2	Value	2	Value	Word-sized field that varies according to request
4	Index	2	Index or Offset	Word-sized field that varies according to request. Typically used to pass an index or offset.
6	Length	2	Count	Number of bytes to transfer if there is a data stage required for this transfer.

Standard Requests and Hub Response

Hubs must support standard device requests like any other USB device. Table 13-2 lists the standard requests and the hubs response to these requests. Refer to Chapter 15 for details regarding the standard requests.

Table 13-2: Hub's Response to Standard Device Requests

Request	Request Field Value	Hub Response
CLEAR_FEATURE	1	Clears the selected feature within the device
GET_CONFIGURATION	8	Returns the configuration value used to configure the device.
GET_DESCRIPTOR	6	Returns the selected descriptor(s).
GET_INTERFACE	10	Optional (Hubs only required to support one interface.)
GET_STATUS	0	Returns status information regarding the state of the device.
SET_ADDRESS	5	Used to assign a unique address to the device.
SET_CONFIGURATION	9	Used to configure a device by assigning the configuration value of the selected configuration descriptor.
SET_DESCRIPTOR	7	Optional (Used to update or modify a selected descriptor.)
SET_FEATURE	3	Sets the selected feature associated with the device.
SET_INTERFACE	11	Optional (Hubs only required to support one interface)
SYNCH_FRAME	12	Optional (Hubs are not required to have isochronous endpoints)

Hub Class Requests

Hubs must also support specific class requests. When the request type field (bits 5..4) in Table 13-1 is set to 01b the request is interpreted as being class specific. The hub class requests are listed in Table 13-3.

Table 13-3: Hub Class Request Codes

Request	Value
GET_STATUS	0
CLEAR_FEATURE	1
GET_STATE	2
SET_FEATURE	3
reserved	4-5
GET_DESCRIPTOR	6
SET_DESCRIPTOR	7

The format and definition of each hub class request is shown in Table 13-4. Only a hub device supports these specific requests. Each of the requests is detailed in the following sections.

Table 13-4: Hub Class-Specific Requests

Request-Type	Request	Value	Index	Length	Data
00100000B	CLEAR_FEATURE (01h)	Feature Selector	Zero	Zero	None
00100011B	CLEAR_FEATURE (01h)	Feature Selector	Port	Zero	None
10100011B	GET_BUS_STATE (02h)	Zero	Port	One	Per Port Bus State
10100000B	GET_DESCRIPTOR (06h)	Descriptor Type and Descriptor Index	Zero or Language ID	Descriptor Length	Descriptor
10100000B	GET_STATUS (00h)	Zero	Zero	Four	Hub Status and Change Indicators

Table 13-4: Hub Class-Specific Requests

Request-Type	Request	Value	Index	Length	Data
10100011B	GET_STATUS (00h)	Zero	Port	Four	Port Status and Change Indicators
00100000B	SET_DESCRIPTOR (07h)	Descriptor Type and Descriptor Index	Zero or Language ID	Descriptor Length	Descriptor
00100000B	SET_FEATURE (03h)	Feature Selector	Zero	Zero	None
00100011B	SET_FEATURE (03h)	Feature Selector	Port	Zero	None

Get/Set Descriptor

The class-specific *Get Hub Descriptor* request provides host software a way to read the hub class descriptor. The "value" field within the setup transaction must be cleared (00h) which is the hub descriptor index number. The format and definition of the hub class descriptor can be found in Table 12-5 on page 188.

The *Set Descriptor* request is optional. This request is used to update the hub descriptor, and is valid only for those hubs that provide a mechanism for updating descriptors.

Get Hub Status Request

The *Get Hub Status* request returns the current hub status, along with state change indicators. Two bytes are returned for status and two bytes for state change during the data stage of the request. The state change byte indicates which status events has incurred a change and the status byte specifies the current status of each status bit. Note that hub status information is global in nature and applies equally to all ports associated with the hub.

Hub Status Fields

Two fields are defined for hub status information as shown in Table 13-5.:

- Local Power Status
- Over-current Indicator

Local Power Status

The Local Power Status field applies only to hub that support both self-powered and bus-powered implementations, or hybrid-powered hubs (i.e. bus interface powered by bus and ports powered by a local supply). This field indicates whether local power to the hub is good or not. Since the USB interface logic is powered by the USB bus, status information can be returned, even if power to the rest of the hub has been lost. The bit definition is:

- 0 = Local power supply good
- 1 = Local power supply lost

If "0" is returned for this bit position then the power to the interface and hub are valid. Note that if power to the bus interface is lost, a time-out will occur when the *Get Hub Status* request is performed, since the hub could not respond. If power to the interface is good then the transaction will complete normally and reports the current status of the local supply.

Over-Current Indicator

The *Over-Current Indicator* applies only to hubs that report over-current protection globally (a summation of all ports). Whether over-current is reported globally or for each ports individually is specified within the hub descriptor's *Hub Characteristics* field (see Table 12-5 on page 188). Definition for this bit field is:

- 0 = All power operations normal
- 1 = An over-current condition exists on a hub-wide basis

If an over-current condition is reported, then power to all ports will have been shut off.

Table 13-5: Format of Hub Status Fields Returned During the Get Hub Status Request

7	6	5	4	3	2	1	0
Reserved (returns zero)						Over-Current Indicator	Local Power Status

15	14	13	12	11	10	9	8
Reserved (returns zero)							

Hub State Change Fields

Two bit fields are defined within the hub state change fields as shown in Table 13-6:

- Local Power Status Change
- Over-Current Indicator Change

Local Power Status Change

This field corresponds directly to the *Local Power Status* bit that reports the current status of local power. If the *Local Power Status* bit is implemented, then this bit must also be implemented and vice versa. This corresponding change bit indicates whether or not there has been a change in the local power since last acknowledged. The bit definition is:

- 0 = No change has occurred to local power status
- 1 = Local power status has changed

If this bit is set then the local power status can be checked to determine the current state of the local power.

Over-Current Indicator Change

This bit field corresponds to the *Over-Current Indicator* bit and must also be implemented if the *Over-Current Indicator* bit is implemented and vice versa. The bit definition is:

- 0 = No change has occurred to the over-current status indicator
- 1 = The over-current indicator has changed

This change bit tells software that their has been a change in the over-current status and the over-current indicator bit should be checked to determine the current state of the current limiter logic. (e.g. Power has been removed to all ports due to the over-current condition.)

Table 13-6: Format of Hub Change Field Returned During Hub Status Request

7	6	5	4	3	2	1	0
Reserved (returns zero)						Over-Current Indicator Change	Local Power Status Change

15	14	13	12	11	10	9	8
Reserved (returns zero)							

Set/Clear Hub Feature Request

The hub class definition of the *Set Feature* and *Clear Feature* requests depend of the value of the feature selector byte. The selector byte defines the hub specific feature that is to be either set or cleared. These features globally apply to the hub, therefore the "index" field of the setup transaction is 00h for hub features. Table 13-7 lists the hub features defined for hub class requests.

Table 13-7: Feature Selector and Index Values for Hub-Specific Requests

	Recipient	Value	Index
C_HUB_LOCAL_POWER	hub	00h	00h
C_HUB_OVER_CURRENT	hub	01h	00h

Hub Local Power Change Request

If software has detected a **Hub Local Power** status change via the *Get Hub Status* request, software acknowledges the request via the *Clear Hub Local Power Change Feature* request. This request clears the change field so that a subsequent change in the hub local power can be detected.

The *Set Hub Local Power Change* request can be used to set the hub local power status bit, causing the corresponding change bit to be set. Although the specification doesn't define the use of the this set feature request, it should be useful for debug purposes to simulate a hub local power change. Note that this request cannot be used to acknowledge a change condition.

Hub Over Current Change Request

The *Clear Hub Over-Current Change* request is used to acknowledge a hub over-current condition that has been detected via the *Get Hub Status* request. This request clears the indicator changed bit thereby, making it possible to recognize a subsequent change in the hub over-current indicator.

The *Set Hub Over-Current Change* request sets the over-current indicator, causing the change to be reflected in the corresponding indicator change bit field. As with the *Set Hub Local Power Change* request, this request appears to have been implemented to support debug efforts.

Get Port Status Request

The *Get Port Status* request is defined in the recipient field of the setup transaction. The Get Hub Status request defines the recipient as the device (i.e. hub), whereas, the recipient of the *Get Port Status* request is defined as "other" (in this case "other" refers to port). The "index" value defines which port is being selected. The request contains a data stage during which the port status and port change indicators are returned.

Like the hub status information, port status information is returned in four bytes. Two bytes are defines for port status field and two bytes for the port change field.

Port Status Fields

The port status fields are shown in Table 13-8 on page 207. Seven bit fields are defined to report the current status of the selected port. Each bit field is discussed in the following sections.

Table 13-8: Format of Port Status Fields Returned During the Get Port Status Request

7	6	5	4	3	2	1	0
Reserved (returns all zeros when read)			Reset Status	Over-Current Indicator	Suspend Status	Port Enabled/ Disabled	Current Connect Status

15	14	13	12	11	10	9	8
Reserved (returns all zeros when read)						Low Speed Device Attached	Port Power

Current Connect Status Field

This field reflects whether or not a device is currently connected to this port. This value reflects the current state of the port, and may not correspond directly to the event that caused the insertion Status Change (Bit 0) to be set.

- 0 = No device is present on this port
- 1 = A device is present on this port

This field is always 1 for ports that have non-removable devices attached.

Port Enabled/Disabled

Ports can be enabled by host software only. However, ports can be disabled by either a fault condition (disconnect event or other fault condition, including an over-current indication) or by host software.

- 0 = Port is disabled
- 1 = Port is enabled

Suspend

This field indicates whether or not the device on this port is suspended. Setting this field causes the device to suspend by not propagating bus traffic downstream. Resetting this field causes the device to resume. Bus traffic cannot be resumed in the middle of a bus transaction. If the device itself is signalling a resume, this field will be cleared by the hub.

- 0 = Not suspended
- 1 = Suspended

Over-Current Indicator

This field only applies to hubs that report over-current conditions on a per port basis. If the hub does not report over-current on a per port hub basis, then this field is RESERVED and returns all zeros.

The Over-Current Indicator when set indicates that the device attached to this port has drawn current that exceeds the specified maximum, and that port power has been shut off. Port power shutdown is also reflected in the Port Power Enable/Disable field.

This field indicates and over-current condition due to the device attached to this port.

- 0 = All power operations normal for this port
- 1 = An over-current condition exists on this port. Power has been shut off to this port

Reset

This field is set when the host wishes to reset the attached device. It remains set until the reset signalling is turned off by the hub and the reset status change field is set.

- 0 = Reset signalling not asserted
- 1 = Reset signalling asserted

Port Power

This field reflects a port's power state. Since hubs can implement different methods of port power switching, the meaning of this field varies depending on the type of power switching used. The hub class descriptor reports the type of power switching implemented by the hub. Hubs do not provide any power to their ports until they are in the configured state.

- 0 = This port is powered OFF
- 1 = This port is powered ON

Hubs that do not support power switching always return a "1" in this field.

Low Speed Device Attached

This field is only relevant if a device is attached.

- 0 = Full Speed device attached to this port
- 1 = Low Speed device attached to this port

Port Change Fields

The port change fields are shown in Table 13-9. Five bit fields are defined to report the status and indicator changes for the selected port. Each bit field is discussed in the following sections.

Table 13-9: Format of Port Change Fields Returned During the Get Port Status Request

7	6	5	4	3	2	1	0
Reserved (returns all zeros when read)			Reset Complete Change	Over-Current Indicator Change	Suspend Change (resume complete)	Port Enabled/ Disabled Change	Connect Status Change

15	14	13	12	11	10	9	8
Reserved (returns all zeros when read)							

Current Status Change

Indicates a changed has occurred in the current connect status of the port. The hub sets this bit when a it detects that the connect status has changed.

- 0 = No change on current connect status
- 1 = Current connection status has changed

This bit is set after RESET if the port has a non-removable device attached.

Port Enabled/Disable Change

This field is set when a hardware event initiates a port disable change (i.e. a disconnect event or other fault condition, including an over-current indication). This bit is unaffected by a host software initiated enable/disable change.

- 0 = No port enable/disable change has occurred
- 1 = Port enable/disable status has changed due to hardware event

Suspend Change (Resume Complete)

This field indicates that a device attached to this port has completed the resume process (i.e. The hub has terminated resume signaling, followed by 3ms of inactivity to allow the device has resynchronized to SOF). This bit is not set when the device enters the suspend state.

- 0 = No change
- 1 = Resume completed

Over-Current Indicator Change

This field only applies to hubs that report over-current conditions on a per port basis. If the hub does not report over-current on a per port hub basis, then this field is RESERVED and returns zero.

This field reports whether or not a change has occurred on the port's over-current indicator.

- 0 = No over-current indicator change for this port has occurred
- 1 = The over-current indicator for this port has changed.

Reset Complete

This field is set when reset processing for this port has completed. Reset complete also causes the port enable status bit to be set and the suspend change field is reset.

- 0 = No change
- 1 = Reset complete

Set/Clear Port Feature

The Set and Clear feature requests may specify a given hub feature or may be associated with an individual port. Hub feature requests are differentiated from port feature requests by the "index" field value of the setup transaction. The index field identifies the port number (port #) that the request applies to. Note that a port number of zero is not permissible, since a hub would interpret the request as a hub-specific rather than a port-specific request. Table 13-10 lists the individual port features that can be set or cleared.

Table 13-10: Feature Selector and Index Values for Port Specific Requests

	Recipient	Value	Index
PORT_CONNECTION	port	00h	port #
PORT_ENABLE	port	01h	port #
PORT_SUSPEND	port	02h	port #
PORT_OVER_CURRENT	port	03h	port #
PORT_RESET	port	04h	port #
PORT_POWER	port	08h	port #
PORT_LOW_SPEED	port	09h	port #
C_PORT_CONNECTION	port	16h	port #
C_PORT_ENABLE	port	17h	port #
C_PORT_SUSPEND	port	18h	port #
C_PORT_OVER_CURRENT	port	19h	port #
C_PORT_RESET	port	20h	port #

The section previous section entitled, "Get Port Status Request" on page 206, defined the status and indicator bits and the status and indicator change bits that are maintained by the hub for each port and returned when a *Get Port Status* request is made. These bits reflect that various port features supported by a hub. The *Set* and *Clear Port Feature* requests provide a method of enabling and disabling particular features and also allows software to acknowledge changes that are detected when the *Get Port Status* request is performed.

Get Bus State

This optional request is defined to facilitate diagnosis of problems by providing bus state information on a port-by-port basis. The information returned is sampled at the last EOF2 point detected at the selected port. Bus state information is returned in a single byte during the data stage of the transfer. The bit definition is shown in Table 13-11 on page 212.

Table 13-11: Format of the Bus State Returned During the Get Bus State Request

7	6	5	4	3	2	1	0
Reserved (returns zero)						State of D+ sampled at last EOF2	State of D- sampled at last EOF2

14 *USB Device Configuration*

The Previous Chapter

The last chapter discussed the control transfer requests defined for USB hubs. Hubs, like all USB devices, support standard requests and also must support hub class specific requests.

This Chapter

This chapter discusses configuration of non-hub devices that are attached to the USB. Device descriptors and other characteristics and features that relate to configuring the device are discussed.

The Next Chapter

The next chapter discusses the standard requests required by USB devices. Each device class may define class-specific requests that are covered in the related device class chapter.

Overview

Prior to configuring a device, the hub to which the device attached must have already been configured and power must be applied to the port. Next, the hub and configuration software must detect the connected device:

- The hub recognizes that a device has been attached by monitoring the D- and D+ port signals.
- The hub sets status information for the port indicating device connect and speed.
- Configuration software reads port status and recognizes a full-speed device is connected.
- Software then enables the port so that the hub will pass bus traffic to the device.

- Configuration software then issues a *Reset Port* request, forcing the device into its default state. In the default state the device is unconfigured and responds only to accesses targeted for device zero and endpoint zero.

Configuration software can now begin the device configuration process. This process is similar to that used when configuring a hub.

- Host queries device's control endpoint (zero) at address zero to determine max payload supported by the default pipe.
- Host assigns unique address to USB device.
- Host reads and evaluates configuration information from descriptors.
- Host verifies that the USB resources needed by the device are available.
- Host issues a configuration value to USB device specifying how it's to be used. When the configuration value is received, the device assumes its described characteristics. Device is now ready to be accessed by client software and can draw the amount of Vbus power described in the configuration.

Reading and Interpreting the USB Descriptors

Device implementers must create descriptors to reflect the characteristics and behavior of the device. This chapter provides the definition and format of the standard descriptors that must accompany every USB device. The standard descriptors include:

- Device Descriptor — describes the number of configurations supported by the device.
- Configuration Descriptors — specifies one or more interfaces and defines certain attributes associated with this configuration.
- Interface Descriptors — defines the number of endpoints related to the interface and defines certain attributes associated with the interface.
- Endpoint Descriptors — specify the attributes associated with a given endpoint along with information needed by host software to determine how the endpoint should be accessed.
- String Descriptors — optional descriptors consisting of a UNICODE string that provides human-readable information that can be displayed.
- Class-Specific Descriptors — a given device class may require additional descriptors as defined by a particular device class specification.

Each descriptor contains a type field that identifies the descriptor as one of the descriptors listed above. Table 14-1 on page 215 lists the type codes that identifies the descriptor. Note that the only device class specific descriptor defined by the 1.0 specification is the hub device class descriptor. Other class descriptors, if required, are defined within the relevant device class specifications.

Table 14-1: Descriptor Type Values

Descriptor Types	Value
DEVICE	1
CONFIGURATION	2
STRING	3
INTERFACE	4
ENDPOINT	5

Device Classes

An important aspect of device configuration is determining which device class a particular device belongs to. A device's class definition provides information used by host and client software to determine how a device is to be controlled and accessed. Host software uses the device class definition to identify the corresponding USB class device driver. The class driver knowing the definition related to its class-specific descriptors can then further evaluate the device to determine specific characteristics of the device.

Devices classes are defined in individual specifications. At the time of this writing the following class specifications had been devised, while others were still being defined.

- HID Device Class — Human Interface Devices
- Communication Device Class
- Monitor Device Class
- Mass Storage Device Class
- Audio Device Class

Chapter 17 provides an overview of each device class.

Device Descriptors

Figure 14-3 defines the device descriptor format and definition. The following sections discuss how host software evaluates the device descriptor during the configuration process. Some fields are not discussed under the following headings since the definition of these field included in Table 14-3 requires no clarification (in the judgement of the author).

Class Code Field

The class code may or may not be defined within the device descriptor since some devices may have a variety of interfaces requiring different class drivers. If a device is accessible by a single device driver, then the class code will be specified in the "device" descriptor. If a device requires more than one class driver to control and access the device, the class codes will be defined within the "interface" descriptors. Their are a many examples of devices of both types and some of these examples are listed below:

Devices with a single class definition are characterized by a single programming interface, such as:

- Hub Device
- Microphone
- Speaker
- Mouse
- Keyboard

Devices characterized by multiple programming interfaces and different class definitions, include:

- Digital USB Telephone — this device can be characterized by two different classes: audio (sender and receiver) and human interface (dialer).
- CD-ROM — this devices can be characterized by several different programming interfaces that have their own device-class definition including, audio, video, and mass storage. Depending on which software application is currently using the CD-ROM, a different USB class driver will be used.
- Composite device — a composite device is a device that has a single interface to two distinctly different functional devices. For example, a keyboard may also have an integrated scanner, and/or a USB headphone jack. Each of these devices would have its own interface descriptor that defines its device class type.

Chapter 14: USB Device Configuration

- Compound device — a compound device is defined by the specification as a hub class device that integrates other functional devices. For example, a USB printer that also includes a hub.

If the device descriptor does not define a class type (class code field =00h), then the interface descriptors will define the class type for each interface being described. Note that the subclass field must also be zero if the class code field is zero.

A class code field containing FFh means that the definition of the descriptor is vendor specific and only the vendor-specific USB device driver would be able to correctly interpret the descriptors and access the device.

Maximum Packet Size 0

This field is used by configuration software to determine the maximum data packet size supported by endpoint zero. When the device is initially accessed it is accessed with the minimum packet size of 8 bytes. If the packet size defined by this field indicates a larger value, then the device contains a larger data buffer that can support the packet size defined. Subsequent accesses to endpoint zero can then be performed more efficiently.

Manufacturer, Product, Serial Number

Optional string descriptors can be included that provide human-readable information related to the manufacturer, product, and serial number of the device. Each of the these fields located at offset 16..14 within the "device" descriptor identify the location of the string descriptors stating the manufacturer and describing the product, and listing the serial number of the device. The value within the description is defined as an index. This index is used by software to access the corresponding string via the *Get Descriptor* request. To access a string descriptor software must specify the descriptor type (01h) and the index number (specified in the descriptor) when performing the Get Descriptor request. Table 14-2 on page 218 shows the format and definition of the Get Descriptor request's setup data. Note that the "value" field specifies the descriptor type and index and the "index" field contains the language ID.

Table 14-2: Definition of Get Descriptor Request Used to Read the String Descriptors

Request-Type	Request	value (2 bytes)	index (2 bytes)	length (2 bytes)	Data
10000000B	GET_DESCRIPTOR (06h)	Descriptor Type and Descriptor Index	Language ID	Descriptor Length	Descriptor

Number of Configurations

A device may define additional configurations to provide flexibility during configuration and enhance the probability that the device can be successfully configured. As an example, a device may normally consume two units of current (200ma); however, if the device is attached to a bus powered USB port, only 100ma of current may be available. In this case the device could not be supported and host software would not enable the device. To avoid this problem a device designer may decide to provide an alternate configuration that reduces the amount of bus current required by the device to 100ma.

The number of configurations field specifies the number of configurations supported. Host software reads the configurations and decides which configuration to select. The specification states that the device driver may be consulted to help determine which configuration to select, but the mechanism for such input from the device driver is not defined.

Table 14-3: Device Descriptor Definition

Offset	Field	Size (bytes)	Value	Description
0	Length	1	Number	Size of this descriptor in bytes
1	DescriptorType	1	Constant	DEVICE Descriptor Type = 01h

Table 14-3: Device Descriptor Definition

Offset	Field	Size (bytes)	Value	Description
2	USB	2	BCD	USB Specification Release Number in Binary-Coded Decimal (i.e. 1.00 is 0x100). This field identifies the release of the USB Specification that the device and its descriptors are compliant with.
4	Device-Class	1	Class	Class code (assigned by USB). If this field is reset to zero, each interface within a configuration specifies its own class information and the various interfaces operate independently. If this field is set to a value between one (1) and 0xFEh (254), the device supports different class specifications on different interfaces and the interfaces may not operate independently. This value identifies the class definition used for the aggregate interfaces. (i.e. a CD-ROM device with audio and digital data interfaces that require transport control to eject CDs or start them spinning.) If this field is set to 0xFF, the device class is vendor specific.
5	Device-Sub-Class	1	SubClass	Subclass code (assigned by USB) These codes are qualified by the value of the DeviceClass field. If the DeviceClass field is reset to zero, this field must also be reset to zero.

Table 14-3: Device Descriptor Definition

Offset	Field	Size (bytes)	Value	Description
6	Device-Protocol	1	Protocol	Protocol code (assigned by USB) These codes are qualified by the value of the DeviceClass and the DeviceSubClass fields. If a device supports class-specific protocols on a device basis as opposed to an interface basis, this code identifies the protocols that the device uses as defined by the specification of the device class. If this field is reset to zero, the device does not use class-specific protocols on a device basis. However, it may use class-specific protocols on an interface basis. If this field is set to 0xFF, the device uses a vendor-specific protocol on a device basis.
7	MaxPacketSize0	1	Number	Maximum packet size for endpoint zero. (Only 8, 16, 32, or 64 are valid)
8	Vendor	2	ID	Vendor ID (assigned by USB).
10	Product	2	ID	Product ID (assigned by manufacturer).
12	Device	2	BCD	Device release number in Binary-Coded Decimal.
14	Manu-facturer	1	Index	Index of string descriptor describing manufacturer.
15	Product	1	Index	Index of string descriptor describing product.
16	Serial-Number	1	Index	Index of string descriptor describing the device's serial number.

Table 14-3: Device Descriptor Definition

Offset	Field	Size (bytes)	Value	Description
17	Num-Configu-rations	1	Number	Number of possible configurations.

Configuration Descriptors

Software reads a configuration descriptor to obtain global information regarding a given configuration option. The following sections discuss the fields that configuration software probes to determine configuration characteristics. Refer to Table 14-4 on page 222 during the following discussions.

Number of Interfaces

As discussed previously, a given device may have two or more interfaces that require different device class drivers. An interface consists of a collection of endpoints through which a given device driver would control and communicate with its device. The NumInterfaces field specifies the number of interfaces that are implemented in this configuration.

Configuration Value

Once configuration software has selected one of the configurations defined by the device, the device must be configured. Each configuration descriptor has a unique configuration value that is used to configure the device. Until the configuration value is written to the device it will not consume more than 100ma of current and is not fully operational.

Configuration software configures a device by using the Set Configuration request. The configuration value is specified within the "value" field of the setup transaction during the Set Configuration request. Refer to Table 15-2 on page 236. Once configured the device takes on the characteristics defined by the selected configuration.

Attributes and Maximum Power

The configuration attributes define how a device is powered and if it supports remote wakeup. A device configuration reports whether the configuration is bus-powered or self-powered. Device status reports whether the device is currently self-powered. If a device is disconnected from its external power source, it updates device status to indicate the device is no longer self-powered.

A device may not increase its power draw from the bus when it loses its external power source beyond the amount of bus power specified in its configuration descriptor.

If a device can continue to operate when disconnected from its external power source, it continues to do so. If the device cannot continue to operate, the device will fail operations that it can no longer support. Host software may determine the cause of the failure by checking status and noting the loss of the device's power source. This information is available via the *Get Status* request (See "Device Status" on page 240 for details).

Table 14-4: Configuration Descriptor Definition

Offset	Field	Size (bytes)	Value	Description
0	Length	1	Number	Size of this descriptor in bytes.
1	DescriptorType	1	Constant	Configuration value = 02h
2	TotalLength	2	Number	Total length of data returned for this configuration. Includes the combined length of all descriptors (configuration, interface, endpoint, and class or vendor specific) returned for this configuration.
4	NumInterfaces	1	Number	Number of interfaces supported by this configuration.
5	Configuration-Value	1	Number	Value to use as an argument to Set Configuration to select this configuration.
6	Configuration	1	Index	Index of string descriptor describing this configuration.

Table 14-4: Configuration Descriptor Definition

Offset	Field	Size (bytes)	Value	Description
7	Attributes	1	Bitmap	Configuration characteristics D7 Bus Powered D6 Self Powered D5 Remote Wakeup D4..0 Reserved (reset to 0) A device configuration that uses power from the bus and a local source at runtime may be determined using the Get Status device request. If a device configuration supports remote wakeup, D5 is set to one (1).
8	MaxPower	1	ma	Maximum power consumption of USB device from the bus in this specific configuration when the device is fully operational. Expressed in 2 ma units (i.e. 50 = 100 ma).

Interface Descriptors

Interfaces defined a collection of endpoints that a given class driver typically manipulates based on the pertinent device class characteristics. Some devices may define a single interface while others may require several. Table 14-5 on page 226 lists the format and definition of the interface descriptor. The following sections further describe the interface descriptors fields that in the author's opinion may require clarification.

Interface Number and Alternate Setting

The "interface number" and "alternate settings" fields within the interface descriptor are used to support the alternate setting feature supported by the USB specification. Devices may define alternate interfaces within the same configuration. The intent is to permit adjustments to a configuration during normal operation, after the initial configuration has been completed. A device that supports alternate settings, will include one or more sets of additional interface and endpoint descriptors that describe the same interface, but that contain alternate settings.

Figure 14-1: Descriptor Tree Containing Alternate Interface Settings

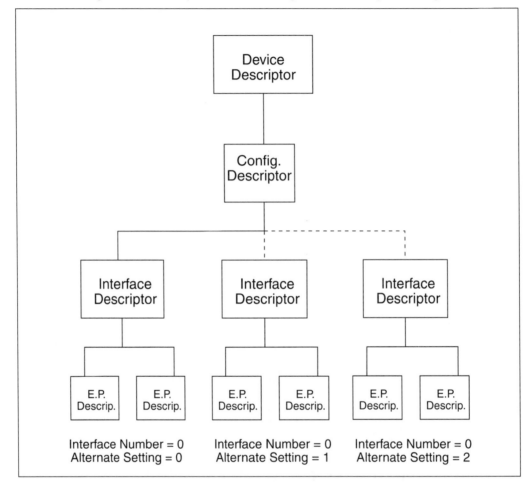

As an example, consider the descriptor tree in Figure 14-1. Note all three interface descriptors have an "interface number" of zero, specifying that each defines settings for interface zero. However, the "alternate settings" field of each interface descriptor is different. During configuration alternate setting zero is used by default. The other settings (one and two) can be chosen after configuration to "fine tune" the configuration. Host software uses the alternate setting value to select the interface of choice, via the Set Interface request (see Table 15-2 on page 236).

When the get Configuration request is made a device returns each primary interface (alternate settings = 0) followed by its associated endpoints, followed by each alternate interface and its associated endpoints. In this way, during configuration host software can detect that alternate settings are present even though they are ignored during configuration.

Number of Endpoints

The number of endpoints required to support the interface is specified at offset 4 within the interface descriptor. This value list the number of endpoints excluding endpoint zero (the default endpoint). The number of endpoints also does not include endpoints associated with alternate settings.

Interface Class and Sub Class

These fields contain values that specify a given device class and subclass that permits software to locate the relevant class driver that will manipulate the endpoints associated with this interface. These values are defined by the individual device class specifications. For example the audio class code is 01h and the sub class codes range from 01-06h and define information such as, whether audio information is pulse code modulated, Dolby Surround, MPEG1, etc. Details can be found in the Audio Device Class Specification.

Protocol

This field is tied to the device class and subclass fields. Some device class specifications may define protocol codes that pertain to a given interface. For example, the audio device class specification defines protocol codes that define whether the audio interface is mono, stereo, quadro, etc. The device class specifications should be consulted to determine the protocol codes and definitions.

Table 14-5: Interface Descriptor Definition

Offset	Field	Size (bytes)	Value	Description
0	Length	1	Number	Size of this descriptor in bytes.
1	Descriptor-Type	1	Constant	Interface descriptor type = 04h
2	Interface-Number	1	Number	Number of interface. Zero-based value identifying the index in the array of concurrent interfaces supported by this configuration.
3	Alternate-Setting	1	Number	Value used to select alternate setting for the interface identified in the prior filed.
4	NumEnd-points	1	Number	Number of endpoints used by this interface (excluding endpoint zero). If this value is zero, this interface only uses endpoint zero.
5	Interface-Class	1	Class	Class code (assigned by USB). If this field is reset to zero, the interface does not belong to any USB specified device class. If this field is set to 0xFF, the interface class is vendor specific. All other values are reserved for assignment by USB.
6	Interface-SubClass	1	SubClass	SubClass code (assigned by USB). These codes are qualified by the value of the InterfaceClass field. If the InterfaceClass field is reset to zero, this field must also be reset to zero. If the InterfaceClass field is not set to 0xFF, all values are reserved for assignment by USB.
7	Inter-faceProtocol	1	Protocol	Protocol code (assigned by USB). These codes are qualified by the value of the InterfaceClass and the InterfaceSubClass fields. If an interface supports class-specific requests, this code identifies the protocols that the device uses as defined by the specification of the device class. If this field is reset to zero, the device does not use a class-specific protocol on this interface. If this field is set to 0xFF, the device uses a vendor-specific protocol for this interface.

Table 14-5: Interface Descriptor Definition

Offset	Field	Size (bytes)	Value	Description
8	Interface	1	Index	Index of string descriptor.

Endpoint Descriptors

The endpoint descriptor defines the actual registers that are implemented within a given device. Table 14-6 on page 228 shows the format and definition of an endpoint descriptor. These descriptors define the capabilities of each register and specify information such as the:

- type of transfer required by this endpoint
- direction of the transfer (IN or OUT)
- bandwidth needed
- polling interval

Configuration software must determine if the USB can support the transfer specified by the endpoint descriptor based on the bandwidth requirements indicated in the MaxPacketSize field. If the endpoint bandwidth requirements exceed the capabilities of the USB, then the device is not configured and the user is notified.

Note that in some cases two or more descriptors may be used to describe a single register. For example, if an input/output register is implemented within the device, endpoint descriptors must be created for transferring data in both directions unless the endpoint is defined as a control endpoint. Control transfers are the only USB transfers that support bidirectional data flow. All other transfers are defined as unidirectional.

For example, if an input/output register is used to transfer information to and from a mass storage device, the register must have two corresponding endpoints: one for transferring data to the register and one for reading data from the register. Based on these two endpoint descriptors, configuration software will establish an IN bulk communications pipe and a separate OUT bulk communications pipe for the mass storage device class driver to use.

Table 14-6: Endpoint Descriptor Definition

Offset	Field	Size	Value	Description
0	Length	1	Number	Size of this descriptor in bytes.
1	DescriptorType	1	Constant	Endpoint descriptor type = 05h
2	EndpointAd-dress	1	Endpoint	The address of the endpoint on the USB device described by this descriptor. The address is encoded as follows: Bit 0..3 the endpoint number Bit 4..6 reserved, reset to zero Bit 7 direction, ignored for Control endpoints 0 OUT endpoint 1 IN endpoint
3	Attributes	1	BitMap	This field describes the endpoint's attributes when it is configured using the ConfigurationValue. Bit 0..1 Transfer Type 00 Control 01 Isochronous 10 Bulk 11 Interrupt All other bits are reserved

Table 14-6: Endpoint Descriptor Definition

Offset	Field	Size	Value	Description
4	MaxPacketSize	2	Number	Maximum packet size this endpoint is capable of sending or receiving when this configuration is selected. For isochronous endpoints, this value is used to reserve the bus time in the schedule, required for the per frame data payloads. The pipe may, on an ongoing basis, actually use less bandwidth than reserved. The device reports, if necessary, the actual bandwidth used via its normal, non-USB defined mechanisms. For interrupt, bulk and control endpoints smaller data payloads may be sent, but will terminate the transfer an may or may not require intervention to restart.
6	Interval	1	Number	Interval for polling endpoint for data transfers. Expressed in milliseconds. This field is ignored for Bulk and Control endpoints. For isochronous endpoints, this field must be set to one. For interrupt endpoints, this field may range from 1 to 255.

Device States

Table 14-7 on page 231 shows the device states that a device goes through during the configuration process. The device states listed in the first row show the typical sequence in state changes from left to right. Note however, that a device can proceed to the suspended state from any other state.

Attached State

Column one in Table 14-7 indicates that the device is not attached to the USB. In this case the state of the device is unknown. The device may be powered if it has its own local power supply or may require power from the bus.

Powered State

Once a device is attached to the USB it may or may not have power applied to it by the hub. That is, some hubs have power switching while others do not. When the device is attached, if the port is not powered, then host software must apply power to the port, detect the device, and enable the port. In this condition the device is powered but must not draw more than 100ma of current.

Default State

The device enters its default state after it has received a reset (both D+ and D- driver low by the hub for 10ms. The device now responds to its default address of zero. Configuration software can use address zero to access the device's descriptors via the default control pipe (always at endpoint zero). The device can also accept control writes allowing an address to be assigned by configuration software.

Addressed State

A device enters its addressed state after receiving a *Set Address* request from configuration software. It now responds only to its new address, not address zero.

Configured State

Once configuration software has determined that sufficient power and bus bandwidth are available to support the device, it can be configured. The configuration value specified within the configuration descriptor that has been selected is written to the device to complete the configuration via the *Set Configuration* request. The device can now draw the maximum current required and is ready to be accessed by the USB device driver.

Suspended State

A device enters its suspend state when the bus remains idle for greater than 3ms. In the suspended state the device must not draw more than 500µa of current. Refer to Chapter 10 for details regarding device suspend.

Table 14-7: Device States

Attached	Powered	Default	Address	Configured	Suspended	State
No	—	—	—	—	—	Device is not attached to USB. Other attributes are not significant.
Yes	No	—	—	—	—	Device is attached to USB, but is not powered. Other attributes are not significant.
Yes	Yes	No	—	—	—	Device is attached to USB and powered, but has not been Reset
Yes	Yes	Yes	No	—	—	Device is attached to USB and powered and has been Reset, but has not been assigned a unique address. Device responds at the default address.
Yes	Yes	Yes	Yes	No	—	Device is attached to USB, powered, has been Reset, and a unique device address has been assigned. Device is not configured.
Yes	Yes	Yes	Yes	Yes	No	Device is attached to USB, powered, has been Reset, has unique address, is configured, and is not suspended. Host may now use the function provided by the device.

Table 14-7: Device States

Attached	Powered	Default	Address	Configured	Suspended	State
Yes	Yes	Yes	Yes	Yes	Yes	Device is, at minimum, attached to USB, has been Reset, and is powered at the minimum suspend level. It may also have a unique address and be configured for use. However, since the device is suspended, the host may not use the device's function.

15 *Device Requests*

The Previous Chapter

The previous chapter discussed configuration of non-hub devices that are attached to the USB. Device descriptors and other characteristics and features that relate to configuring the device were also discussed.

This Chapter

This chapter discusses the standard requests required by USB devices. Each device class may define class-specific requests that are covered in the related device class chapter.

The Next Chapter

Host software consists of three layers: the USB Device Driver, the USB Driver, and the Host Controller Driver. The next chapter discusses the role of each of these layers and describes the requirements of their programming interface.

Overview

All USB devices must respond to a variety of requests called "standard" requests. These requests are used for configuring a device, for controlling the state of its USB interface, along with other miscellaneous features. Device requests are issued by the host using the control transfer mechanism. Prior to configuration a device responds to its default address of zero. This permits configuration software to request the contents of any device's descriptors (from endpoint zero) using device address zero during configuration.

Additionally, devices may also support class-specific requests. Except for hub devices, these class requests are defined by the device-class specifications and are not included within the main portion of the specification. Similarly, a device may support vendor-specific requests that pertain to a given vendor's implementation.

Control transfers, used to transmit device requests, consist minimally of a setup stage and a status stage, but may also include a data stage, depending on the type of request being performed. The setup stage consists of setup transactions as illustrated in Figure 15-1. The eight byte data payload of a setup transaction defines the type of request being issued by the host. This chapter discusses only the standard device requests. Refer to the particular device class chapter for information related to class-specific requests.

Figure 15-1: Format of Setup Transaction that Specifies the Device Request Being Performed

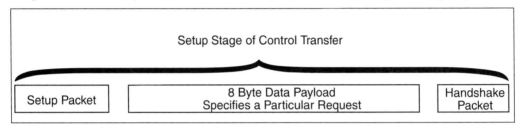

Standard Device Requests

When a control transfer is initiated, the setup stage of the transaction specifies the particular request to be performed by the device. The format of the setup data is shown in Table 15-1, while Figure 15-2 defines the contents of the setup data for each of the standard request types.

Note that in Figure 15-1 bits 5 and 6 of byte zero are 00b indicating that the specific request is a standard request type. The second byte (the request field) defines which standard request is to be performed, while the definition of the other fields are dependent upon the request specified. For example, the CLEAR_FEATURE request defines the "value" field as the feature selector. Figure 15-3 lists the specific features that the request applies to. The following sections describe each of the standard requests.

Note that the last column in Figure 15-2, labeled "Data," indicates whether the request requires a data stage during the control transfer. For example, the *Get Configuration* request uses the data stage to transfer the configuration value. Many requests however can be performed without a data stage.

Table 15-1: Format of Data Payload during Setup Transactions

Offset	Field	Size	Value	Description
0	Request-Type	1	Bit-map	Characteristics of Request D7 Data xfer direction 0 = Host to device 1 = Device to host D6..5 Type (h) 0 = Standard 1 = Class 2 = Vendor 3 = Reserved D4..0 Recipient (h) 0 = Device 1 = Interface 2 = Endpoint 3 = Other 4..31 = Reserved
1	Request	1	Value	Specific Request
2	Value	2	Value	Word-sized field that varies according to request
4	Index	2	Index or Offset	Word-sized field that varies according to request. Typically used to pass an index or offset.
6	Length	2	Count	Number of bytes to transfer if there is a data stage required for this transfer.

If the request contains fields with illegal values or values not supported, the endpoint to which the request is directed will automatically enter the stalled state. Host software must clear the stall condition using the *Clear Stall* request. A control endpoint must continue accepting setup transaction even if it is stalled. If the default control endpoint fails to respond to a setup transaction, the device must be reset to clear the condition.

Table 15-2: *Standard Device Requests*

Request-Type	Request	value (2 bytes)	index (2 bytes)	length (2 bytes)	Data
00000000B 00000001B 00000010B	CLEAR_FEATURE (01h)	Feature Selector	Zero Interface Endpoint	Zero	None
10000000B	GET_CONFIGURATION (08h)	Zero	Zero	One	Configuration Value
10000000B	GET_DESCRIPTOR (06h)	Descriptor Type and Descriptor Index	Zero or Language ID	Descriptor Length	Descriptor
100000001B	GET_INTERFACE (10h)	Zero	Interface	One	Alternate Interface
100000000B 100000001B 100000010B	GET_STATUS (00h)	Zero	Zero Interface Endpoint	Two	Device Interface, or Endpoint Status
00000000B	SET_ADDRESS (05h)	Device Address	Zero	Zero	None
00000000B	SET_CONFIGURATION (09h)	Configuration Value	Zero	Zero	None
00000000B	SET_DESCRIPTOR (07h)	Descriptor Type and Descriptor Index	Zero or Language ID	Descriptor Length	Descriptor
00000000B 00000001B 00000010B	SET_FEATURE (03h)	Feature Selector	Zero Interface Endpoint	Zero	None
00000001B	SET_INTERFACE (11h)	Alternate Setting	Interface	Zero	None
10000010B	SYNCH_FRAME (12h)	Zero	Endpoint	Two	Frame Number

Set/Clear Feature

The *Set* and *Clear Feature* requests provide a method of enabling and disabling a set of features defined by the feature selector value. Two features are defined for the standard device requests as shown in   Figure 15-3.

Table 15-3: Feature Selectors

Feature Selector	Recipient	Value
DEVICE_REMOTE_WAKEUP	device	1
ENDPOINT_STALL	endpoint	0

Device Remote Wakeup

Some devices may be designed to wake the system in the event of a global suspend or to wake a hub port that has been selectively suspended. (See   Chapter 10 for details regarding suspend.) The *Set Feature* request, with *Device Remote Wakeup* selected, enables a device to signal wakeup to the hub. The *Clear Device Remote Wakeup* request prevents a device from signaling remote wakeup to the hub. Whether a device's ability to signal remote wakeup is currently enabled or disabled is reported to software via the *Get Status* request.

EndPoint Stall

Software has the ability to stall a given endpoint or to clear a stall condition. The *Set* and *Clear Endpoint Stall* request defines which endpoint within the device is being targeted via the "index" field of the setup transaction. A stall bit is defined for each endpoint that indicates whether the endpoint is currently stalled or not. The stall bit is read in conjunction with the *Get Status* request.

Set/Get Configuration

Host software configures a device by selecting one of the configurations defined within the device's descriptors and assigning the corresponding 8-bit configuration value to the device. The *Set Configuration* request is used by software to assign the configuration value. Conversely, software may inquire which configuration has been assigned to a device, using the *Get Configuration* request. Note that the configuration value is transferred during the data stage of the control transfer.

Set/Get Descriptor

Device descriptors are read using the *Get Descriptor* request. The optional *Set Descriptor* request is supported by devices that provide a way to add new or update existing descriptors. In either instance, a specific descriptor and an index within the descriptor can be targeted. The standard *Set/Get Descriptor* requests support only the device, configuration, and string descriptors. Each of these descriptors has an associated value that defines the descriptor type as shown in Table 15-5. The interface and endpoint descriptors can only be read via the Get Configuration Descriptor request and are returned following the selected configuration descriptor.

Host software initially accesses the device descriptor to determine the maximum data payload that a device's default control pipe supports. The device descriptor specifies the maximum data payload supported by a the default control pipe (endpoint 0). Host software can determine the maximum payload for endpoint 0 by issuing a *Get Descriptor* request with the values shown in Table 15-4. The high byte within the "value" field contains the descriptor type (01=device descriptor) and the low byte contains the descriptor index. The device will return the contents of the device descriptor starting at the index specified. The descriptor contents are returned during the data stage of the control transfer.

Table 15-4: Contents of Setup Transaction During Get Descriptor Requests

Request Type	Request	Value (2 bytes)	Index (2 bytes)	Length (2 bytes)	Data
10000000B	GET_DESCRIPTOR (06h)	01h=Device Descriptor 07h=Index	Zero or Language ID	Descriptor Length	Descriptor Contents

Note that if a string descriptor is specified, the index value will contain the language ID. For all other descriptor types the index is cleared (zeros).

Table 15-5: Descriptor Types That Can Be Specified Via Standard Get/Set Descriptor Request

Descriptor Types	Value
DEVICE	1
CONFIGURATION	2
STRING	3

Set/Get Interface

The *Set* and *Get Interface* requests are used to specify an alternate settings to be used in some selected configurations. That is, some devices may have an interface that contains mutually exclusive settings. In this case, the interface descriptor will provide a value used to select the alternate setting. The setting must be selected using the *Set Interface* request. The host can determine which alternate setting has been selected by using the *Get Interface* request.

Get Status

The host can obtain status information from a device via the *Get Status* request. Status information is returned in the data stage of the control transfer. Host software can specify the status information from three separate layers associated with the device:

- **Device Status** — provides global status that applies to the entire device.
- **Interface Status** — returns all zeros. Interface status is defined as reserved.
- **Endpoint Status** — provides information pertaining to the selected endpoint.

The recipient of the request is specified in the *Request Type* field of byte zero as shown in Table 15-1 on page 235. The status information is returned in little endian format for the selected recipient as described below. Since the interface status information is reserved, only the device and endpoint status information is included.

Device Status

Table 15-6 illustrates the information returned to the host when a *Get Status* request is made and device is specified as the recipient.

Table 15-6: Device Status Information Returned during Get Status Request

7	6	5	4	3	2	1	0
Reserved (reset to zeros)						Remote Wakeup	Self Powered

15	14	13	12	11	10	9	8
Reserved (reset to zeros)							

Self Powered Bit

The self powered bit reflects whether the device is currently bus-powered (0) or self-powered (1). This field may not be changed by the *Set Feature* and *Clear Feature* requests.

Remote Wakeup Bit

This bit reflect whether the device is currently enabled or disabled to generate resume signaling to wake up the hub port. By default this bit is cleared (0) after reset, thereby disabling remote wakeup. Host software can set and clear this bit using the *Set and Clear Device Remote Wake Feature* request.

Endpoint Status

Table 15-7 illustrates the information returned when an endpoint is specified as the recipient of the request. The endpoint number is specified in the "index" field of the setup transaction. The low byte contains the endpoint number and the transfer direction (IN or OUT) that it supports. Endpoint status information consists of only the stall bit and all other bit positions are defined as reserved.

Stall specifies whether the endpoint is currently stalled (1) or not (0). This bit can be changed using the *Set* and *Clear Endpoint Stall Feature*. The stall field always returns to zero after a *Set Configuration* or *Set Interface* request.

Table 15-7: Endpoint Status Information Returned during Get Status Request

7	6	5	4	3	2	1	0
Reserved (reset to zeros)							Stall

15	14	13	12	11	10	9	8
Reserved (reset to zeros)							

Sync Frame

This request is used by isochronous endpoints that use implicit pattern synchronization. Isochronous endpoints may need to track frame numbers in order to maintain synchronization. Isochronous endpoint transactions may vary in size according to a specific pattern that repeats. The host and endpoint must agree on which frame the repeating pattern begins. The host uses the *Sync Frame* request to specify the exact frame in which the repeating pattern begins. The data stage of the Sync Frame request contains the frame number in which the pattern begins. Having received the frame number, the device can start monitoring each frame number sent during the SOF.

Part IV

USB Host Software

16 *USB Host Software*

The Previous Chapter

The previous chapter discussed the standard requests required by USB devices. Each device class may define class-specific requests depending of the device class definition.

This Chapter

Host software consists of three types of components: the USB Device Drivers, the USB Driver, and the Host Controller Driver. This chapter discusses the role of each of these layers and describes the requirements of their programming interface.

The Next Chapter

The next chapter introduces the concept of device classes and discusses each device class that was defined at the time of this writing.

USB Software

Host software provides the interface between USB device drivers (or client drivers) and the devices that they must communicate with. USB device drivers are unaware of the USB implementation. That is, they have no knowledge of the characteristics, capabilities, or limitations of the USB nor the USB device. Consequently, USB host software must accept transfer requests made by USB device drivers and perform the requested transfers based on the requirements of the USB. The following general capabilities are supported by a USB system.

- USB Interface Control
- Configuration Services
- Bus and Device Management

- Power Control
- Device Data Access
- Event Notification
- Collection of status and activity statistics
- Error Detection and Handling

USB software is based on the device framework established by the USB specification. This framework describes the logical view that each software element has of the USB devices. The relationships between the USB software layers and their view of USB devices is reviewed below. Refer to Figure 16-1 on page 247.

Function Layer

Transactions performed over the USB are initiated by USB device driver (Client Drivers). During configuration, the hub client accesses the bus, and when accessing other USB devices, the client drivers may be class-specific or vendor-specific. No matter which USB client drivers wishes to access a given USB device, it must use host software to request its IO transfer be performed over USB (via an IO Request Packet, or IRP). These clients only have knowledge of the device interface (consisting of a collection of endpoints) that they wish to manipulate. Therefore a USB client driver's visibility to USB is limited to:

- the interface within their device
- class-specific descriptors that have been pre-defined to help them determine specific characteristics of their interface
- the mechanisms provided by host software to access and control their function

Device Layer

Client initiated transfers must be performed according to the characteristics of the USB and the capabilities of the target USB device. USB host software exists to support USB clients by providing services that they can use to initiate transfers and control their devices.

Host software also ensures that the bus can support all devices attached to the USB. The host software views each device through its standard device descriptors. These descriptors provide the necessary information to determine which driver will use this device and how much of the bus bandwidth is required. With this knowledge, host software can establish the communications pipes that the clients will later use when they access their interface.

Host software must also forward IRPs to the Host Controller Driver (HCD), which has specific knowledge of the host controller design. The HCD passes the IRPs on to the host controller is a form that it understands.

Interface Layer

This layer is represented by the host controller (including the root hub), the USB cable(s), and the device's USB interface. These components actually transmit control and data information to/from the USB devices.

Figure 16-1: Device Framework — Software's View of Hardware

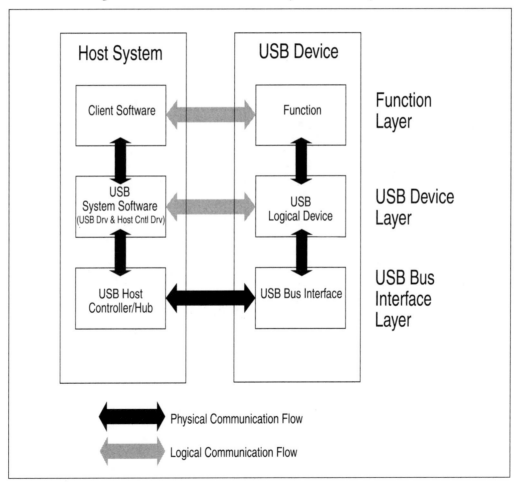

The Software Components

The three software components that comprise the host USB software solution are illustrated in Figure 16-2 on page 249. The primary functions associated with each layer include the following (note however that the exact division of responsibility is not precisely defined by the specification):

USB Client Drivers — client drivers are the software entities that control a given USB functional device. Client drivers must exist for each type (class) of function attached to the USB. These drivers are unaware of the details associated with the USB transfer mechanisms and must rely on USB host software to manage their transfer requests based on the capabilities and limitations of the USB. The intended implementation of client drivers is based on device class definitions. Client drivers view the USB devices as a collection of endpoints that can be accessed to control and communicate with its function.

USB Driver (USBD) — The USB driver has knowledge of the devices requirements (via device descriptors), as well as knowledge of the USB's capabilities. With this knowledge the USBD must divide IRPs into USB and device-sized chunks. The USBD also supports USB device configuration by ensuring that the USB resources required by each device can be supported. It also establishes communications pipes for each endpoint detected during configuration, but only if the necessary USB bandwidth is available. The USBD provides a programming interface called USBDI (USB Driver Interface), giving client drivers a way to request transfers be performed to or from their USB function. A variety of client services are provided by the USB Driver to assist the USB Client in controlling and accessing its function.

USB Host Controller Driver (HCD) — two implementations of USB Host Controllers have been defined: the Open Host Controller and Universal Host Controller. Consequently, two Host Controller Drivers must be implemented if each controller is to be supported by host software. The Host Controller Driver provides the low level support for the USB by converting IRPs into individual transactions to be performed via the USB. The programming interface between the USB Driver and the Host Controller Driver is implementation specific and is not addressed by the USB specification.

Note that the USB specification does not define the exact division of duties that the USBD and HCD are responsible for. Subsequent chapters define the basic requirements of their programming interfaces, however the exact implementation of these interfaces is operating system dependent.

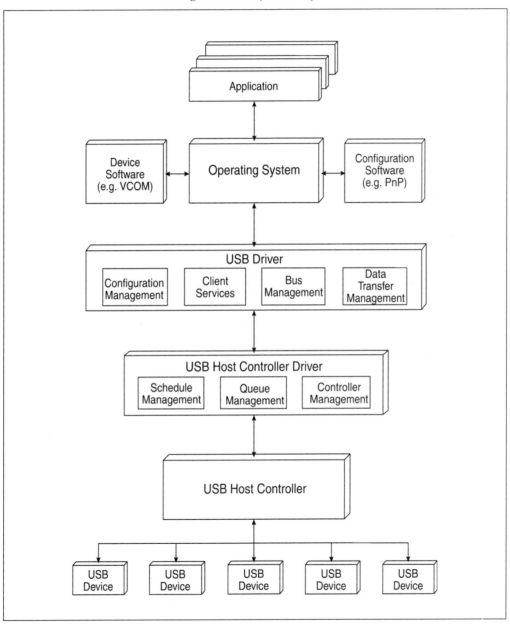

Figure 16-2: Software Layers

USB Driver (USBD)

The USB Driver is involved in the following functions:

- Configuration Management
- Bus Management (Tracking and allocating bus bandwidth)
- Data Transfer Management
- Providing Client Services (the USBDI)

Each of these USBD functions are described below.

Configuration Management

Host software must support automatic configuration of USB devices. The actual software elements involved in configuration and the sequence of steps taken to perform the configuration vary. Configuration begins with the root hub and proceeds one port at a time until all devices have been detected and configured.

Configuration activities rely on access to the default control endpoint within each device. The USBD initializes the default control pipe before configuration begins. This pipe is used repeatedly during the configuration process. The actual software components involved in configuration varies depending on the implementation, however, conceptually the components involved can be thought of as the:

- hub client driver
- configuration software
- USBD

USB Elements Requiring Configuration

USB configuration involves configuring three distinct elements:

- Device Configuration — Device configuration involves accessing the device's descriptors, determining the USB resources required by the device (i.e. power and bus bandwidth), allocating these resources by establishing communication pipes for each endpoint, and assigning the configuration value for the selected configuration. Device configuration is discussed in "Part III" of this book.
- USB Configuration — The communications pipes established during device

configuration cannot be used until the pipes are initialized by the device driver using the pipes. During initialization, the device driver must set the policy for the pipe. Setting the policy means defining how the pipe is to be used by the device driver. For example, the service interval must be established, the maximum data transfer used by the client, etc. Once the policy for a pipe is set it is ready to be used.

- Function Configuration — The device driver for a given USB device may have additional configuration to complete that the USB software is completely unaware of. This configuration is typically related to a particular device class or might be part of a vendor-specific device and driver.

Once a configuration has been established, the USBD permits modification of the configuration, by adjusting setting associated with a given interface, or by selecting an entirely different configuration.

Allocating USB Resources

Host software must be able to determine if a device just attached to the USB can operate based on the available USB resources. Host software tracks two USB resources:

- Power
- Bus Bandwidth

It is the responsibility of software to ensure that the device has the necessary resources prior to configuring it for operation.

Verifying Power

Some devices may require more USB bus power than is available at a given port. This can occur when a high powered device is attached to a bus powered hub port. By reading a hubs standard descriptors, configuration software can determine the amount of power that is available at a given USB port (minimum current allowed is 100ma). Software can also determine the amount of current required by a device that is attached to a port by reading its descriptors. Note that descriptors can be read because a device cannot draw more than the 100ma of current (the guaranteed amount of current available).

If the device requires more current than the port can supply, then software must not configure the device and should report power shortage to the user.

Tracking and Allocating Bus Bandwidth

The USBD must determine if the USB can support a given pipe before it is setup for communicating with a device's endpoint. Each endpoint descriptor contains the bus bandwidth needed to support the endpoint. The bandwidth specified by the endpoint descriptor includes only the data payload size and does not include overhead time. Consequently, the USBD must calculate the execution time required to transfer the data over the bus. Once total execution time has been calculated, then the frame schedule must be checked to see if the new pipe can be supported.

Several parameters must be known in order to calculate the bus bandwidth requirement for a given pipe, including:

Number of data bytes — This information is read from the MaxPacketSize field within the endpoint descriptor.

Transfer type — Isochronous and interrupt transfers require guaranteed bandwidth, while control transfers have a guaranteed 10% bus reservation. Bulk transfers have no guaranteed bandwidth during any given frame. Transfer type also determines the amount of overhead associated with the transaction. For example, isochronous transfers are not accompanied by handshake packets. The overhead includes the:

- token packet — sync bits (8) + PID (8) + Address (11) + CRC (5) +EOP (2) = 34 bits
- data packet overhead — sync bits (8) + PID (8) + CRC (16) + EOP (2) = 34 bits
- handshake (if required) — sync bits (8) + PID (8) + EOP (2) = 18 bits

Transfer type is encoded into the Attribute field within the endpoint descriptor.

Host recovery time — The time needed for the host controller recover from the last transmission and prepare for the next. This parameter is host controller implementation specific.

Hub low speed setup — If the transaction targets low speed device, then the time required for the preamble packet delivery and the hub delay associated with enabling the low speed ports must be included.

Bit stuff time — Bit stuffing time must also be calculated. Since bit stuffing is a function of the data stream, which is unknown to host software, a worst case theoretical maximum number of additional bit times is included for bit stuffing (1.1667 * 8 * number of bytes).

Depth in topology — The round-trip time required to send packets to a device and receiver the response depends on the number of cable segments the transmission must cross. The maximum round-trip delay is specified as 16 bit times. Software may either use this worst case value when calculating transaction time or may determine where in the topology the target device resides and specify the delay based on the number of cable segments the transmission must cross (70ns one-way trip delay per cable segment).

Once the total bus time required to support the pipe has been calculated, if the pipe can be support, the USBD establishes the pipe and adds the transaction to the frame schedule.

Bus Bandwidth Reclamation

Since the bandwidth calculations in many instances are based on worst case values (e.g. bit stuffing), there will normally be bus bandwidth remaining after all scheduled transactions have completed during a frame. Host controllers can be designed to reclaim this leftover bandwidth and perform additional transactions to utilize the bus more efficiently. Control and bulk transfers are candidates for reclamation. Since isochronous and interrupt transfers are scheduled they will already have completed. How a host controller implements bus bandwidth reclamation is implementation dependent.

Bus Management

The USBD must allow a client to become the master client on the USB. A master client can adjust the number of bit times within a frame. The master client may add or subtract one bit time to the current USB frame to adjust the SOF interval. Some endpoints require that they synchronize their internal clock to the USB data rate based on the 1ms SOF. However, a device may not be able to synchronize its internal clock to the 1ms SOF. A client driver accessing such a device can adjust the SOF interval so that it can synchronize the SOF to its internal clock.

Note that the USBD supports only one master client. If a client is unable to become the master, then it must be able to synchronize to the host by adjusting its data flow.

Data Transfer Management

Each pipe that is setup during configuration is defined for a specific endpoint within a functional interface within a device. A given interface and therefore each endpoint within an interface is managed by exactly one software client driver. A client must initialize a pipe before it can be used. During pipe initialization, the client specifies the policy for that pipe. The policy defines the exact amount of data to be transferred per IRP and the maximum service interval (if required). The client may also request notification of status information (e.g. completion status) from the USBD. The client must also specify the location of its memory buffer where data read from the endpoint is to be stored or where data to be written to the endpoint resides.

The USBD may need to break the IRP into chunks that can be supported by both the endpoint (buffer size) and the constraints associated with the USB protocol.

Providing Client Services (The USB Driver Interface)

The USB driver must provide a programming interface (USBDI) that is used by client software to control and access USB devices. Via these mechanisms USBD provides a variety of client services. A given implementation of a USB driver must provide the following software mechanisms.

- Command Mechanisms — Command mechanisms allow clients to configure and control USBD operation and to configure and generically control a USB device. Some of the commands may utilize the pipe mechanisms.
- Pipe Mechanisms — Pipe mechanisms allow USBD clients to manage device specific data and control transfers. The pipe mechanism does not permit direct access the device's default pipe, since it is owned by the USBD.

Pipe Mechanisms

Two basic types of pipes are supported by USB implementations:

- Default Pipes (owned by USBD) — Default pipes are used principally to access a device's configuration information. The USB driver is responsible for setting up and managing accesses via the default pipes, unless the USBD uses the default pipe to fulfill some portion of the request.

- Client Pipes (message and stream pipes) — A client pipe is any pipe not owned and managed by the USBD. The client uses pipes to transfer information to and from USB function endpoints. A client is responsible for providing the buffering needed to support the data transfer rate. All four types of pipes (based on the four transfer types) are supported.

Client Pipe Requirements

USBD Client Pipe mechanisms are required to support the following functions. These functions are intended to provide clients with a high-speed/low overhead method of data transfer:

- Aborting IRPs
- Queuing IRPs
- Managing pipe policy
- Requesting master client status (Adjusting S.O.F.)

Command Mechanisms

Command mechanisms allow a client to access and control a USB device. For example, read and write accesses can be made to a device's data and control endpoints. The command mechanisms provide the following generic types of access/services. The USBDI must provide a mechanism for the following actions:

- Interface state control
- pipe may be reset
- pipe may be aborted
- Retrieve descriptors
- Get current configuration settings
- Adding devices (Hub client)
- Removing devices (Hub client)
- Managing status
- Sending class commands
- Sending vendor commands
- Establishing alternate settings
- Establishing a configuration
- Establishing the max packet size
- Setting descriptors

Part V

USB Device Class

17 *Device Classes*

The Previous Chapter

Host software consists of three layers: the USB Device Driver, the USB Driver, and the Host Controller Driver. The previous chapter discussed the role of each of these layers and described the requirements of their programming interface.

This Chapter

This chapter introduces the concept of device classes and discusses their role within the USB. This chapter discusses the first five class types that were defined. These class are discussed to provide the reader with a sense of the information defined for each class and the USB mechanisms that they use. A detailed discussion of device classes requires in-depth knowledge in the associated field such as telephony and audio.

The Next Chapter

The next chapter introduces the Universal Host Controller defined by Intel. The transfer mechanism is discussed and the transfer descriptors built by the Universal Host Controller Driver are detailed.

Overview

Device classes are intended to permit a device driver design that can manipulate a set of devices that have similar attributes and services. A given class definition can further describe the individual characteristics of particular device types within the class, thereby providing the USB device driver with the information it needs to manipulate the device as required.

Device class definition relates to a functional interface used to access and control a particular class of device. Figure 17-1 on page 261 illustrates a USB CD-ROM device with two interfaces. Devices that support two or more functions are called composite devices and require an individual interface for each function. A mass storage class driver is required to use the CD-ROM for reading files from a program disk, while the Audio Class Device Driver is required to play a music CD. Each driver accesses the collection of endpoints that constitute the programming and data interface(s) for the device class.

Note that the USB components that are device class specific are the functional interface and the USB device driver. The descriptors associated with a device specify several items that relate to device class definitions, including:

- Device Class Code field — from the device descriptor (if device contains a single functional interface), and/or from each functional interface descriptor.
- Sub Class Code field — the definition of this field is device class specific.
- Protocol field — this optional field may be defined for a given device class and sub class to define some element of the programming interface supported by the device.

The device class code fields can be used by host software to locate the appropriate device driver needed to access a device's functional interface. All other standard descriptor information is related to USB specific information that the host software can interpret without knowledge of the device class definitions.

Note also that some device class specifications define additional descriptors that host software has no particular knowledge of. These descriptors are intended for the class-specific device drivers to detect device attributes and characteristics required to access the device.

In summary, class definitions help establish a common grouping of devices that a common class driver could accommodate and allows a device to describe its capabilities to the host and USB class device driver. Class codes provide a mechanism for USB host software to identify the appropriate device driver that is designed to manipulate a given USB device's functional interface. The individual class specifications describe specific characteristics and attributes that devices within the class may support and defines the control mechanisms used by a USB Class device driver to access and manipulate its function.

Figure 17-1: CD-ROM Supporting Mass Storage and Audio Interfaces

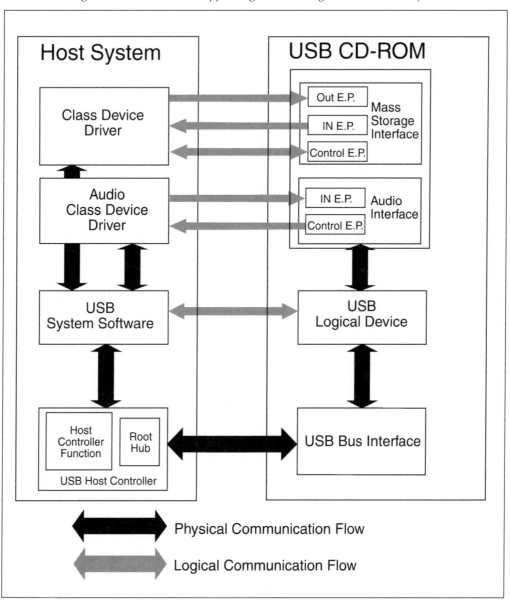

Device Classes

Initially five major classes of devices were identified to support a relatively wide range of common functional devices on USB, with the intention of adding other device classes as required. The initial classes are:

- Audio Device Class — Devices that are the source of sink of real-time audio information.
- Communications Device Class — Devices that attach to a telephone line (not local area networks).
- Display Device Class — Used to configure monitors under software control.
- Human Interface Device Class (HID) — Devices manipulated by end-users.
- Mass Storage Device Class — Devices used to store large amounts of information (for example, floppy drives, hard drives, and tape drives).

At the time of this writing the device class specifications were in various states of completion. Since these definitions are still evolving no attempt is made to provide detailed information in this book.

Other device classes are in the definition stage or were being considered at the time of writing. These include:

- Image Device Class — Devices that deal with images (either still or moving) New group. May split into "still" and "video classes
- Physical Interface Device Class (PID) — Devices that provide tactile feedback to operator. Examples include: Joystick with variable resistance for simulating increased stick forces and turbulence. Split off from HID class.
- Power Device Class — Devices that provide power to system or to peripherals. Example devices include: Uninterruptable Power Supplies and Smart Batteries. Can be either stand alone device or integrated into the interface.
- Printer Device Class — May be merged with storage device class.

The following sections describe the major features of the initial five device classes discussed previously.

Audio Device Class

The audio class specification defines standardized audio transport mechanisms used to propagate and control digital audio. A major focus of the audio class is synchronization of the audio data stream to ensure no distortion of the sound.

Chapter 17: Device Classes

Each audio function has its own device interface that is used to access and control the function. Audio devices are those devices that interact with USB-compliant audio data streams. Audio devices are grouped into subclasses as listed below:

- 8-bit Pulse Code Modulated (PCM) Audio Data
- 16-bit PCM Audio Data
- 16-bit Dolby Surround Data
- IEC958 Audio Encoded Data
- MPEG1 Audio Encoded Data
- AC3 Audio Encoded Data

Each of these subclasses have protocol codes that further define the audio device. The subclass codes and protocol codes are defined in Table 17-1. Note that the protocol codes only apply to certain subclasses and that some protocols can apply to more than one subclass. The definition for AC3 encoded data was not completely defined at the time of writing.

Table 17-1: Audio Subclasses and Protocols

Subclass Code	Subclass Name	Protocol Code	Protocol Name
01h	8-bit Pulse Code Modulated (PCM) Audio Data	01h 02h	Mono Stereo
02h	16-bit PCM Audio Data	01h 02h 03h 04h	Mono Stereo Quadro Stereo & Stereo
03h	16-bit Dolby Surround Data	02h	Stereo
04h	IEC958 Audio Encoded Data	05h 06h	IEC958 Consumer IEC958 Professional
05h	MPEG1 Audio Encoded Data	07h 08h	Layer 1 Layer 2
06h	AC3 Audio Encoded Data	TBD	TBD

Standard Audio Interface Requirements

The standard endpoints required by an audio includes the following:

- Control Endpoint Zero — used to manipulate settings and to retrieve the state of the audio function.
- Interrupt Endpoint — used to obtain status information.
- Isochronous Endpoint — one or more isochronous endpoints for audio data transfers. Note that a synchronization endpoint may accompany an isochronous endpoint.

The number of isochronous endpoints required is specified for each audio subclass/protocol combination defined in Table 17-1. For example, all PCM audio data subclass/protocol combination require a single isochronous endpoint except for the 16-bit PCM Stereo & Stereo interface which requires two isochronous endpoints.

Synchronization Types

The audio device class specification defines three methods that isochronous endpoint can use to ensure synchronization between itself and the host:

- Asynchronous — Isochronous endpoints using asynchronous synchronization sent or receive audio data at a rate that is locked to an external clock or a free running internal clock. The device cannot synchronize the transfer rate to the USB clock (based on the 1ms Start of Frame).
- Synchronous — Devices whose isochronous endpoints have their own sense of timing and need to synchronize their audio data rate to the USB's SOF of frame. Two methods are defined to accomplish this:

  1. Synchronize the sample clock to the 1ms SOF.
  2. Adjust the SOF until it is synchronous to the sample clock

- Adaptive — These devices have a specific range of rates at which they can send or receive audio data, permitting them to synchronize to the rate imposed at their interface by SOF timing.

Audio Class-Specific Descriptors

The audio class specification defines a class-specific interface descriptor and class-specific endpoint descriptors. These class-specific descriptors are in addition to the standard interface and endpoint descriptors. Devices are configured based on the standard endpoint descriptor information, that is, bus bandwidth is allocated based on the requirements specified within the descriptors. Once the audio class driver loads it must obtain additional information from the device to completely understand the properties supported by the device and the method used for data synchronization. See the audio class specification for details regarding the format and definition of these class-specific descriptors.

Audio Class-Specific Requests

The audio class specification defines class-specific requests that control various audio properties. In general, the properties can be divided into the following two groups:

- Audio Control Properties — This category of requests control the audio function such as volume and tone. These properties are controlled via the audio control blocks defined by the audio class specification. The audio control block contains parameters that can be manipulated by software via the class-specific requests.
- Endpoint Properties — These properties control various aspects of the audio data transfers such as, sampling frequency. These properties are manipulated by changing the endpoint the characteristics of the isochronous audio data endpoint.

The set of properties that all standard USB audio devices should support are termed general properties. However, the audio class specification permits other vendor implementations to define additional properties. A class-specific request called the *Get/Set System Exclusive* properties is provided as a mechanism for controlling vendor-defined properties. Refer to the audio class specification for details regarding the definition and use of the audio class-specific requests.

Communication Device Class

Any USB device that connects to a telephone line falls within the definition of a communications class device. At the time of this writing, two subclasses had been defined:

- Telephony Interface
- Vendor-Specific

However, numerous protocols are defined within the telephony subclass as shown in Table 17-2. These protocols specify the control protocol used to control the communications function.

Table 17-2: Telephony Protocol Types and Codes Used by Telephony Devices

Protocol Code	Description	Related Reference Document
00h	Not defined	NA
01h	Common AT commands (Hayes compatible)	V.225ter
02h	Alternative PSTN modem command set	V.25bis
04h	Serial ISDN Terminal Adapter Control	V.120
08h	In-Band DCE control	V.ib
10h	ISDN TA control	Q.931
20h	Reserved	NA
40h	Other standard DCE control protocol not defined by the audio class specification. The control protocol used for this device is defined in string descriptor.	NA
80h	Manufacturer-proprietary DCE control protocol is used. The protocol used is described in a string descriptor.	NA

Communications Device Interfaces

USB communications class devices have interfaces that vary depending on their characteristics. The endpoints that might be used also with the typical used of these endpoints is defined below:

- Control Endpoint Zero — Used to send information that is not time sensitive and that requires relatively little bus bandwidth. This ensures that the control pipe does not become saturated with some of the extremely long command sequences required by some control protocols.
- Interrupt Endpoint — Used to report device-generated events (i.e., on/off hook and user key presses) and communications network events such as incoming call notification. May also be used to determine interface availability and related data formats.
- Isochronous Endpoints — Isochronous are used for transmitting and receiving data to ensure a constant bit rate that is required for real time communications that requiring low latency.
- Bulk Endpoints — This endpoint is used when the data consists of bursts that are not as time sensitive, such as data to and from a conventional modem.

Communications Class-Specific Descriptors

Two types of class-specific descriptors are defined for communications devices. These descriptors include:

- Class-specific Configuration Descriptors
- Class-specific String Descriptors (also called Protocol Descriptors since they define aspects of a device based on it protocol code)

Please refer to the specification for details regarding the format and definition of these descriptors.

Communications Class-Specific Requests

The following class-specific requests are defined by the communications device class specification. These are:

- Send Encapsulated Command

- Get Encapsulated Response
- Report Format (encapsulated protocol message)
- Notification of Interface Availability
- Select Interface Protocol Command
- Get Interface Command

Please refer to the specification for details regarding the format and definition of these requests.

Display Device Class

This device class defines the mechanism used to control display settings, such as brightness, contrast, and color. Traditionally, these controls have been implemented via manual controls on a hardware control panel. The USB display function permits these adjustments to be made under software control.

The display class and subclasses are defined within the Device Descriptor as illustrated in Table 17-3.

Table 17-3: Display Class Standard Device Descriptor Definition

Offset	Field	Size (bytes)	Value	Description
4	DeviceClass	1	Class	Class code = 04h for display class
5	DeviceSubClass	1	SubClass	Subclass code: • 01h = CRT • 02h = Flat Panel Display • 03h = 3-D Display

The Standard Display Device Class Interface

USB display device require only the default control endpoint for passing control information to the display. Only one configuration and one interface is defined by this class. Note that since no endpoint other than the default endpoint is used, the interface descriptor specifies no endpoints.

Chapter 17: Device Classes

Display Device-Specific Descriptors

A USB display device uses three device-specific descriptors:

- Display Descriptor — The display descriptor defines which controls are supported by this device, and specifies the displays characteristics. This information is based on the *VESA Extended Display Identification (EDID)* specification. This descriptor is read via the *Get Display ID* request.
- Display Status Descriptor — This descriptor provides status information on a variety of display settings, along with the horizontal and Vertical frequency used by the display. This descriptor is read via the *Get Display Status* request.
- Display Control Descriptor — This descriptor is used to determine the possible values that can be set for each controls supported and its current setting. A separate Display Control descriptor exists for each control, defined by control codes in the specification. The control code to be referenced is specified in the *Get Max* and *Get Current* requests which return the contents of the descriptor.

Device-Specific Requests

Seven device-specific requests are defined for display class devices:

- Get Display ID
- Get Max
- Get Current
- Set Current
- Get Display Status
- Degauss
- Set Display Power Mode

These requests provide the mechanism for obtaining status regarding the current settings of the display and for changing the display settings. See the Display Device Class specification for details.

Mass Storage Device Class

Mass storage devices differ from most device classes in that they may also be used when booting the operating system. This requires that the system BIOS must be able to initialize and access USB storage device. The mass storage definitions then must be supported both by device drivers and the system ROM. Several type of mass storage device are defined by the USB Mass Storage Device Class specification. Five subclasses have been defined:

- General Mass Storage Subclass — This subclass defines devices that are normally access storage media in a random fashion.
- CD-ROM Subclass — CD-ROM of course are read only. These drives may also contain interfaces beyond the mass storage interface, to support audio and video applications (not related to the mass storage class).
- Tape — Tape drives are unique due to the streaming nature of the data written to and read from the drive. Sending data on time is important since the tape drives stores data linearly as the tape moves past the heads. If data is not available on time, data corruption occurs and time consuming retries are required.
- Solid State — These devices have no moving parts to control, but require special commands to perform the time consuming writes, since a write follows an erase operation.

A devices class code and subclass codes are specified in the interface descriptor. Table 17-4 shows the mass storage device class code and subclass code field within the interface descriptor.

Table 17-4: Mass Storage Class Code and Subclass Code

Offset	Field	Size (bytes)	Value	Description
5	InterfaceClass	1	Class	Class code for mass storage device = 01h.
6	InterfaceSubClass	1	SubClass	SubClass code for mass storage devices defined as: 01h = General Mass Storage 02h = CD-ROM 03h = Tape 04h = Solid State 05 - FEh Reserved

Standard Mass Storage Interface

The standard interfaced used by mass storage devices (except CD-ROM) consists of three endpoints:

- Control endpoint (default endpoint zero) not defined by interface.
- Bulk transfer endpoint supporting IN transactions.
- Bulk transfer endpoint supporting OUT transactions.
- Interrupt transfer endpoint.

Control Endpoint

Mass storage device drivers and devices use the device's default control endpoint to deliver commands to the mass storage function. These commands are send using SCSI command structures. The device typically responds to the command when the host subsequently accesses the endpoint specified (or targeted) by the command. For example, depending on the command, the device might return status when the interrupt endpoint is accessed, or transfer data to or from the media when the host accesses one of the bulk transfer endpoints.

Bulk Transfer Endpoints

Bulk transfer endpoints are used to transfer read from and write to the mass storage media. Since bulk transfers are unidirectional, separate bulk endpoints are required for reading and writing.

Interrupt Endpoint

The interrupt endpoints returns status information when requested by the storage class driver to determine the completion status of a command that has been previously issued to the mass storage device.

General Mass Storage Subclass

The general mass storage subclass is designed to support devices with removable media. However, hard drives are also included in this subclass and are view as devices that have their media permanently locked. The device specifically supported by this subclass include:

- Floppy Drive
- Magneto-Optical

- Zip (floptical)
- Syquest
- Hard Drives

Access to all these devices is very similar since they support random read and write operations in a block/sector oriented fashion. The SCSI command protocol is supported by these devices and used to issue commands via the default control endpoint. For backward compatibility, some of these device (e.g. floppy drive) must work with media from older operating systems, such as DOS that use cylinders, heads, and sectors (CHS) to address the device. These device must be capable of determining and reporting device geometry associated with the media. In this way, CHS information can be translated by BIOS and/or the operating system into a logical blocks.

CD-ROM Subclass

The interface associated with a CD-ROM requires a different combination of endpoints than used by the other subclasses. This is due to the CD-ROM's ability to store CPU data (code and data within files), audio, and video. CD-ROMs must support and mass storage and audio interfaces, and may optionally include an audio/video interface. These additional interfaces might include isochronous endpoints and must be accessed and manipulated by other class drivers (i.e., audio class driver). The specification defines the interface number that must be defined within the interface descriptor's "interface number" field for each interface supported by a CD-ROM. Since the mass storage and audio interfaces are required there will be at least two interfaces defined by a CD-ROM. The interface numbers are:

- 00h = Mass Storage interface
- 01h = Audio interface
- 02h = Audio with Video interface

The CD-ROM mass storage interface uses the same endpoints, with the exception that the bulk OUT endpoint. The bulk OUT endpoint is not needed since data can only be read from the media. The interrupt endpoint for CD-ROMs is used only to report media change.

CD-ROMs are sector/block oriented devices, but unlike the general subclass devices, the sector sizes can be much larger. CD-ROM sector sizes can vary from 2,000 bytes to over 3000 bytes in contrast with the typical 2048 sector size for the general subclass devices.

Tape Subclass

Devices within this subclass are those that have removable media and require streaming data. The nature of streaming tape access is that is may take an extended amount of time to seek the information requested, hence the term pseudo-random access is used to describe access to tape.

USB tape devices supports the Advanced Technology Attachment Packet Interface (ATAPI) for tape of the QIC-157 standard.

Solid State Subclass

Solid state mass storage devices typically require that a memory block be erased prior to data writes. Solid state devices are specified to transfer data only and do not require any isochronous endpoints. The interface uses portions of the SCSI-2 protocol defined for "Direct Access Storage and Optical Memory Device's." These interface supports a subset of the SCSI command set. Refer to the specification for details regarding the SCSI commands support by solid state storage devices.

Class and Device-Specific USB Requests

The programming interface used by mass storage devices includes use of the default control endpoint to deliver commands to the device. The commands are sent via USB control transfers. These devices support the standard requests defined by the USB specification, but also support class-specific and sub-class specific requests that are defined by the Mass Storage Device Class specification.

One class-specific request is defined for mass storage devices, and is used to send sub-class specific (or device specific) commands. This request is defined as the *Accept Device-Specific Command* (ADSC) request. This request is defined as request number zero. When issued, the device-specific command is sent during the data stage of the control transfer. The format of the command depends on the subclass of the mass storage device as follows:

- General Mass Storage — ANSI X3.131, *Small Computer Systems Interface-2*
- CD-ROM — SFF-8020i, *ATA Packet Interface for CD-ROMs*
- Tape — QIC-157, *ATA Packet Interface for Tape*

- Solid State — *QIC-157, ATA Packet Interface for Tape* and SCSI command set (with modifications)

Human Interface Device Class

The Human Interface Device (HID) class pertains to devices that are manipulated by humans to control some facet of a computer's operations. Devices within this class might consist of the following types:

- Keyboards and pointing devices
- Front-panel controls
- Controls associated with devices such as telephones (dialer), VCR remote controls, and game simulation devices.
- Devices that may not control the operation of a device, but provide data in a format similar to other HID devices.

Like mass storage devices, some HID devices may need to be used in the boot process. Therefore, it is necessary to support these device in system BIOS, by including a firmware-based HID client capable of accessing the boot input device.

Other class definitions define device subclasses and protocol definitions that characterize the device and specify protocols that the device uses. This provides software with the information it needs to access the device. The HID class specification does not use this same approach. It was determined that such an approach would be too restrictive and create an ever growing list of new subclasses and protocol definitions as new devices were introduced. As a result, HID devices use the so-called, entity descriptor to characterize devices and define protocols.

Entities specify a set of low-level parameters that can be combined to describe the characteristic behavior of a device. In this way, a device can be described by choosing the entities that describe its input and output characteristics. Several groups of entities have been defined to characterize various aspects of an HID device. Refer to the HID class definition for details regarding the entities descriptors.

Part VI

Host Controllers and Hub: Example Implementations

18 *Universal Host Controller*

The Previous Chapter

The previous chapter introduced the concept of device classes and discussed their role within the USB. It reviewed the first five class types that were defined. These class were discussed to provide the reader with a sense of the information defined for each class and the USB mechanisms that they use. A detailed discussion of device classes requires in-depth knowledge in the associated field such as telephony and audio.

This Chapter

This chapter introduces the Universal Host Controller defined by Intel. The transfer mechanism are discussed and the transfer descriptors built by the Universal Host Controller Driver are detailed.

The Next Chapter

The next chapter discusses the Open Host Controller design, specified by Compaq, Microsoft, and National Semiconductor.

Overview

The Universal Host Controller (UHC) and the Universal Host Controller Driver (UHCD) are responsible for scheduling and executing IRPs forwarded from the USB driver. The UHC also integrates the root hub function that is compliant with the USB hub definition. The root hub integrated into the UHC has two USB ports. The following sections describe the mechanism used by the UHC to schedule and generate transactions via the USB.

The UHC is integrated into the Intel PIIX3 PCI ISA Expansion Bus Bridge and later chips. It is implemented as a PCI master and is capable of performing transactions to and from memory to fetch and update data structures built by the UHCD.

Universal Host Controller Transaction Scheduling

The sequence of transactions scheduled and performed during each 1ms frame is illustrated in Figure 18-1. Note that the periodic transfers are scheduled first (isochronous and interrupt) followed by the control and bulk transfers. The periodic transfers can take up to 90% of the bus bandwidth and control transfers are guaranteed at least 10% of the bandwidth.

The UHCD schedules transactions by building a series of transfer descriptors that are linked to form the collection of transactions that are to be performed during a given frame. This is known as the frame list and is located in system memory.

Figure 18-1: Universal Host Controller Transfer Scheduling

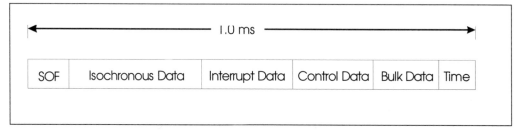

Universal Host Controller Frame List Access

Figure 18-2 illustrates the mechanism used by the UHC to access the frame list from memory. The components involved are:

- Start of Frame (SOF) Counter — This counter decrements with each 12 MHz clock cycle. When the counter expires the frame counter is incremented and the next frame begins. This clock is also the source of USB bit timing for transmissions initiated by the root hub.
- The SOF Modify Register — This register can be used to adjust the number of bit times contained in each frame. This changes the interval at which frames are started. The modify register supports the master client feature that allows a single client driver to adjust SOF timing to permit the USB

frame rate to synchronize to its isochronous transfer rate. The default value results in 1ms frame generation.

- Frame Counter — The frame counter increments at each frame time to select the next sequential entry in the frame list. Each entry contains a pointer to the first transfer descriptor.
- Frame Number Register — The UHCD programs the constant start frame number into this register to define the initial entry point within the frame list. This value once loaded into the frame counter is incremented by the SOF Counter.
- Frame List Base Address Register — The UHCD identifies the base address of the 4KB frame list.

The frame list is an array of up to 1024 entries corresponding to a particular frame. Each entry contains a pointer to a linked list of data structures that contain the information needed by the host controller to build a transaction that will be forwarded to the root hub for transmission over the USB. The UHC reads and interprets each transfer descriptor and generates the transaction described for each descriptor.

Figure 18-2: Frame List Access

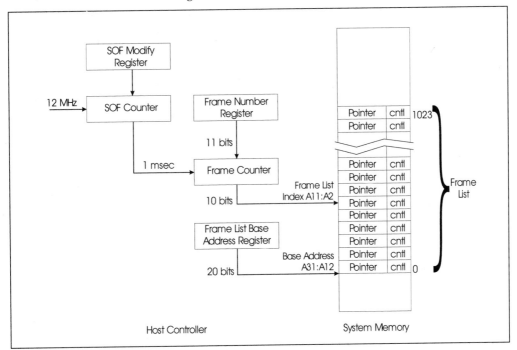

UHC Transfer Scheduling Mechanism

Figure 18-3 illustrates the frame list and the linked list of transfer descriptors that define the transactions to be performed by the UHC. This illustration presumes that many different devices are attached to the USB and that all transfer types are being used by these devices. The order in which the transfer descriptors are linked determines the order that each transaction will be transmitted over the USB. Note that the frame list entry points to transfer descriptors defined for isochronous transfer endpoints. The non-isochronous transfers are queued to permit retries in the event of a failed transaction, whereas isochronous transactions cannot be retried.

Each queue head (QH) and associated transfer descriptor (TD) list are associated with a given transfer type. The first queue is allocated for interrupt transfers followed by the control transfer queue and finally bulk transfer queues. When all scheduled transactions have completed, the host controller can reclaim the remaining bus bandwidth by performing additional control and bulk transfers.

Bus Bandwidth Reclamation

Bus bandwidth reclamation can be implemented such that when all scheduled transactions have completed, the UHC can use the remaining frame time to perform additional transactions. This requires that the last QH is the list points back to the beginning of the control and bulk queues. Each QH also has a termination bit that when set terminates the transfer sequence and no reclamation occurs.

The UHC tracks frame timing to monitor the amount of frame time left for scheduling additional transactions. A sample point (called PreSOF point) permits the UHC to determine is there is sufficient time to start the next transaction before the end of packet. The PreSOF point can be selected for 32 or 64-byte packets under software control. If the packet cannot complete in the remaining time it is not performed.

Figure 18-3: Transfer Mechanism and Execution Order

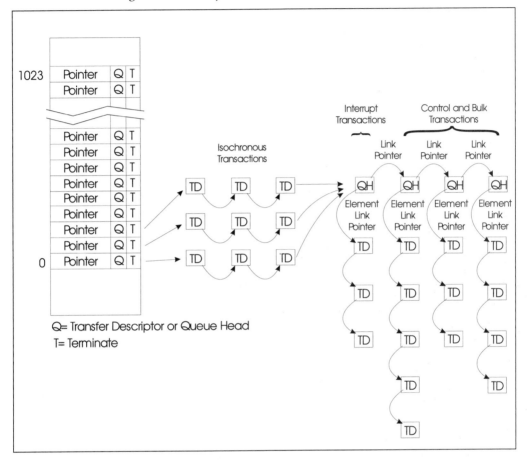

Transfer Descriptors

This section defines the contents of the transfer descriptors and the queue heads. Figure 18-4 illustrates the contents of a transfer descriptor. In general, transfer descriptors contain the information needed by the UHC to generate a transaction and report status including:

- Transfer Type (isochronous and other)
- Type of Token Packet (IN, OUT, SETUP)
- Direction of Transfer

- Size of Data Packet
- Data Toggle Bit
- Memory Buffer Location
- Completion Status

The transfer descriptor consists of four double words (DW0 - DW3). Each DW within the transfer descriptor is defined in tables Table 18-1 - Table 18-4, respectively.

Figure 18-4: Transfer Descriptor Format

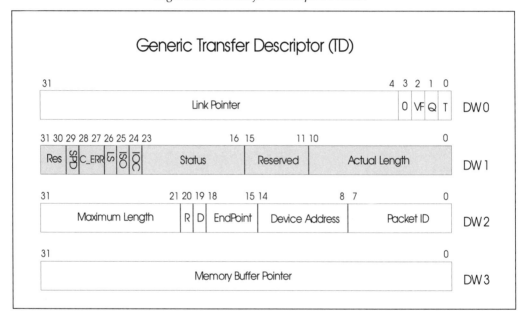

Table 18-1: Definition of Fields (DW0)

Bit	Field Name	Description
0	T	Terminate — Link pointer is valid (0) or not valid (1).
1	Q	QH (Queue head) or TD (Transfer Descriptor) select — Informs UHC that link points to QH (1) or TD (0).

Table 18-1: Definition of Fields (DW0)

Bit	Field Name	Description
2	VF	Vertical First — Specifies a depth first (1) or breath first (0) method of process TDs.
31:4	Link Pointer	Points to another TD or QH (address bits 31:4)

Table 18-2: Definition of DW1

Bit(s)	Field Name	Description
10:0	Actual Length	Actual length of the transfer that is written by the UHC after the transaction has completed.
23:16	Status	Status information posted by the UHC, indicating completion status including: • Active — set by software to enable execution of a transaction by UHC. Cleared by UHC to indicate that descriptor should not be executed when encountered in schedule again. • Stalled — set by UHC to indicate an endpoint stall has been encountered. • Data Buffer Error — set by UHC to indicate that it has encountered a data buffer overflow or underflow. • Babble Detected — UHC has detected a babble condition when executing this TD. UHC also sets stalled bit since this indicates a serious failure. • NAK Received — set by UHC when NAK is returned by target. • CRC/Timeout Error — set by UHC if a bus time-out or CRC error has been detected.

Table 18-2: Definition of DW1

Bit(s)	Field Name	Description
24	IOC	Interrupt on Complete — UHC should generate an interrupt at the end of frame in which this TD completed.
25	ISO	Isochronous Select — this TD is isochronous (1)
26	LS	Low Speed Device — Preamble packet must be used
28:27	C_ERR	Error Counter — two bit field used to indicate number of error that have occurred when executing this descriptor. UHC decrements count when each error is detected. (not decremented for babble or stall).
29	SPD	Short Packet Detected — this bit enables the detection of short packets resulting from queued transactions that access the target (IN transactions).

Table 18-3: Definition of DW2

Bit(s)	Field Name	Description
7:0	Packet ID	Specifies which type of token packet to use: IN, OUT, or SETUP.
14:8	Device Address	Address of device being accessed by this TD.
18:15	EndPoint	EndPoint of device being accessed by this TD.
19	Data Toggle	Determines which data packet the UHC should send or expect. (always 0 for isochronous transfers)
31:21	Maximum Length	Specifies the maximum number of data bytes allowed for this transfer. Maximum value is 1280 (4FFh)which is the longest packet that is guaranteed to fit into a single frame (does not include PID or CRC).

Table 18-4: Definition of DW3

Bit(s)	Field Name	Description
31:0	Memory Buffer Pointer	Points to the beginning of the memory buffer to be used during this transaction. The buffer must be at least as long as the value maximum length field in DW2.

Queue Heads

Queue heads identify a linked list of transfer descriptors that have been queued. A queue head contains a pointer to the first TD to be executed (called a QH element link pointer) and a pointer to the next QH (called a link pointer). The QH also has a termination bit that permits software to terminate frame transactions without bus bandwidth reclamation. Figure 18-5 illustrates the format of a QH. For a description of each field, see table Table 18-5 and Table 18-6.

Figure 18-5: The Queue Head Link and Element Link Pointers

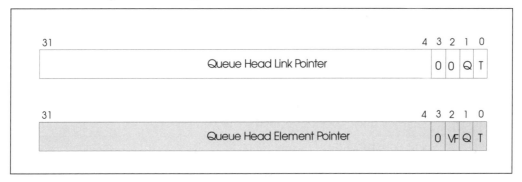

Table 18-5: Queue Head Link Pointer Definition

Bit	Name	Description
0	T	Terminate — 1 = last QH (pointer is invalid, discontinue processing after execution all TD within this Queue. 0 = Pointer is valid (process next descriptor).
1	Q	QH/TD Select — 1=QH, 0=TD. Defines the definition of the next descriptor that the link pointer references, so that decoding can be performed correctly.
3:2	Reserved	Reserved — must be written as 0s.
31:4	QHLP	Queue Head Link Pointer — specifies the address of the next descriptor to be processed in the horizontal list.

Table 18-6: Queue Head Element Link Pointer Definition

Bit	Name	Description
0	T	Terminate — 1 = Terminate (no valid queue entries). 0 = Pointer is valid (process next TD).
1	Q	QH/TD Select — 1=QH, 0=TD. Defines the definition of the next descriptor that the link pointer references, so that decoding can be performed correctly.
2	VF	This bit is ignored by UHC.
3	Reserved	Reserved — must be written as 0s.
31:4	QELP	Queue Element Link Pointer — specifies the address of the next TD or QH to be processed in this queue.

Chapter 18: Universal Host Controller

UHC Control Registers

The UHC maps its registers into PCI I/O address space. These registers are accessed by the UHCD to control various aspects of the UHC's operation. Refer to Table 18-7. Note that the base address is programmed by the PCI configuration software during PCI enumeration.

Table 18-7: UHC I/O Registers

I/O Address	Register Access	Register Description
Base + 00-01h	R/W	USB CommandRegister — Writes to this register cause the indicated controller action. Bits fields defined are: • **Max Packet** selects 32 or 64 byte packet size for bus bandwidth reclamation. • **Configure Flag** indicates that configuration is complete and has no affect on hardware. • **Software Debug** used to enable and disable the debug feature. Related to Run/Stop bit field. • **Force Global Resume** causes the host controller to broadcast resume signalling. • **Enter Global Suspend** causes all downstream USB transaction to cease, resulting in global suspend. • **Global Reset** forces the UHC to send 10ms of reset over the USB • **UHC Reset** causes internal timers, counters, state machines, etc. to their default states. • **Run/Stop** permits the host controller to single step USB transactions. Used in conjunction with Software Debug bit.
Base + 02-03h	R/WC	USB Status Register — This register provides various status states. The status bits are defined below: • **HC Halted** indicates that the host controller has stopped executing. Caused by Run/Stop bit or as a result of an internal error. • **UHC Process Error** indicates that a fatal error has occurred when processing a TD. UHC automatically sets the Stop bit to halt further TD execution. • **PCI Bus Error** indicates that a serious error has occurred during a PCI transaction, causing execution to stop. • **Resume Detect** set by the UHC when is detects a remote wakeup from the USB while in suspend. • **USB Error Interrupt** indicates that a USB transaction has resulted in an error condition. • **USB Interrupt** is set when a TD completes and the TD's IOC bit is set.

Table 18-7: UHC I/O Registers

I/O Address	Register Access	Register Description
Base + 04-05h	R/W	USB Interrupt Enable — Enables and disables the following sources of interrupt: • **Short Packet Interrupt Enable** • **Interrupt On Complete Enable** • **Resume Enable** • **Time-out/CRC Enable**
Base + 06-07h	R/W	Frame Number — Contains the current frame number and frame list index value.
Base + 08-0Bh	R/W	Frame List Base Address — Contains the base address of the frame list in memory. Programmable only on aligned 4KB boundaries.
Base + 0Ch	R/W	Start of Frame Modify — Contains a value that is added to the start value of the SOF counter to adjust the number of bit times within a frame. Default value is 64 which is added to the SOF counter's default of 11936, thereby yielding a count of 12000 or 1ms SOF intervals.
Base + 10-11h	R/WC	Port 1 Status/Control — This register controls the state of root hub port 1 and reflects port status change conditions. The bit fields are: • **Suspend** indicates whether the port is currently suspended or not. • **Port Reset** indicates whether the port is currently reset or not. • **Low Speed Device Attached** indicates the speed of the attached device. • **Resume Detect** indicates that a remote wakeup has been signaled by a USB device. • **Line Status** these two bits reflect the state of the D+ and D- logic levels to support debug efforts. • **Port Enable/Disable Change** indicates that the port has been disabled due to either a device being disconnected or babble or LOA detected on the port. • **Port Enabled/Disabled** indicates whether the port is currently enabled or disabled. • **Connect Status Change** indicates that a device has either been connected or disconnected from the port. • **Current Connect Status** indicates whether a device is currently attached to the port.
Base + 12-13h	R/WC	Port 2 Status/Control — same definition as Port 1

19 *Open Host Controller*

The Previous Chapter

The previous chapter introduced the Universal Host Controller defined by Intel. The transfer mechanism was discussed and the transfer descriptors built by the Universal Host Controller Driver were detailed.

This Chapter

This chapter discusses the Open Host Controller design, specified by Compaq, Microsoft, and National Semiconductor.

The Next Chapter

The provides a brief review of a sample USB hub based on the Texas Instrument TUSB2040 hub.

Overview

The Open Host Controller (OHC) and the Open Host Controller Driver (OHCD) are responsible for scheduling and executing IRPs forwarded from the USB driver. The OHC also integrates the root hub function that is compliant with the USB hub definition. The root hub integrated into the OHC has two USB ports. The following sections describe the mechanisms used by the OHC and OHCD to schedule and generate transactions via the USB.

Open Host Controller Transfer Scheduling

Figure 19-1 on page 290 illustrates the sequence of transfers performed by the Open Host Controller. Note that a reservation can be made at the beginning of the frame (for non-periodic transfers) to support the 10% bandwidth guarantee for control transfers and to ensure that some non-periodic transfers (control and bulk) get performed during each frame. Next, the periodic transfers (interrupt and isochronous) are performed and can take up to 90% of the bus bandwidth, if time remains then additional non-periodic transfers can be scheduled.

The OHCD schedules transactions by building a series of transfer descriptors that are linked to form the collection of transactions to be performed during a given frame. This is known as the frame list and is located in system memory.

Figure 19-1: USB Transfer Scheduling

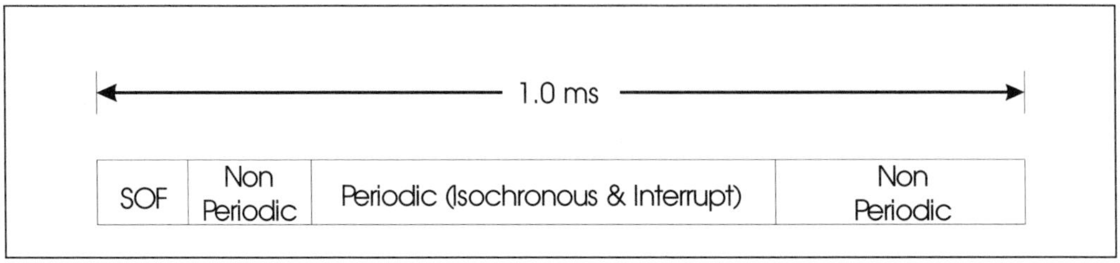

The Open Host Controller Transfer Mechanism

Figure 19-2 on page 291 illustrates the mechanism used to generate transactions during each consecutive frame. The OHCD builds descriptors and places them into an area of memory called the host controller communications area (HCCA). These descriptors include Endpoint Descriptors (EDs) and Transfer Descriptors (TDs). The OHCD assigns an ED to each endpoint in the system. The ED contains the address and endpoint number, thus providing information the controller needs to communicate with the endpoint. Each ED is represented as a circle in Figure 19-2. A queue of TDs is linked to each ED that represent the transactions that are pending completion for that endpoint.

EDs of a giver transfer type are linked together and pointed to by a register within the controller. Notice that there is a register that points to each of the non-periodic transfer types (control EDs and bulk EDs), and a separate register (HCCA register) that points to the linked list of isochronous transfers (interrupts and isochronous) that points to one of 32 entries points for processing interrupts and isochronous transfers. register pointed to by Head pointers to the list of EDs

Figure 19-2: The Transfer Scheduling Mechanism

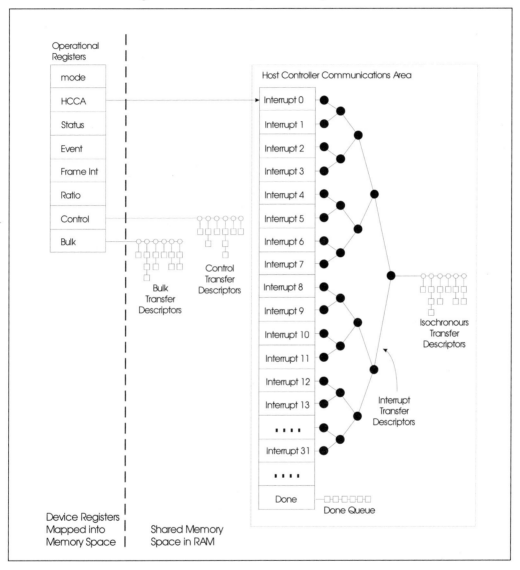

The OHC traverses the ED list is the order that is illustrated in Figure 19-1. The controller begins by accessing the control and bulk descriptors where it left off at the end of the previous transfer. After a predetermined interval that is programmed into controller, it discontinues non-periodic transfers and proceeds to the periodic transfers via the HCCA register. Note that interrupts are scheduled differently from the other transfer types. The HCCA register increments at the end of each frame to point at the next linked list of interrupt TDs, which are scheduled for completion during the current frame. The end of the interrupt list always links to the beginning of the isochronous EDs. Once the isochronous transfers have completed, the controller is free to continue processing control and bulk transfers where it left off, if sufficient time remains within the current frame.

The OHC links transfer descriptors to the "Done" queue after is has completed successfully or if an error has occurred when performing the TD. The OHCD can then check the done queue for completion status information.

The ED and TD List Structure

All transfers are all scheduled using the standard TD list structure as illustrated in Figure 19-3. The head pointer is the OHC register for control and bulk transfers. A different interrupt head pointer is selected for each frame as the HCCA register value increments. The interrupt head pointer is located in the HCCA memory area. Isochronous EDs simply link from the last interrupt ED in the current interrupt list. TDs are enqueued to each ED as IRPs are requested by USB device drivers. An endpoint that is currently idle will not have any TDs enqueued.

Interrupt and Isochronous Transfer Processing

Processing the interrupt and isochronous ED list begins with the interrupt header pointer for the current frame. The list is traversed sequentially, until one transaction associated with the first TD has been performed for each endpoint in the list.

Control and Bulk Transfer Processing

At the beginning of a frame the control and bulk queues are processed until the "remaining" field of the HcFmRemaining register is less than or equal to the "start" field of the HcPeriodicStart register. More control transfers are performed than bulk transfers based on a ratio of control to bulk transfers specified within the "ControlBulkServiceRatio" field of the HcControl register. The controller performs these transfers based on a round robin sequence tied to the ratio (e.g., three control transfer followed by one bulk transfer). If sufficient time remains within the frame after completing the periodic transfers, the controller returns to the control and bulk lists, and continues processing where it left off.

The Done Queue

When the OHC completes a transfer, the TD is linked to the Done queue and written back to the HCCA. In this way, the OHCD can search the Done queue to determine which transactions have been de-queued by the controller and what their completion status is.

Figure 19-3: Transfer Queues

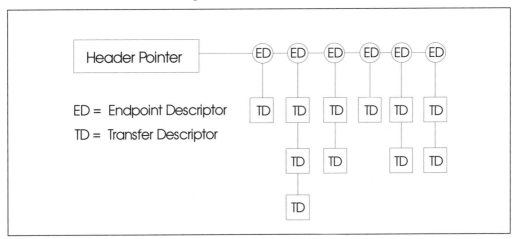

Interrupt Transfer Scheduling

Figure 19-4 illustrates conceptually how the interrupt EDs are linked to ensure that interrupt transactions occur during the specified polling interval. The HCCA pointer register specifies the base address of the HCCA area in memory where a list of 32 interrupt header pointers reside. The five least significant bits of the frame number are used as an index into the interrupt header pointer list. Each frame a different sequence of interrupt transaction are performed based on the ED links from the selected interrupt header pointer.

The interrupt EDs are linked such that they appear in the list for every nth frame that represents its polling interval. For example, interrupts with a polling interval of 32ms would be linked into only one interrupt header pointer. Since a given header pointer is accessed once every 32 frames the interrupt transaction occurs once every 32ms. At the other extreme, a interrupt endpoint with a polling interval of 1ms, would be linked into every interrupt header pointer list. In this way, interrupt transactions can be scheduled at intervals of 1ms, 2ms, 4ms, 8ms, 16ms, or 32ms.

Figure 19-4: Interrupt Scheduling

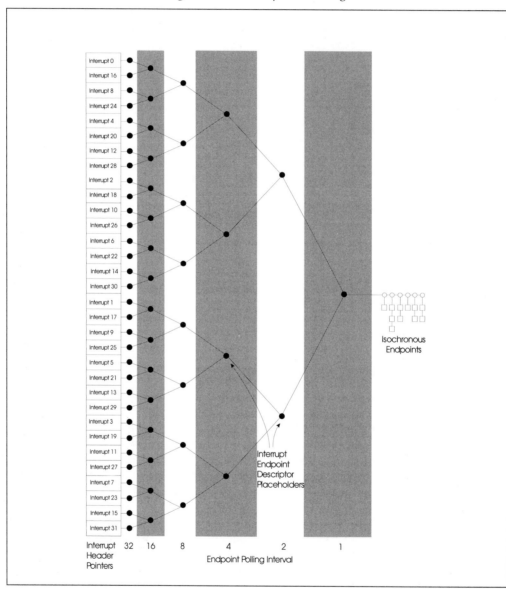

EndPoint Descriptors

Endpoint descriptors exist for every endpoint on the USB and provide information related to the location (device address and endpoint number) and characteristic of the endpoint. In addition, the ED contains pointers to the TD list when there have been transfers enqueued by the OHCD. Figure 19-5 illustrates the format of the ED and Table 19-1 through Table 19-4 define each bit field within the descriptor.

Figure 19-5: Endpoint Descriptor Format

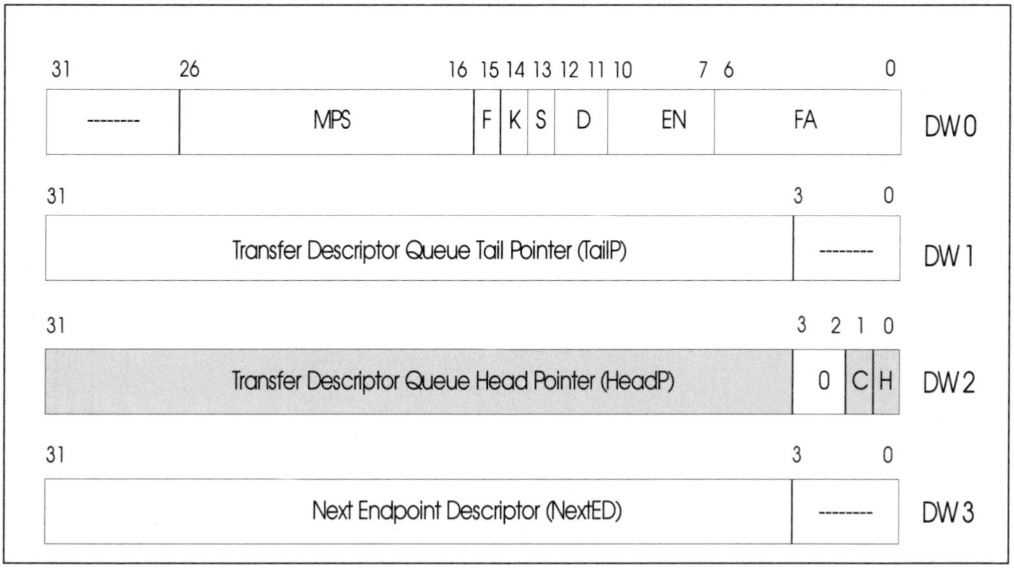

Table 19-1: Definition of Endpoint Descriptor Fields (DW0)

Bit	Field Name	Description
6:0	FA	Device Address — USB device containing the target endpoint.
10:7	EN	Endpoint Number — Address of target endpoint within device.

Table 19-1: Definition of Endpoint Descriptor Fields (DW0)

Bit	Field Name	Description
12:11	D	Direction — Direction of transfer, encoded as follows: 00b = get direction from TD 01b = OUT 10b = IN 11b = get direction from TC
13	S	Speed — Specifies cable speed of the endpoint. 0 = full speed (12 Mb/s) 1 = low speed (1.5 Mb/s)
14	K	Skip — When set the host controller continues to the next ED without processing any TDs associated with this ED.
15	F	Format — Defines the format of the TDs linked to this ED. 0 = interrupt, bulk, or control TD format 1 = isochronous TD format
26:16	MPS	Maximum Packet Size — Specifies the maximum packet size supported by this endpoint.

Table 19-2: Definition of Endpoint Descriptor Fields (DW1)

Bit	Field Name	Description
3:0	"-------"	Not Defined — These fields can be used by the host controller driver for any purpose, and are ignored by the host controller.
31:4	TailP	Transfer Descriptor Queue Tail Pointer — Points to the last TD in the queue associated with this ED. If TailP and HeadP are the same value, then the ED contains no TDs that the host controller can process. If they are different values, the TDs specify a valid memory buffer to transfer information to or from.

Table 19-3: Definition of Endpoint Descriptor Fields (DW2)

Bit	Field Name	Description
0	H	Halted — When set, this bit indicates that processing of the TD queue has halted, usually due to an error incurred when processing the TD queue.
1	C	Toggle Carry — This bit contains the value of the toggle bit when it must be transferred from one TD to the next.
2	0	A field with zero must be written as a zero by the host controller driver.
31:4	HeadP	Transfer Descriptor Queue Head Pointer — Points to the next TD is the list to be processed for this endpoint.

Table 19-4: Definition of Endpoint Descriptor Fields (DW3)

Bit	Field Name	Description
3:0	"-------"	Not Defined — These fields can be used by the host controller driver for any purpose, and are ignored by the host controller.
31:4	NextED	Next Endpoint Descriptor Pointer — Points to next ED descriptor in the linked list. If zero this indicates the end of the linked list.

Transfer Descriptors

Transfer descriptors are enqueued when an IRP is transfer to the OHCD. The TD contains the specific information needed to perform the transfer, such as the memory buffer location where OUT data resides or where IN data will be placed. A given transfer will likely take numerous frames to complete and completion status is reported in the TD. Two forms of transfer descriptor are defined:

- General TD
- Isochronous TD

The general TD is used for all transfers other than isochronous. Device Drivers that support isochronous transfers typically request additional transfers before the first has completed and provides buffering so that data rate matching can be performed. The isochronous TDs support this mechanism.

General Transfer Descriptor

The general TD format is illustrated in Figure 19-6 and the contents of each field is defined is Table 19-5 through Table 19-8.

Figure 19-6: Transfer Descriptor Format

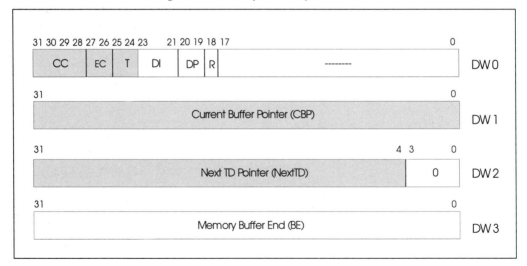

Table 19-5: Definition of Transfer Descriptor Fields (DW0)

Bit	Field Name	Description
17:0	"-------"	Not Defined — These fields can be used by the host controller driver for any purpose, and are ignored by the host controller.
18	R	Buffer Rounding — If zero, this bit specifies that the last data packet from an endpoint must exactly fill the defined data buffer. If one, then the last data packet may be smaller than the defined buffer without causing an error condition.
20:19	DP	Direction/PID — The Packet ID is for this transfer is specified within this field, which also defines the direction of transfer. The field is encoded as follows: 00b = Setup (to endpoint) 01b = OUT (to endpoint) 10b = IN (from endpoint) 11b = Reserved
23:21	DI	Delay Interrupt — Contains a delay count that specifies the number of frames that the host controller must wait before generating an interrupt, indicating that the TD has completed successfully. If this field contains "11b," then there is no interrupt associated with completing the TD.
25:24	T	Data Toggle — The least significant bit of this field contains the data toggle state. This value is only valid when the most significant bit of this field is "1." If the msb of this field is "0," then the toggle bit must be obtained from the Toggle Carry within the ED.
27:26	EC	Error Count — This field contains the error count associated with transaction error that have occurred when processing this transfer descriptor. This field is incremented each time a transmission error occurs. When the value increments to three, the error type is recorded in the error condition code field (bits 31:28) and the endpoint is halted. When the TD completes before three errors occur this field is reset to zeros.

Table 19-5: Definition of Transfer Descriptor Fields (DW0)

Bit	Field Name	Description
31:28	CC	Error Condition Code — Specifies the type of error that has occurred when executing this TD.

Table 19-6: Definition of Transfer Descriptor Fields (DW1)

Bit	Field Name	Description
31:0	CBP	Current Buffer Pointer — This field points to the physical address of the next memory location that will be accessed to transfer data to or from the endpoint. A value of zero indicates that all bytes for this TD have been transferred.

Table 19-7: Definition of Transfer Descriptor Fields (DW2)

Bit	Field Name	Description
3:0	0	A field with zero must be written as a zero by the host controller driver.
31:4	NextTD	Next Transfer Descriptor — Points to the next transfer descriptor is the list for this endpoint.

Table 19-8: Definition of Transfer Descriptor Fields (DW3)

Bit	Field Name	Description
31:0	BE	Memory Buffer End Address — This field contains the physical address of the last byte in the memory buffer for this transfer descriptor.

Isochronous Transfer Descriptor

Figure 19-7 illustrate the format and contents of the 32 byte isochronous transfer descriptor. Since isochronous endpoints have a timing element to ensure data rate matching, the isochronous transfer descriptor can perform, track, and buffer up to eight consecutive frames of data.

The descriptor contains a starting frame number (in the StartingFrame field) consisting of 16 bits that determines when the isochronous transfer should begin. The OHC subtracts this 16 bit starting frame value from the lower 16 bits of the actual frame count to determine when the transfer should begin. If the result is negative the controller recognizes that the starting point has not been reached and progresses to the next ED. However, when the starting frame and current frame numbers match, the OHC starts the transfer with a frame reference of zero. Data is placed in a buffer specified by the BufferPage0 and Buffer-End fields. The exact location within the buffer where data is placed is defined by the Offset0 field. Data from the next frame is placed in the buffer specified by Offset1, etc.

Following each data packet transfer, the offset value in the TD is replaced with completion status information, called the Packet Status Word (PSW). The upper four bits define the condition code and the remaining bits indicate the size of the transfer.

Each field within the isochronous TD is described in Table 19-9 through Table 19-13.

Figure 19-7: Isochronous Transfer Descriptor

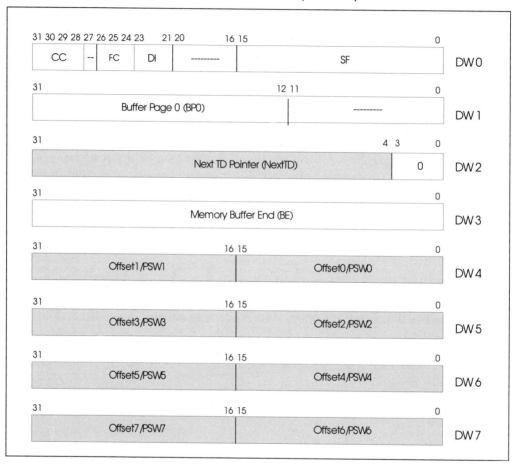

Table 19-9: Definition of Isochronous Transfer Descriptor Field (DW0)

Bit	Field Name	Description
15:0	SF	Starting Frame — contains the lower 16 bits of the frame number in which the isochronous transfer is scheduled to begin.
20:16	"----"	Not Defined — These fields can be used by the host controller driver for any purpose, and are ignored by the host controller.

Table 19-9: Definition of Isochronous Transfer Descriptor Field (DW0)

Bit	Field Name	Description
23:21	DI	Delay Interrupt — Contains a delay count that specifies the number of frames that the host controller must wait before generating an interrupt, indicating that the TD has completed successfully. If this field contains "11b," then there is no interrupt associated with completing the TD.
25:24	FC	Frame Count — Number of data packets (frames) of data described by this TD. 0= one frame and 7= eight frames.
27	"----"	Not Defined — These fields can be used by the host controller driver for any purpose, and are ignored by the host controller.
31:28	CC	Error Condition Code — Specifies the type of error that has occurred when executing this TD.

Table 19-10: Definition of Isochronous Transfer Descriptor Fields (DW1)

Bit	Field Name	Description
11:0	"----"	Not Defined — These fields can be used by the host controller driver for any purpose, and are ignored by the host controller.
31:12	BP0	Buffer Page 0 — Points to the physical page number where the data buffered starts for this transfer descriptor.

Table 19-11: Definition of Isochronous Transfer Descriptor Fields (DW2)

Bit	Field Name	Description
4:0	0	Reserved must be written as zero.
31:5	NextTD	Next Transfer Descriptor — Points to the next isochronous TD in the linked list.

Table 19-12: Definition of Isochronous Transfer Descriptor Fields (DW3)

Bit	Field Name	Description
31:0	BE	Buffer End — Points to the end of the data buffer provided for isochronous data.

Table 19-13: Definition of Isochronous Transfer Descriptor Fields (DW4-7)

Bit	Field Name	Description
15:0 31:16	OffsetN	Offset 0-7 — Specifies the offset within the data buffer where the data from this frame is to be stored.
15:0 31:16	PSWN	Packet Status Word 0-7 — Used to report completion status after the packet has been placed in the memory buffer. Also specifies the actual size of the data packet transferred.

The Open Host Controller Registers

The control registers are mapped into PCI memory address space via the PCI configuration base address register. These registers can be grouped into functional groups as follows and as illustrated in Figure 19-8:

Host Controller Control and Status — these registers define the operating mode of the host controller, reflect current status of the host controller, provide interrupt control and status, and reflect error status conditions.

Memory Pointers — these registers provide pointers to the data structure that are required to communicate with the host controller driver and perform transactions based on the transfer descriptors that reside in memory.

Frame Counter and Control — frame timing status and control are provided by this set of registers, and govern SOF timing and control events that are tied to frame timing intervals.

Root Hub Status and Control — these registers are dedicated to the root hub function. Two sets of registers are included to control the two ports.

Please refer to the Open Host Controller specification for a detailed description of these registers.

Figure 19-8: Open Host Controller Registers

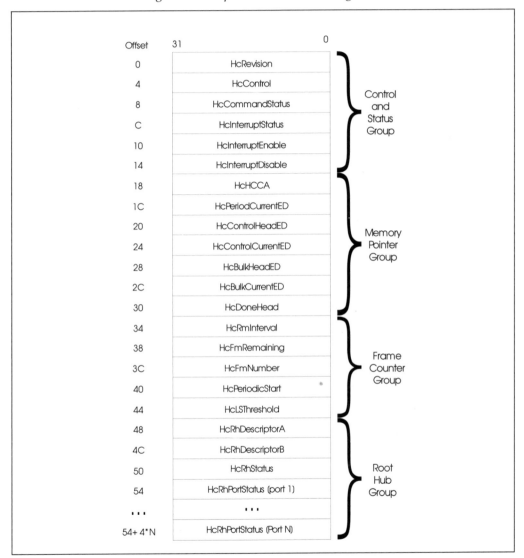

20 *The TUSB2040 Hub*

The Previous Chapter

This chapter discusses the Open Host Controller design, specified by Compaq, Microsoft, and National Semiconductor.

This Chapter

This chapter provides a review of the Texas Instruments TUSB2040 USB hub.

Overview

The TUSB2040 is a four port hub CMOS device based on the USB 1.0 specification. A seven port hub (TUSB2070) is also available. Key features of the hub include:

- Uses the Intel Serial Interface Engine (SIE)
- Supports both bus- and self-powered modes of operation
- Includes integrated USB transceivers
- Supports full-speed and low-speed operation on all ports
- Supports suspend and resume operation
- 3.3Vdc operation
- 48MHz Crystal Input
- Available in a 28 pin DIP package

Figure 20-1 illustrates the functional blocks that comprise the hub. Some hub designs are based on microcontrollers, however the TUSB2040 employs a state machine design.

Timing for the chip is obtained through the 48MHz crystal inputs. The following sections discuss the major elements of the TUSB2070 implementation.

USB System Architecture

Figure 20-1: Block Diagram of TUSB2040 Hub

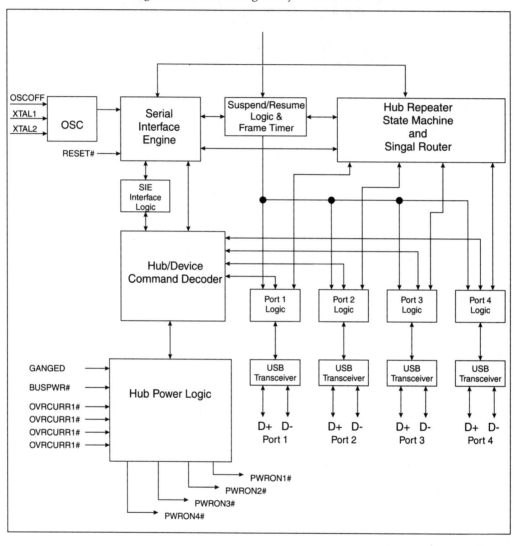

Power Control

The TUSB2040 can be implemented as a self-powered or bus-powered hub. This is accomplished by strapping the BUSPOWER# pin to ground (bus powered) or tying it to 3.3Vdc (self powered). Power switching and over-current protection can be implemented with either individual port protection or ganged protection. This selection is made by tying the GANGED pin to ground (individual power switching and over-current protection) or to 3.3Vdc (ganged switching and current protection). These variations are discussed and illustrated in the following sections.

Self-Powered with Individual Port Control

Figure 20-2 on page 310 illustrates a self-powered implementation with individual port power switching and over-current protection. Individual port power switching and over-current protection is provided by four TPS2014s. Power is applied to the port when the PWRON# pin is asserted, causing the corresponding TPS2014 to switch 5Vdc to it output pin. If a TPS2014 detections an over-current condition, it asserts its OC# (Over-Current) pin, thereby notifying the TUSB2040 hub that an over-current has occurred. The hub will switch power off to the port and set status indicating the over-current condition.

Note that in this example implementation the TUSB2040 is powered by the USB even though it is self-powered. This permits USB software to access the hub even if the local power-supply is turned off, giving software the opportunity to detect the no-local power condition and report it to the user.

The SN75240 transient suppressors reduce in-rush current and voltage spikes.

Figure 20-2: TUSB2040 Implemented as Self-Powered Hub with Individual Port Power Switching and Over-current Protection.

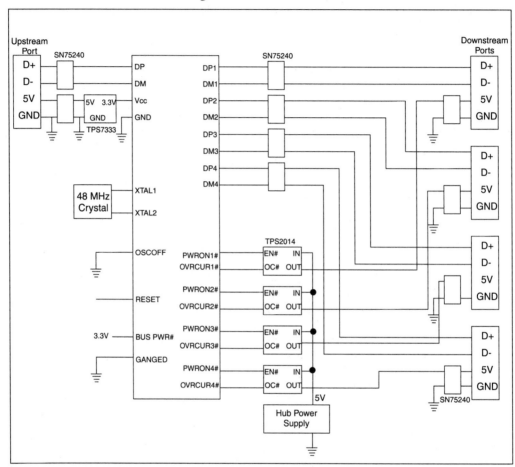

Self-Powered Hub with Ganged Port Control

Figure 20-3 on page 311 illustrates the TUSB2040 implemented as a self-powered hub, but cost can be reduced by using a single TPS2015 to perform ganged power switching and over-current protection. The TUSB2040 is configured for ganged operation when the GANGED pin tied to 3.3Vdc.

Figure 20-3: Self-Powered Hub Implemented with Ganged Power Switching and Over-Current Protection

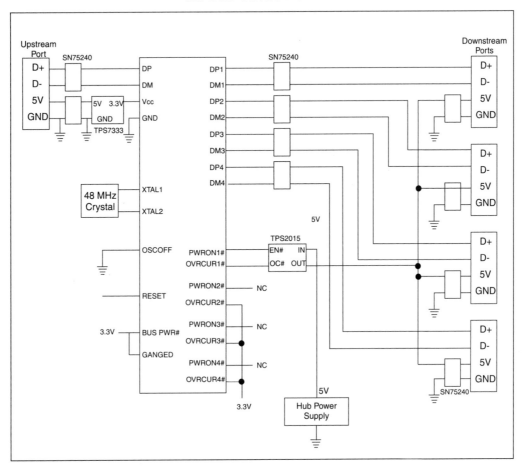

Bus-Powered Hub with Ganged Port Control

When the BUSPOWER# pin is tied to ground, the TUSB2040 is configured for bus-powered operation. The USB cable power applied to the input of the TPS2015 and is routed to the ports. Figure 20-4 on page 312 illustrated a bus-powered configuration with ganged power switching and over-current protection.

Figure 20-4: TUSB2040 Configured for Bus-Powered Operation and Ganged Power Switching

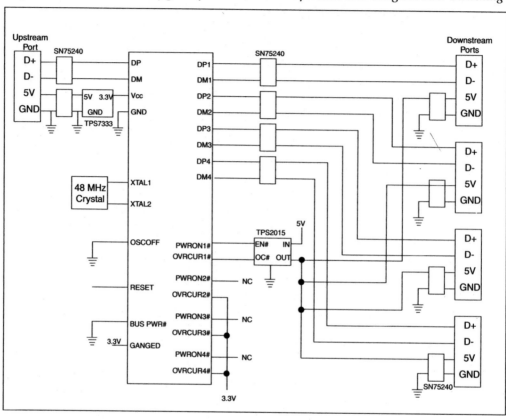

Appendix: FuturePlus USB Preprocessor

Overview

With this versatile product, designers can use their HP logic analyzer as a passive USB analyzer. The FuturePlus protocol-sensitive logic and USB Transaction Inverse Assembler, coupled with the advanced triggering and system performance software of HP's logic analyzers, give the user a powerful tool in debugging, testing, and verifying compliance of USB peripherals and USB-based systems.

Capabilities

- Passive USB bus analysis
- Complete USB serial to parallel decode
- Automatic detection and operation at high-speed (12Mbits/s) or low-speed (1.2Mbits/s), including dynamic speed changing
- Automatic USB reset detection
- Address and end point specified in token packet held until transfer completes
- Allows for easy triggering, store qualification and performance monitoring of specific end points
- Supports the full USB specification
- Supports all types of data transfers, including isochronous transfers
- Supports dynamic hot swapping
- Use your existing HP logic analyzer
- Requires only 2 pods
- Complete configuration files and USB Transaction Inverse Assembler supplied for your HP logic analyzer
- Uses HP's enhanced triggering capabilities, cross-domain analysis, store qualifiers, and system performance software for complete USB performance monitoring

Implementation

The USB preprocessor provides two functions: 1) Provides an electrical and mechanical interface from the Universal Serial Bus to Hewlett-Packard logic analyzers for passive bus monitoring. 2) Provides test points to measure the power and signal fidelity of the USB bus.

State Analysis Mode

The software included with the FSUSB contains complete configuration files and a FuturePlus USB Transaction Inverse Assembler for your HP logic analyzer. In State Analysis mode, the analyzer master clock is derived from the USB Protocol. The USB serial data is converted to parallel data in the preprocessor regardless of high or low speed operation. Any USB resets are automatically detected. Since the address and end point specified in the token packet are held until the transfer is complete, triggering, store qualification and performance monitoring of specific end points is easy! The enhanced triggering capabilities of your HP logic analyzer allow you to trigger on: (1) any address and end point, (2) any data pattern, (3) any data CRC, (4) any USB error (CRC fail, serial bit stuff error, and missing frames), (5) bad or invalid PID's, or any combination of these. Store qualifiers allow the user to store any combination of: (1) any address and end point, (2) any data pattern, (3) any data CRC, (4) any PID type, or any combination of these. All USB cycles and transaction identifiers (SOF, OUT, IN, SETUP, DATA0, DATA1, ACK, NAK, STALL, and PRE) are decoded by protocol-sensitive clocking logic and presented as separate bits to the logic analyzer. These packet identifiers will allow the user to: (1) store all USB traffic, (2) store only certain packet types, (3) store only packets to and from a certain function. The FuturePlus Transaction Inverse Assembler makes analyzing the resulting stored USB traffic easy and accurate. Another good feature: the electrical power for the FSUSB circuitry is drawn from the logic analyzer, not your USB bus!

Timing Analysis Mode

The FSUSB provides timing or analog analysis of the actual bit stream. Using this mode, the user can correlate the data in the bit stream to the actual decode of the data. Here are the signals that are accessible for timing measurements: clk12, mdata, lbc_idle_state, pid_state, sof_or_adr_state, sof_or_ep_state, crc_state, pre_data_state, data_state, sof_tick.

Cross-Domain Analysis

Are you analyzing data in multiple domains? Simply use this preprocessor to monitor the USB, and then use another FuturePlus Systems preprocessor to monitor your other bus. FuturePlus has preprocessors for the PCI, ISA, VME, VXI, PMC, and SIMM buses. You can create your own custom measurement system, cross-domain trigger between buses, and view data from multiple buses simultaneously in the same display. In a similar fashion, you could connect a preprocessor for your host processor to another logic analyzer card. You could then use HP's Software Analyzer (B4620A) to view source code, code execution, and the corresponding USB packet transfers simultaneously.

Index

A

Access Bus 21
ACK 99, 102
acknowledge packet (ACK) 95
adaptive synchronization 76
address assignment 172
asynchronous synchronization 76
Audio Class-Specific Descriptors 265
Audio Class-Specific Requests 265

B

babble 129, 130, 132
babble error 130
bandwidth allocation 172
bit stuff errors 110, 112
bit stuff time 252
bit stuffing 63
bulk transfer 72
Bulk Transfers 41
bus bandwidth 173, 250, 252
bus bandwidth reclamation 253
bus bandwidth, bulk 81
bus bandwidth, control 81
bus bandwidth, interrupt 80
bus bandwidth, isochronous 78
bus powered hubs 35
bus time-out 114
bus turn-around time 114
bus-powered device 142
bus-powered hub 139

C

cable delay 114
cable power 57
class-specific descriptor 46
Clear Hub Feature request 192
Clear Hub Local Power Feature request 193
Clear Hub Over-Current Change request 206
Clear Port Feature request 193, 211

client driver 30
client pipes 255
command mechanisms 254, 255
Communication Device Class 266
Communications Class-Specific Descriptors 267
Communications Class-Specific Requests 267
Communications Device Interfaces 267
communications pipe 72
compound device 140
Configuration Descriptor 45
configuration descriptor 45, 177, 180
configuration sequence 168
configuration value 173, 181
control transfer 72, 80
control transfer stages 80
Control Transfers 41
CRC 88, 110, 111
current budge 136
current during configuration 139
current limiting 137, 141
Cyclic Redundancy Check (CRC) 85

D

D 60
D- 61
D+ 60, 61
data packet 44, 85, 94
data packet errors 113
data stage 80
data toggle 116
DATA0 116
data0 packet 94
DATA1 116
data1 packet 94
default control endpoint 168
default control pipe 170, 176
default control port 176
default device address (zero) 172
default pipe 176

Index

default pipes 254
depth of topology 253
descriptor 176
descriptors 24
device attachment 60
device configuration 250
Device Descriptor 45
device descriptor 45, 177, 178
device detachment 61
Device Framework 38, 45, 247
device layer 246
Differential 0 69
Differential 1 69
differential amplifier 68
differential data 59, 64
differential driver 65
differential signaling 64
Display Device Class 268
Display Device Class Interface 268
Display Device-Specific Descriptors 269
DMA channel 38
DMA channels 11
downstream (away from the host) 36

E

e USB driv 31
end of frame (EOF) 130
end of packet (EOP) 69
endpoint 41
endpoint descriptor 45, 177, 252
endpoint zero 24, 168
endpoints 24
enumeration 167
EOF1 130
EOF2 130, 132, 212
EOP 70, 85, 88, 132
EOP2 191
Error checking mechanisms 109
error recover, interrupts 80
error recovery, bulk 82
error recovery, isochronous 78

F

false EOP 115
Firewire 21
frame 31, 32, 41, 74
frame list 31
full speed cable 56
full-speed device detection 60
full-speed driver 66
function configuration 251
function layer 49

G

ganged power switching 138, 187
GeoPort 21
Get Bus State request 212
Get Descriptor request 176
Get Hub Descriptor request 186, 202
Get Hub Status request 192, 202, 203, 206
Get Port Status request 192, 193, 206
global suspend 153

H

half-duplex 64
handshake packet 85, 95
handshake packet errors 113
handshake packets 44
HCD 247, 248
high-speed devices 50
host controller 27, 32
Host Controller Drive 29
host controller driver 42
host recovery time 252
hub class descriptor 186
hub class request 201
hub client 170
hub configuration 175
hub controller 33, 35, 36
hub delay 114
hub descriptor 176
hub functions 33

hub low speed setup 252
hub port states 194
hub repeater 37
hub repeater state machine 132
hub request 198
hub resume state 164
hub state change 204
hub state machine 132
hub status change endpoint 170
Hub Status Endpoint Descriptor 185
hub suspend state 152
Human Interface Device Class 268
hybrid powered device 148
hybrid powered hub 146
hybrid-powered 181

I

I/O Request Packets 30
idle state 62, 67, 69
IEEE 1394 21
IN packet 91
IN token 89
IN transaction 98
initiating global suspend 153
input sensitivity 68
insufficient bus current 143
interface descriptor 45, 177, 182
interface layer 247
interrupt transfer 71
Interrupt Transfers 41
IRP 30, 31, 41, 73, 246, 254
IRQ 11, 12, 38
isochronous transfer 72, 76, 101
Isochronous Transfers 41

J

J state 61, 62, 69

K

K state 61, 62, 69

L

Legacy 12
legacy 11
legacy connectors 15
legacy hardware 19
legacy I/O 11, 14
legacy interrupts 12, 13
legacy software 19
LOA 132
LOA error 130
LOA errors 130
local power status 203
loss of activity (LOA) 130
low speed cable 55
low speed driver 66
low-power device 142
low-speed cable 38
low-speed device detection 60
low-speed devices 38, 50
low-speed transaction 97

M

Mass Storage Device Class 269
master client 253
max. data packet size, bulk transfers 81
max. data packet size, control transfers 81
max. packet size, interrupt transfers 80
max. packet size, isochronous transfers 78
maximum packet size 185
message pipes 255

N

NAK 100, 103
No Acknowledge packet (NAK) 96
NRZI 59, 62, 63
number of interfaces 180

O

OHC Done Queue 293
OHC Endpoint Descriptors 290

Index

OHC HCCA 290
OHC Interrupt Transfer Scheduling 293
OHC Transfer Descriptors 290
OHC transfer queues 293
Open Host Controller (OHC) 32, 289
Open Host Controller Driver (OHCD) 289
Open Host Controller Transfer Scheduling 289
OUT token 89, 92
OUT transaction 102
Over-Current Indicator 203
over-current protection 137, 187

P

packet 85
packet errors 110
packet ID 85, 87
Packet ID (PID) checks 110
packets 44
PID check 90, 110
pipe mechanisms 254, 255
pipe policy 254
plug and play 18
policy 251
port change fields 209
port change indicators 206
Port Power Mask 188
port status 206
port status fields 207
power switching 138
power switching mode 138, 187
power verification 251
preamble 50
preamble packet 38, 87, 97
propagation delay 56

R

remote wakeup from global suspend 155
remote wakeup from selective suspend 158

repeater 35
Reset 70
reset 172
resource allocation 250
resume from global suspend 153
resume from selective suspend 157
resume signaling 155
resume state 69
Root Hub 29
root hub 32, 33

S

selective suspend 157
self-powered device 148
self-powered hubs 145
serial interface engine (SIE) 36
series A connector 54
series A plug 54
series A receptacle 54
series B connector 55
series B plug 54
series B receptacle 54
Set Address request 172
Set Configuration request 181
Set Descriptor request 202
Set Hub Local Power Change request 206
Set Hub Over-Current Change request 206
Set Port Enable Feature 193
Set Port Enable Feature request 171
Set Port Feature request 211
Set Port Power Feature request 187, 191
setting the policy 251
SETUP packet 94
setup stage 80
SETUP token 89
setup token 93
single-ended receivers 65, 68
single-ended zero 162
slew rate 66
slew rate, full speed driver 67

Index

slew rate, low speed driver 66
SOF 90, 253, 264
SOF token 89, 130
special packet 87
STALL 101
Stall packet (STALL) 96
standard descriptors 177
start of frame (SOF) 31
start of packet (SOP) 69
status change endpoint 171, 176, 184
status stage 81
stream pipes 255
string descriptor 46, 177
suspend 23, 151
suspend state 152
synchronization types 264
synchronous sychronization 76

T

The Universal Host Controller (UHC) 277
tiered star topology 51
toggle bit 117
token 85
token packet 85
token packet errors 112
token packets 44
transfer descriptor contents 39
transfer descriptors 32
transfer type 185
transfer types 41

U

UHC bus bandwidth reclamation 280
UHC Control Registers 287
UHC frame list 278
UHC queue heads 285
UHC transfer descriptors 278
UHC Transfer Scheduling 280
UNICODE 177
Univeral Serial Bus (USB) 21
Universal Host Controller (UHC) 32

Universal Host Controller Driver (UHCD) 277
upstream (toward the host) 36
USB bandwidth 41
USB bus interface layer 47
USB client driver 31
USB client drivers 248
USB configuration 250
USB Device Drivers 29
USB device drivers 30
USB device layer 48
USB Driver 29, 49, 248, 250, 252
USB driver 29, 41, 42, 254
USB enumeration 167
USB enumerator 186
USB features 23
USB host controller 27
USB Host Controller Driver 49
USB host controller driver 31
USB host controller driver (HCD) 31
USB hub 34
USB Hubs 29
USB ports 35
USB signaling states 69
USB transfer 39
USBD 248

V

voltage drop budget 137

W

Wait For End Of Frame 2 (WFEOF2) 132
Wait For End Of Packet (WFEOP) 132
Wait For Start Of Frame (WFSOF) 132
Wait For Start Of Packet (WFSOP) 132
WFSOF 160, 164
WFSOP 152, 162

The PC System Architecture Series

The PC System Architecture Series is a crisply written and comprehensive set of guides to the most important PC hardware standards. Each title illustrates the relationship between the software and hardware, and thoroughly explains the architecture, features, and operation of systems built using one particular type of chip or hardware specification.

MindShare, Inc. is one of the leading technical training companies in the computer industry, providing innovative courses for dozens of companies, including Intel, IBM, and Compaq.

> *"There is only one way to describe the series of PC hardware and architecture books written by Tom Shanley and Don Anderson: INVALUABLE."*
> —*PC Magazine's* "Read Only" column

ISBN 0-201-40994-1

ISBN 0-201-37964-3

ISBN 0-201-40997-6

ISBN 0-201-40995-X

ISBN 0-201-48535-4

ISBN 0-201-40996-8

ISBN 0-201-30974-2

ISBN 0-201-40991-7

ISBN 0-201-30973-4

ISBN 0-201-40992-5

ISBN 0-201-41013-3

ISBN 0-201-40990-9

ISBN 0-201-55447-X

ISBN 0-201-46137-4

http://www.awl.com/cseng/series/mindshare/

♦ Addison-Wesley